Preserving Patients:
Anecdotes of a Junior Doctor

Tom Parsons

CW00859153

To Mum.
For introducing the pleasure of reading and writing.

Introduction

I am not a writer so I am not sure why I have written a book. Does writing a book make you a writer? Making an omelette does not make you a chef, more an unambitious cook. Riding a horse does not make you a jockey it makes you a horse rider, or if you are American and require further delineation; horseback rider. Playing the piano doesn't make you a pianist, at least not the way I do it. So what makes you a writer? Hopefully not just financial success. Perhaps it is the ability to sit in a coffee shop pretentiously tapping away on an Apple Mac whilst sipping a macchiato? Maybe that is where I went wrong.

I am a doctor and everyone knows what a doctor is. We diagnose and treat diseases, we practise medicine. There are no half measures when it comes to being a doctor. You cannot dabble at being a doctor; not unless you want to be arrested and imprisoned.

But what about Chiropractors, Osteopaths, Homeopaths, Naturopaths, Shamans, Aroma therapists, Faith healers and Reiki practitioners? They all profess to diagnosing and managing disease. Maybe I am the homeopath's equivalence to a writer. Nevertheless there is something unique to practising medicine as a doctor. Despite everything, patients continue to trust doctors with their bodies and their minds. They tell us facets of themselves that, occasionally, they have never told another, truths that have never been declared, fears never expressed and desires never fulfilled. We are trusted with explicit details, intimate physical examinations, painful interventions and life-threatening operations. But a patient doesn't give their trust away for free. Trust comes with certain expectations.

Researchers have probably investigated what patients perceive as being critical to their healthcare experience; what they expect from their doctor. Usually it is along the lines of having a doctor who actually listens to them, who is caring and compassionate and explains pertinent issues adeptly. Undoubtedly by displaying the above, by consulting attentively with empathy and compassion, the doctor will cement this trust placed in them. This doctor-patient relationship is a pillar of medicine, a fundamental tenet and, as the name suggests, is unique to doctors and their patients.

I would argue that now, and ever increasingly, the primary expectation, almost demand, of a patient to their doctor is to get better. It doesn't seem to matter how banal the disease or how severe, the expectation remains absolute. Whether the patient's disease is entirely their own fault has no impact on their expectation. Patients also have no patience in the pursuit of this expectation. As though their susceptibility to disease and their own mortality is just an inconvenience. The severity (or banality) of the disease appears to have little impact on how long they are prepared to wait. You can't wait for routine appointment as, by the time it arrives, you'll 'probably be better by then'. The 'fix' must also be immediate. If this isn't possible they will skip over the healthcare provider and seek another because they have a 'disease' and therefore an expectation. Often they will have an idea what is wrong with them and feel they just require the necessary health professional to execute their requirements; perhaps like a hairdresser perfecting the appropriate shade of blonde. Often these fixed ideas are as absurd as they are unshakeable and immovable and failure to instigate that referral, prescribe that antibiotic or identify that 'problem' results in the patient complaining or seeking solutions from another healthcare provider.

I reckon, in the most part, we do pretty well. No matter the problem, no matter how serious or trivial we can battle with patients ideas, match expectations and deliver appropriate diagnosis and management so ultimately make people 'better'. But here's the rub; we can't every time. We are human and fallible. We nuance certain aspects of your history (what you tell a doctor) due to our own individual biases and specialisations. We take shortcuts. We fail to recognise certain signs (examination findings) and see ones which aren't there. We can select the wrong investigation, order needless investigations that result in more anxiety or fail to request any investigation when one is required. Furthermore we are working in a public funded, overstretched service with ever increasing demands made year on year. What this means is that some people, some of the time, will get the wrong diagnosis and/or the wrong treatment. So does it matter if the doctor explains what they are doing, delivers their diagnoses with aplomb and empathy but is fundamentally wrong in what you came to see them for? They have failed in that core expectation; to be made better quickly.

But even when a doctor is incorrect this doesn't mean that they are wrong or 'negligent'. A diagnostic hypothesis is there to be refuted or confirmed. If the diagnosis is refuted an alternate diagnosis is hypothesised and tested. These are the difficulties and complexities of medicine. What makes it more difficult is that all the components of diagnosis and management are constantly changing as new evidence is published, appraised, reviewed and recommended. Now there are over 25 million research citations on medical databases with not enough hours in the day, even if all you did was read research, to keep up with articles published daily pertaining to your specialist area. This leads to the publication of endless, constantly updating guidelines for managing specific conditions. Despite your ever increasing expectations you become increasingly complicated with ever more interweaving disease processes each with their own complex management.

Undoubtedly the complexity of medicine will reach the point where we struggle to keep up. For the population we already need computers to manage our huge workload. To ensure scan results don't go unnoticed, blood results missed and delays in diagnosis averted. For the individual we already use computers constantly to fact check, calculate risk scores and check medication doses. Surely eventually the computer will actually become more efficient in assimilating all the various facets of your health problems? Can the computer therefore better match your expectations? What if the computer can take over all together? They will be able to select the relevant points of your history without bias and cross reference them with databases to bring up a list of potential diagnoses. They could select and then utilise information from diagnostic tests which they could probably, in the most part, perform and read with better accuracy than a doctor. They could review information from your previous medical problems and your current medications with better accuracy than either you or your doctor could recall or record. They will never make prescribing errors, never get the dose wrong. Finally

4

they could cross reference this with millions of research articles to deliver the best, most up to date management. If the management required is an operation or procedure the computer and robotics will probably be able to deliver it with greater precision than a human. If you require lifesaving treatment an automated vehicle will come and get you and take you to the nearest hospital so a robot driven by Artificial Intelligence (AI) can provide lifesaving care. They might even be able to personalise your treatment depending on your individual genetic makeup. Furthermore they will be the gold standard; the best available and infallible. There won't be any medical negligence lawyers (hoorah) as the computer will never be wrong, or the margin of error will be known and insured against for when the outcome is poor. They will be the equivalent of driverless cars; I'm not saying things won't ever go 'wrong' but there will never be a 'mistake'.

But what about the compassion and empathy? A computer will never be able to empathise with human emotion. If the primary expectation is for accurate, standardised diagnosis and treatment then would patients be content to forgo humans from the process? The entire concept of entrusting another human being with your medical information will be lost to software, computer codes and sophisticated algorithms saved on secure servers with perhaps a mortal at the end to provide that human touch; a hug and a tissue.

Often the trust that exists between doctors and patients is itself fallible. Doctors occasionally lie to patients and patients often lie to doctors. Patients malinger or exaggerate symptoms to obtain disability payments or privileges, to avoid work, to avoid incarceration, to access controlled medications or just to be taken seriously. Patients lie about their maladaptive behaviours and will often underplay their symptoms to prevent restrictions on their employment or just because of wilful self-deception. They lie to maintain self-esteem, they lie for autonomy and they lie out of sheer embarrassment. No matter how sophisticated the algorithms and artificial intelligence a computer will always struggle with this aspect of the doctor-patient relationship. But would patients lie to the computer? Would a computer be able to take an impartial facts based judgement on issues pertaining to employment or benefits? Patients currently will happily divulge to a search engine what they will not disclose to their doctors so perhaps the (perceived) anonymity of an AI delivered consultation is worth the lack of empathy. Until they can work out how to trick you that the computer is actually displaying empathy.

So this brings me to why I have written this book. If you accept, as I have, the ascendancy of AI and therefore, for the vast majority, computer delivered healthcare then the concept of a patient-doctor interaction as we know it presently will be defunct within a generation. In the very least it will be altered irrevocably to how today's medicine is practiced. Perhaps the only saving grace for the medical profession is the complete ineptitude of NHS in all matters pertaining to IT. More on that later.

Presently the doctor-patient relationship remains the cornerstone of clinical medicine and remains the reason why I practice medicine. There is no better feeling in the world than the gratification from a patient who you have made better. So my reasons for writing this book is to give an insight into this unique relationship. To understand the doctor-patient relationship you must understand the context in which it exists; the National Health Service. I'll start at the beginning; the doctors 'Foundation Programme'. I think it worth mentioning that I have no particular political motives, my aim is not to influence you on the future direction of health policy. I am not banging the drum for any particular team although I do reserve the right for an occasional whinge.

Finally confidentiality remains the basis on which the doctor-patient relationship is built. Therefore whilst this book is based on reality, any similarity to real life people or their medical conditions is pure coincidence. All inspiration is based only loosely on medicine I, or many others, have seen, or heard. These encounters thrown up in the air with a large glug of embellishment and a sprinkle of hyperbole have been meshed together badly into a strange shaped and bizarre flavoured sausage. I hope it eats well.

Whilst the best efforts have been attempted to ensure medical accuracy no one should apply the principles described in this book to real life without first consulting their doctor. She or he really does know best and they will listen to you empathetically, seek to understand your concerns, pay homage to your ridiculous ideas and exceed your expectations. Until the robots arrive.

Tom Parsons
July 2017

Foundation Year 1

Medicine

Medicine is not only a science; it is also an art. It does not consist of compounding pills and plasters; it deals with the very processes of life, which must be understood before they may be guided.

Paracelsus
16[th]Century

First Day

Every junior doctor remembers their first day. Most approach it with a due sense of apprehension and humility. Not me. I was ready. There was no hiding in the cupboard in the event of the cardiac arrest bleep going off. I was going to sprint there to arrive first on the scene. I'd quickly assert control, equipped only with my conceit and freshly memorised Advanced Life Support algorithms. Panicking nurses would be quickly induced to calm and then probably fall in love with me. Patients would wake up following the swift delivery of a shock and immediately shower me with chocolates, bottles of wine and probably name their firstborn after me. I was as keen as a razor's edge probably covered in mustard.

I had taken my time in obtaining my medical degree, enjoying the scenic route. Normally it takes five years to train as a doctor, six if you take a year out to do some science of dubious quality. In order to get into Medical School you need to get yourself a full quota of top grades at A-level, play the violin to grade 8 standard, wipe grannies' arses in your spare time and have the full complement of Duke of Edinburgh awards. I spent most of my time during my 6th Form years trying to get the opposite sex to spend time with me, preferably alone and naked. When the opposite sex colluded against me, deciding that they didn't want to lose our 'friendship' in some sort of homage to Dawson's Creek, I generally felt too misunderstood to waste my time studying and instead indulged in prolonged periods of sulking and brooding. The end result from spending one's time making mix-tapes for my betrothed on an old fashioned tape-deck, and rebelling against any form of teacher or parental discipline, was a clutch of incredibly unimpressive A-levels. Any notions I had of becoming a doctor, which I occasionally mentioned, just to please my Nana who thought all doctors were lesser deities and so consequently rewarded me with five pounds, were quickly dispelled. With my grades I would be lucky to attend the local polytechnic to study Car Park attending or worse still; Psychology. Despite this, my poor long suffering mother and father were still desperate to rid themselves of my brooding, sulking rebellious company, so much so, that I was definitely going to go to (any) university to get a (any) degree, in something. Anything. And not in my home town as my father succinctly put it; 'Going to a university in your home town is like going to a brothel and not getting laid.' In other words they were banishing me to Scotland.

Five years later, the time it would take to train an 18 year old to become a doctor, I had just about managed an undergraduate Bachelor of Science degree in Physiology. This included two unintentional gap years largely due to my insistence in trying out nearly every degree in the social and natural sciences departments coupled with a somewhat lackadaisical approach to revision; particularly in the interesting field of invertebrate zoology. As time progressed my acquired work ethic increased in an inversely proportional pattern to the time I spent drinking, trying to get women to sleep with me, brooding and being misunderstood. A rather excellent couple of physiology lectures reviewing the large volume of trial research being propelled out in the field of cardiovascular pharmacology had thrust my thinking back towards medicine.

Buoyed with having a plan of action, for once, I ramped up the workload, added in a sprinkling of work experience which, in retrospect, did little to illuminate my ignorance of what a doctor does day-to-day and applied for a place. The Labour government, what with the European Working Time Directive massively curtailing the number of hours doctors were legally allowed to work per week, had had to recruit several thousand extra doctors and open several new medical schools to train them in (ring any bells?). As luck would have it this reached a climactic the year I applied. I managed, even with my dreadful A-level results, a cobbled together degree in Physiology and a charming performance at interview, to sneak a place. I am unsure whether supply exceeded demand that year but the Medical school did completely change their interview and admission procedures the following year. I have successfully convinced myself that this was nothing to do with me.

Without exaggerating, the first two pre-clinical years at medical school are tough. But I arrived expecting to be hit with a sledgehammer of biochemistry, anatomy and physiology. I had even

11

forked out a small fortune in textbooks in anticipation. I was somewhat surprised therefore to be sat, in the first fortnight of a medical degree, in a draughty church hall, in a deprived inner city centre, drinking tea and biscuits with Geoff. Geoff was a post-doctoral sociology lecturer undergoing research into health barriers for ethnic minorities. He had long brown hair which he occasionally swept back into a pony tail. This seemed to accentuate his enormous nose that looked like it could be used to open a tin of peaches in an emergency survival situation. He had a small patch of hair under his lower lip (I believe this is known as a 'soul patch') that looked like he had repeatedly failed at shaving. He wore two thumb rings, tight black jeans, hand knitted jumpers, read the Guardian in the lunch hour and wrote an online left-wing blog.

Geoff was a module leader on one of the 'pink modules' we had in the first term of the first year of medical school. The term 'pink modules' derived from how the medical school actually highlighted the social science modules in pink on our packed timetables. The pink label also seemed to have taken on a derogatory connotation reflecting a perceived lack of intellectual complexity or importance in comparison to the heavyweight scientific subjects.

Geoff would describe in great detail the evidence pertaining to the literature behind the psychosocial and socioeconomic factors underpinning health inequalities. Believe it or not but poor health is not just due to a diet of fast food, cheap cigarettes and turbo-charged cider but actually about people's aspirations, stresses, locus of control and societal pressures. Having adopted my parents' mostly Conservative views, reading about health inequalities by Black, Marmot and Acheson[1] was equally confusing and revealing. I remember asking the pony-tailed one:

---

[1] Douglas Black, Donald Acheson and Michael Marmot were notable doctors and epidemiologists who all, at the behest of the government, produced reports into health inequalities. Health inequality is where people, usually due to being poorer, die younger and live their lives in worse health.

'Geoff, I understand the importance of the social determinants for health and that wealthy alcoholics will live longer than poor alcoholics but I don't understand how I can influence this as a future doctor at the coalface?'

'Doctors have great influence in society so hopefully in the future you will have the power to do this,' Geoff replied.

As first year medical students we all felt very pleased with this; us doctors as influential members of society. We were going to be powerful citizens directly influencing their patient's locus of control. I didn't really know what it meant but it sounded smashing. Now that I am a doctor I can confirm that this is complete horseshit. Politicians change policy, not doctors and we all know how politicians do not listen, not one iota, to doctors. Unless of course a doctor becomes a politician and then their views are considered messianic unless they differ from those of the health secretary in which case they are ignored. If I may quote from the Telegraph: 'In our democracy, different people have different roles to play. Politicians should decide how public services are run, then answer for their decisions. Public servants should provide those services. It is not the job of doctors to dictate health policy; their job is to treat patients.' So whilst I see the socio-economic and psychosocial effects on patient's health daily and now understand what that means, I am practically impotent in addressing their root causes. Sorry Geoff.

The pace of lectures, group workshops and assignments continued to ramp up coupled with the ever increasing volume of information to learn and process. The range was vast from the anatomy of the brachial plexus (a network of nerves that provide the arm with movement and sensation) to the Kreb's cycle (how cells actually get their energy). By the end of the first year we were begging to be sat in a church hall drinking stewed tea with Geoff drawing lists of sociology terms on giant posters in felt-tips. Coupled with a strong dedication to pretending to play Medics rugby (so I could attend the post-match drinking sessions) spare time was at a premium. Examinations to check our progress seemed to precipitate almost monthly bouts of epochal stress that made me feel like I was suffering from a pre-menstrual disorder. Just when you felt your little neurons were completely saturated you burst through pre-clinical exams and into clinical medicine; the latter half of the medical degree. Suddenly all the basic anatomy, physiology and biochemistry learnt in draughty lecture theatres and University dissection rooms seemed completely detached as you received your first hospital placements. Now you were in the clinical world of linoleum floors and that universal peculiar hospital smell that you are unsure whether to attribute to the food or incontinence. We cycled through medicine, general surgery, orthopaedics, paediatrics, obstetrics and gynaecology, general practice and psychiatry. I saw little boys who wet the bed in enuresis clinic, old ladies who wet the bed in uro-gynae clinic and middle aged men that wet the bed in prostate clinic. I delivered babies and talked to psychotics in the middle of a bipolar effective episode. I learnt how to perform an anaesthetic, scrubbed in for hernia repairs and presented patients on post take ward rounds. My flat mate and I spent several hours putting in the largest peripheral venous cannulas we could in each other, usually on a Thursday evening, after returning from the pub. The alcohol had the added benefit of negating the pain when your clumsy flatmate inserted a needle into your median nerve but also, when he finally managed to hit claret, could be used to infuse fluids overnight as a hangover prophylaxis. The hospital training was excellent in the most part and usually delivered by senior registrars and consultants. I relished it, and by the time it came to the final examinations; that final hurdle to cross, with a bit of extra book work, I felt prepared.

Despite telling a rather perturbed pregnant women, who was chugging along with her normal pregnancy, that in fact her baby had intrauterine growth retardation and we should check this with an ultrasound I got through clinical finals and written finals with no issues. All new doctors start work in August and I officially became a doctor in mid-July. The medical school, again quite perceptively, had requested but not mandated, a period of two weeks of shadowing for all us new-starters. They were planning on mandating it the year following but wanted to give it a trial run first; probably to work out the logistics rather than assess any added benefit. Many of my medical school colleagues strategically decided to completely ignore this latest medical school edict and planned on taking a two week holiday before their lives as working members of society started. I was absolutely delighted to finally be given the opportunity to share my newly acquired plethora of knowledge with anyone but my father. Whilst my health advice freely distributed to my old man had achieved no tangible healthcare benefit, he had, on the back of it, managed to annoy his GP who had now labelled him, officially, as a hypochondriac. Besides I wanted to at least give the illusion that I knew what I was doing before I started. I could perhaps get a grip of the computers and systems? I therefore contacted the hospital in which I was going to start work in August and arranged shadowing for the last three days of the timetabled fortnight. Surely that would be sufficient to learn the ropes. Besides, I had booked a holiday.

So the concept of shadowing is, I'm sure, not alien to most. You meet the person who is doing the job now and learn the ropes from them in a sort of accelerated apprenticeship. These days a formal shadowing period is mandatory for all newly qualified UK doctors about to start their first job as a Foundation Year 1 doctor. In the first two years doctors change jobs, and often hospitals, every 4 months. Whilst more senior doctors provide consistency the most junior doctors are just supposed to learn how everything works on the first day of their new job following changeover. Whilst the role is the same, the process is completely different. Every hospital orders even the simplest investigations differently. Even the continuation sheet, the blank pieces of headed paper which form the majority of the patient notes, is found in a different place on every ward resulting in a rather tedious new game, every four months, which I can only describe as a combination of 'fetch' and 'hide and seek'. Having spent my last 10 days of freedom from the yoke of perennial employment ordering rum cocktails and perfecting my suntan, I arrived early in the morning at the little district general hospital on the first Monday of August for three days of shadowing. I was shortly to be a fully contributing, tax paying member of society at the rather advanced age of 27.

Hospitals are traditionally divided into large inner-city teaching hospitals and smaller district general hospitals, which usually serve the surrounding villages and townships. Larger hospitals provide many more services and expertise and generally suck up the complex and difficult medical problems. The district general hospitals therefore tend to refer their more complex patients to the larger teaching hospitals but are usually just as busy and more commonly provide better teaching opportunities, due to being less well staffed, for junior doctors. I would be starting off in a district general hospital located maybe 10 miles from a big city teaching hospital. I managed to find the ward which would be my base for the next 4 months when not on-call. My first rotation was in acute medicine and so my base ward was the Clinical Decisions Unit; a 20-26 bedded unit (depending on whether they opened the extra capacity) on the top floor of a ubiquitous hospital tower block. Usually the majority of patients admitted to hospital ended up there from the Acute Medical Unit where they were either treated and discharged or were stabilised before moving on to a different ward.

'Can I help you?' said a small rotund lady in her late 50s in a dark blue uniform. Her question despite offering help was probably closer to 'who are you and why are you here?'

It is always tempting when an officious looking nurse asks you this question to answer: 'No thank you' and wait for them to ask the question they really want to: 'who are you and why are you here?'

'I'm Tom, one of the new doctors starting this week, I'm here for my shadowing,' I said a little defensively.

'Oh, I think Jane has been waiting for you. I'm Anne and I'm the ward manager.'

'Hi, err Tom,' I repeated awkwardly.

Anne walked me around the corner where a slim ginger girl was sat in blue scrubs on the desk swinging her legs.

'Heyyyyy' she said elongating her greeting, 'you must be the new house officer?'

'Yes, Tom.'

'So bit of an issue Tom,' she started, 'so sorry. Bit shit. The other house officer is off on long term sick and they haven't been able to get a locum, slash,' Jane performed a slashing motion with her hand whilst continuing to nonchalantly swing her legs, 'couldn't be bothered to get a locum.' She seemed almost pleased to be telling me this.

'Right.'

'So you are kind of it today,' she extenuated the 'it' and carried on swinging her legs. A pregnant pause followed as it dawned on me that my shadowing period was rapidly evolving into two days of unpaid work.

'It?'

'Yep, there is no one else to cover the ward'

'Are you not here?'

'Love to, but I'm just finishing nights. Sorry I'm a bit', she paused to think of a word, 'fractious,' she added, 'I'm on my fourth can of Red Bull and 5th night on call.'

'Right.' I purposefully raised an eyebrow in protest.

'Listen let me take you down to Jo the medical workforce lady,' Jane said. 'They can at least try and get a doctor to cross cover from a different ward to give you a hand.' She sounded quite uncertain. 'Then I can give you a quick once over how the ward works. It's Dr Masood this week on-call and he is a bit...,' she paused again to consider her word, 'particular.'

She skipped past me, caffeine fuelled, and marched down the corridor. I struggled to keep up as she strode through several doors and passages into the bowels of the hospital. She fired questions from over her shoulder and I tried to reciprocate in between having to break into a trot every few steps to keep up. We descended down several flights of stairs before Jane finally pushed through a plastic sheet and seemed to burst free of the main hospital building. We skirted along the wall before crossing the consultant car park filled with expensive German cars. We entered the door of, what looked to be, a collection of port-a-cabins connected together. I walked past several office spaces where secretaries were turning on their computers and swigging cups of coffee as they prepared to start another day in this glorious institution of our nationalised health system. We finally approached a closed door.

'Ah,' Jane said, 'it's a Monday. She isn't here on a Monday.' She set off back through the corridors across the car park and back into the main hospital building with me trailing behind her like a loyal sheep dog. We returned to the ward and sat down next to one of the computers.

'This is a bit rubbish Tom but if I at least give you a quick tutorial on the computers you can get cracking. I mean you get this all in the induction on Wednesday but you won't be able to do much for the next two days unless,' she paused and typed in her password and username into the log-in page, 'anything,' she muttered incoherently. The computer booted up and we waited. 'Sorry the computers are a little slow.' I wasn't sure who she was apologising to. 'So if I give you my passwords you can use them until you get your own. To log onto the main system my password is 'drjane1'.'

'Okay, easy to remember.'

'You'll need to write them down as there are a few more.'

'Right.' I grabbed a piece of paper out of the printer and wrote drjane1.

'To log on to order blood tests or X rays you'll need this programme.' She clicked on a desktop icon and the programme slowly loaded. 'My password for this one is drjane4.'

'Why four?'

'All the programmes require passwords. It is fine when you start because you just have the same password for them all. They all expire at different times though and you have to put in a different password every time you renew it.'

'Got it. DrJane4,' I repeated scribbling it on my piece of paper.

'This one here,' she hovered over the desktop application with the mouse cursor, 'is for viewing the X-rays. That one is 'drjane7'. I won't open it as it takes ages to load. And this one is for viewing blood tests and scan reports but not X-rays. That one is drjane9,' she paused and tickled her chin, 'or is it 8?'

'I'll try both.'

'Okay the last one is for e-prescribing.'

'E-prescribing?'

'Yep, all the prescribing is done on the computers now. It is actually kind of useful as you can change a prescription from any trust computer so if you are the other side of the hospital and a nurse, say, wants some paracetamol prescribing you can just do it without walking all the way over.'

'Oh cool. Probably useful for IV fluids and stuff too.'

'No all IV fluids and syringe drivers are still on paper charts.'

'Oh.'

'And it also takes ages to log in so if you just want to change one thing it can be a pain.'

'Right.'

'So I can give you my password for this too but just tell the consultant when he arrives as I don't think you are really allowed to prescribe on my log-in. He might be able to get hold of a locum log-in for you.'

Jane continued helpfully explaining things and I heard the noise of her rapid caffeine fuelled details but I felt my mind already wandering. I was ready. Sure, this was supposed to be a formative experience for me but the NHS needed me. There was no hiding in the cupboard. I was as keen as a razor's edge covered probably in some sort of condiment. I was here to save lives. I am a doctor.

Second day

I am a shit doctor. In fact I am not even a doctor. I am an administrative assistant with a medical degree. I am the equivalent of training an astronaut to spacewalk only to send him to Cape Canaveral to do the photocopying. Doctors diagnose and treat people. I don't do this. I find notes. I scribe for my consultant. I pull the curtain around the patient's bedside on ward rounds and then pull it back when the consultant is finished. I load up the drug charts, X-rays and blood tests for the consultant's perusal on computer systems that could be no more unnavigable if they were in Dutch. I request the blood tests and bleed the patients when the phlebotomist writes 'patient being washed' on the top of my request and decides not to bother coming back. I chase the results from the blood tests that I perform and the ones the phlebotomist occasionally does too. I insert peripheral venous cannulas. I insert them again when they mysteriously, according to the nurses, 'fall out'. I prescribe drugs, not of my own volition but because the consultant tells me to. I then change my prescription when the pharmacist tells me the dose is wrong.

I order scans and investigations, which I often cannot fathom any clinical reason for, but have to convince the radiologists that not only is it absolutely essential for the management of my patient but must be done today. I get shouted at by my consultant when I tell him that the radiologist says the scan isn't indicated. I go back to the radiologist to say it is indicated and this is why. I get abuse from the radiologist that I am a woeful doctor with all the clinical acumen of a dead fish. I agree and the radiologist agrees to perform the scan. I then take the request form (a piece of paper) to the radiographers. I then chase the radiographers when the scan doesn't happen immediately. I then chase the radiologist to report the scan.

I ask every other specialty in the hospital to review my patients, at the behest of my consultant, even though I am not quite sure why their review is required. If the specialist isn't based at my hospital I phone another hospital. I stay on hold for 30 minutes and then get told there is a fax referral form. I spend twenty minutes looking for the referral form and then fax it. I then fax it again when it hasn't been received/was lost/the fax machine didn't send it. I phone the other hospital's team back when they have received the fax (again spending 15 minutes on hold). When they tell me they don't need to come to see the patient but request some investigations I phone them back (anything to listen to that magnificent on-hold music) to update them on the results of the investigations. When my consultant is annoyed that I obviously didn't make the gravity of the situation clear to the specialist I phone them back again.

I fix printers. I fail to fix the printer. I phone the information technology helpdesk to fix the printer. I spend another 15 minutes on hold. A man comes to service the printer a week later. Several hours following I attempt to fix the printer again. I fail again. I give up and decide to print at a different computer on the adjacent ward. I try and fix that computer. I phone the IT helpdesk again. I spend more time on hold.

I even occasionally interact with a patient but only to perform all manner of unpleasant procedures on them from sticking a tube down their nose to a finger up their bum.

Finally, I write lengthy and tedious discharge summaries on patients I don't even know, using only the notes that I can't decipher due to the NHS' absolute reliance on a somewhat antiquated mode of recording facts known as 'handwriting'.

Whilst at medical school we were judged by how well we performed in exams; both clinical and written. Now I am judged by how quickly I can organise an MR (magnetic resonance) scan for an octogenarian who might have had a mini-stroke. I am judged by how well I can remember every patient's blood test results as the IT system runs at the speed of a quadriplegic sloth and my consultant is too impatient to wait for me to log in and read the result to him. Any attempt at using any initiative is quickly clamped down on:

'What are the blood test results?' the command would bark.

'I didn't repeat them today.'

'Why?' the consultant would ask accusingly.

'Well they were normal yesterday.' I would say under your breath, 'and normal the day before, and the day before that and the day before that.' I have absolutely no doubt, in fact, I would bet my kidney on it (ironically which is what I'm testing the function of) that they will be normal again today.

'This patient is on diuretics and needs daily blood tests,' the consultant would snarl.

So despite the patient being an elderly frail lady admitted to hospital because she was unable to cope at home. Despite her severe dementia which means she has to be essentially restrained to be bled. Despite having had several normal blood tests (as well as several failed attempts) and as a consequence her body surface area is now one giant bruise, despite the poor old dear reaching this terminal juncture you definitely want another blood test? But you found yourself instead mumbling:

'I'll make sure they are done today.' And you would add it to your burgeoning jobs list.

'Let me see the X-ray?' you would hear him shout irritably. And then you would stand, the full team, consultant in the centre, registrar dutifully by his side with me the house officer peering in from the wings, clutching notes and lists and scan requests trying to operate the CoW[1]. Our forced proximity was heightened by the awkward silence interrupted only by the metronomic tap of the consultant's foot as the X-ray took a whole cretaceous period to load up on the screen. And then finally:

---

[1] CoW is a computer on wheels. This can be as simple as a laptop on a piece of fibreboard attached to the deconstructed base of an office chair or a more elaborate IT solution. It is usually the former. Our trust renamed the CoWs to WoWs; workstations on wheels following a rather unfortunate incident. There were two CoWs on our ward; one with a larger screen known as big CoW and one with a smaller screen known as little CoW. When the senior consultant called from across the ward that he wanted the big CoW on the ward round and the rather obese ward sister replied 'coming' a patient's relative (who I believe worked as a sexual discrimination lawyer) complained to the management. This was quickly followed with the edict from high that all CoWs were to hitherto be known as WoWs. Everyone still refers to them as CoWs. Including the fat ward sister.

'Hang on a minute. That looks different from last time,' the consultant would declare. Everyone would look at each other in fake bemusement. By now we had lost the will to live never mind care. 'I wonder whether we should repeat it?' the consultant would add.

The registrar and I would glance at each other to try and discern whether this was a request, rhetorical question or a query he wanted us to answer. Then the registrar would notice that I had clicked on the wrong patient and we were looking at Mrs Biggins' X-ray in bed 14 by mistake.

'Are you capable of performing this simple task Dr Pearson or do I have to find you something which is more befitting your limited capabilities?' The scathing remark would reverberate. Meanwhile red faced with embarrassment I would wonder whether now would be the appropriate time to remind my learned superior that my name is Parsons. 'How are you feeling?' he would ask when we finally got to the patient.

'Go away you moron,' the reply would ring out from the crumpled heap of skin and bone lying in the bed.

'Hmm… is she demented?' the consultant would ask with careful deduction?

Tempting though it was, to suggest that she appears lucid, you would instead opt for a further re-cap and close scrutiny of the patient's notes from the very beginning of their admission; an indecipherable set of hieroglyphics that spanned months. And then finally we would land at his last ward round, usually the day before yesterday. 'Ah yes, she is a terminally demented nursing home resident, awaiting social services placement.' he would say, 'I remember now.' And with that another little part of you would perish when you realised that you had another thirty odd of these to go before the ward round could be considered complete. 'Shall we move on?' And the whole charade would recommence at the next patient's bedside. 'Wait.' The commanding instruction would shout. We would all look up like Meer cats sensing danger. 'We haven't checked the observation chart.' And off I would scurry, unleashed from my trap, to try and locate where the nurses had hidden the observation chart and the metronome of foot tapping would start up again.

23

As time progressed the sense of disempowerment and boredom is joined with aching feet, a dry mouth and a keen hunger. A bubbling frustration would form threatening, at any point, to explode in a rant of expletives at your consultant followed by repeatedly hitting my forehead against the closest immovable object. The drugs trolley perhaps. I felt like the first proper clinical decision I was going to make as a doctor would be to section myself to avoid the rest of the ward round. If only I could find the section forms in the ward filing cabinet which was so disorganised it could be hiding the lost Ark of the Covenant.

When the ward round was finally over I would find myself again queuing outside the radiologists' office to be shouted at for a procedure I didn't want, order or understand because my consultant insisted it must be done, again and today. The patient's health apparently, their life even, invariably hinged on this one test and tomorrow would not do.

'Do you realise what time it is?' the radiologist would ask.

'Yes I am aware it is 4 o'clock.' I am sufficiently intellectually developed enough to at least understand the concept of time. It's just whilst you've been sat in the dark all day, I have only just finished the ward round. Getting the radiologist to agree to perform the scan required turning the patient's history into the most creative work of fiction since Tolkien sat down one afternoon and decided to write a story about a small person. Naturally when the porter came to take the patient for this concocted 'emergency' scan the patient, at death's door you understand, was outside having a fag. The porters buggered off and they missed the scan slot.

'Well can I not get it re-arranged?' You would plead with the booking clerks.

'Not today you can't love, I'm all booked up, I can do next Wednesday?'

'Next Wednesday!? No way, I'll be crucified. Please?' you would beg. 'You must have something sooner?'

'Okay, okay, listen I can put them on the reserve list for tomorrow. But only because it's you.'

'Thank you. Thank you, Thank you.' It was like a Death Row reprieve. I had long ago taken to prostituting myself to middle aged booking clerks in order to get things done; male or female.

And just when you think you've cracked it, just when you might finally be seen to be a 'good' doctor in the eyes of your consultant, the MRI machine would break down again. A non-functioning imaging machine is not a valid excuse for not being able to obtain a scan. It will be my lack of initiative to blame, not the machine. Not even the contractors are culpable despite earning triple what I do per hour and milking every last pence by being slower in repairing the bloody thing than a parkinsonian tortoise who, unlike all other tortoises, does not subscribe to the theory that slow and steady wins the race.

Ah but what about the on-calls? Surely it gives you some reprieve from the tedium of ward work? Sure, occasionally the house officer gets a go at clerking, but usually when on-call they have to do ward cover. This means that instead of covering just your own ward, you get to cover everyone else's too. At night you would prowl the hospital in the early hours. Endless monotonous tasks would descend on you with the touch of a button by a militant senior nurse via a wireless network to your PDA: a system, I can only presume, designed to be worse than the dreaded bleep where you can at least bat away some of the rubbish over the phone. Undoubtedly this tracks your progress around the hospital like Pac-Man gobbling his tasks or the most dreadful ever version of Pokémon Go. All done under the auspices of some anecdotal evidence that it improves patient care or makes my life easier but probably being used to assess which doctors aren't working hard enough.

'Of course it has nothing to do with monitoring and auditing how quickly jobs are completed or whether that position will be gapped next rotation,' the managers would tell us on the mandatory training days I would have to attend on my days off which I wasn't allowed to claim back as study leave.

Every doctor remembers their first day, because the days after merge into one endless ward round of administration. Because you are not judged on what you know, your rapport with the patient or your diagnostic acumen but your ability to get a scan result, write prompt discharge summaries, get social services here and get your patients out of hospital to keep up with the ever increasing demand at the front door. I am a shit doctor.

When the chips are down

'Oh Kwashiorkor?' he chuckled.

Chuck was a Ghanaian doctor who came over to the UK. I'm not sure Chuck was his real name but he seemed to like it. Whilst he had been a doctor for many years, and was the equivalent of a consultant in Ghana, he was working as a senior house officer; the grade above me. He was diligent, compassionate and had an excellent knowledge of the diagnosis and management of infectious diseases from his experiences in working in several states in Africa where such diseases are common. Naturally he hoped for a better life for his family and in return he assisted in filling the gaping holes in the provision of acute care which continue to plague the NHS. Despite that he wasn't in a training job and had considerably less opportunities for progression than British graduates, he went about his craft with a permanent smile, chuckling at everything, however banal. The exception to this was any attempt at humour directed towards him which he would reply with a quizzical look, a raise of his eyebrows, a shrug and then return to the permanent grin. I'm not sure whether it was a cultural lack of understanding, just a general lack of understanding or whether I told crap jokes. This reversed humour polarity seemed to manifest in any social interaction with Chuck. I could tell the bloke I was off to lunch and he would laugh sidesplittingly.

'Hello Mrs Hemmingway,' I heard Chuck saying in his undulating African tones from behind the curtain. 'I'm just going to feel your belly?'

'Get off me you golly-wog bugger,' the delirious 94 year old Mrs Hemmingway shouted. Chuck pacified her and emerged from the curtain with an embarrassed shrug. The nurse left behind proceeded to deliver Mrs Hemmingway a fierce lecture on ethnicity and diversity. 'Well I don't care if it's not very nice I don't want to be fiddled with by any bugger.'

Chuck and I were on-call together. It was my first set of 'clerking on-calls' as opposed to just covering the wards. This meant I finally had a chance to take a history, examine patients and form a diagnosis; the pillars of clinical medicine. It also meant a short reprieve from the tedium of my base ward; the Clinical Decisions Unit. During your clerking on-calls you would see all the new admissions transferred to the medical team from the Emergency Department or those sent in from their GP. Clerking new admissions involved taking a full history, examining the patient which hopefully culminated in a diagnosis. You could then request some discriminating investigations and start treating the problem. The consultant on-call would come round twice a day and you would 'present' the case to them. The consultants usually took a potted history again, quickly examined the patients once more and ensured everything was correct. More importantly they decided who really needed to come into hospital and who could be managed, if possible, as an outpatient. Inpatient beds are precious resources these days.

In the AMU at this hospital there was a walled rectangular station in the centre of the unit. The inside perimeter of this central rectangle was lined with desks where the clerking doctors sat to do their paperwork along with the nurse in charge and the ward administrator. The desks were littered usually with notes, reference books, folders, investigation request forms, coffee cups and decimated tins of chocolates occasionally gifted by thankful patients. This central reservation was surrounded on all sides by cubicles of unwell patients referred from the Emergency Department. The rectangle had just had installed high frosted glass walls which made it somewhat of a refuge, safe from the prying eyes of patients or the tapping feet, cross-armed stare of their relatives. A posture, if you are unfamiliar with it or have never performed it, is simply decoded as 'how much longer do I have to wait' and is usually accompanied with an increasing volume of muttering, 'tutting' with accompanying facial tic. During particular busy times patients would often encircle the entrance to our little clubhouse like hungry demons; wanting to, but unwilling to, cross over the hallowed boundary, as though in fear of spontaneous combustion. The particularly desperate would adopt siege tactics forcing negotiation, ceasefire and a full and expansive clarification of their relatives' medical problems complete with a full explanation of what all these medical terms mean. Whilst many of you might think that you have a right to this explanation, try telling this to the other sick patients who have been deprived of a doctor for an hour for the purposes of your enlightenment.

In less busy more sanguine times though it was the designated place where doctors could write up their notes, check X-rays, drink coffee and talk about last night's X-factor performances. The computers, despite being incapable of checking the results of any medical investigation, are quite good at checking the cricket scores. Mostly it is somewhere out of the hustle-bustle where one can gather one's thoughts and where I, as the most junior of junior doctors, could seek the opinion of my more senior colleagues like Chuck.

These eagerly sought alternative views are typically odd enquiries about the best investigation for a patient or what drug to prescribe. Should we recommend in our management plans that the patient needs to be admitted? Can the patient feasibly go home? Hospitals really are dangerous places. For the elderly and demented, hospital is a place of hard floors which brittle bones don't bounce on. It is where glasses and false teeth go missing and bright lights and unfamiliarity increases the waxing confusion of dementia. The dire food leaves you starving and constipated. The quite preposterously undermanned nursing staff leave you sat in your own excrement. Then someone like me, as the junior doctor, can make a total hash of your medication which your GP has been conscientiously tweaking for the past ten years. Or, worse still, someone fails to make that important inpatient referral or to spot the impending sepsis caught from the warm ripe cauldron of some of the fiercest bacteria in existence, resistant to many of our antibiotics (except the ones that give you hosing diarrhoea and are so toxic that daily blood levels must be taken to ensure you don't leave hospital with your kidneys melted or even more deaf than when you arrived). One must always be careful when admitting a patient to hospital; once you're in, you tend to stay in. Many a patient has skipped into hospital through the front door and been carried out the back in a wooden box due to our medical mischief. Hospitals are dangerous places.

This was my 4th day on-call which usually come every 5 weeks or so as a block of 5 days. Despite the 13 hour shifts and the hard work, I was enjoying myself and for once learning something, other than how to fix a printer. Over the past few days our little rectangular harbour in the middle of the department had become a little forum of education. No question was too stupid for Chuck and he encouraged you to talk about your patients so all could learn. It had happened twice this week already where one of the doctors would chirp up to another, in a blasé type of way, 'I've got an interesting one here.' Or, 'I've just seen this one…' Doctors busily writing notes, or checking X-rays or blood results all stopped what they were doing and listened; all eager to learn.

There are unwritten rules to this naturally. Firstly you really can only pipe up about a patient who has presented with something rare or different or exciting or perhaps even something mundane but in an amusing fashion; any X-rays of an object self-inserted in a body cavity were always worth a look for instance. Providing the on-call group with a running commentary on the magnificence of your daily mundane toil is tedious and so generally frowned upon. Finally, as doctors are essentially all ultra-competitive geeks, the proposer of an interesting case must, under no circumstances, turn their advice or opinion into a game of belligerent curative top-trumps of who knows the most.

'Hi,' I said addressing the sister-charge. She was busy trying to scan notes and get some patients out of the department and to the ward. Allegedly the Emergency Department were beating on the door to transfer patients before they breached the hallowed four hour target,

'Yep,' she said trying to keep her irritation out of her voice. She had been a nurse for twenty years and I was a first year doctor in my first month of work.

'I can't find the notes for cubicle 8,' I explained, 'I looked in the slot and……' She cut me off by thrusting them at my chest wordlessly. 'Thanks, I said meekly.

I read the ED three line clerking:

35 year old male
PC- Abdominal swelling

HPC- several days of increased abdominal swelling, no pain.

Imp ? Constipation.

Plan- admitted medics, blds, cannula.[1]

The patient's name was Graham McPhee. I made my way over to cubicle 8 and popped my head around the drawn curtain.

'Hello doc,' hailed a voice almost cheerily. I looked at the notes and looked up the patient and then looked down at the notes. DOB 4/9/1975. I looked up again. Must have the wrong cubicle- he looks 60.

'Sorry sir,' I apologised, 'wrong cubicle.' I quickly took my leave before I was asked any difficult questions like when they were going to be seen or where the toilet was; both of which I did not know the answer to. I walked back to the ward sister.

'Graham McPhee,' I read looking at the sheet, 'what cubicle is he in again?'

She looked at me, rolled her tongue over her bottom teeth and below her bottom lip. She was undoubtedly attempting to infer I was retarded.

'That one,' she said in a palsied voice pointing at the one I had just come out of two feet behind me. Perhaps her equality and diversity mandatory training had expired.

'Oh.' I looked at the sheet again as she brushed past me muttering something inaudible. I seethed inwardly and smiled. 'Sorry, thanks for all your help.' I said not bothering to keep all sarcasm from my tone. I walked back to the cubicle.

'Mr McPhee?' I said.

'Yes.'

---

[1] PC meant presenting complaint, HPC; history of presenting complaint and Imp; clinical impression or diagnosis (not that the patient was a constipated but small homunculus). Blds meant routine blood tests and cannula being a plastic tube that is put in your vein for a short period for the purpose of giving intravenous medications or fluids.

'Lovely,' I said warmly, 'I've found you'

'Yes, that's me, you want me then after all?'

'Well 'want' belies certain fallacious connotations,' I smiled. He looked back at me vacuously. I didn't explain. 'So how can I help?'

'He's all blown up.' A deep voice boomed from the corner behind me.

I turned around to see an elderly lady sat in the corner. Her hair was peroxide blond and the texture of wire-wool pulled back into a somewhat haphazard ponytail exposing the truthful grey roots. Wild hairs escaped from the front seemingly defying gravity as though powered by a charge of static electricity. She wore a matching tracksuit in brand but not colour; a white top and black bottoms seemingly meshed together by the presence of complementing stains of varying longevity. The look was topped off with a pair of well-worn white trainers and bilateral sovereign rings. Before I attended my equality and diversity mandatory training it would have been tempting to hypothesis that the presence of a 'sovvy ring' coupled with the scraped back hair of the Croydon Facelift as 'chav positive' signs.

'Hi Tom's my name, and you are?'

'I'm Graham's mother.'

'Lovely to meet you,' I courteously replied making a small bow of my head. I stalled as I tried to remember what I had just said. 'Oh yes…blown up. What do you mean blown up?'

'My stomach,' Graham replied.

'Yeah it's his stomach,' the voice echoed from behind me. I looked around again.

'Do you mean it has increased in size?' I clarified, 'become distended?'

'Yep,' Graham concurred.

'Tell me about it?' I ordered keeping my questions as open as possible.

'It got big over the past few days dinnit?' The voice from behind me boomed again. I felt just the slightest hint of impatience wash over me.

'Let's see if Mr McGhee can tell us in his own words,' I smiled again at her.

'It's McPhee.'

'Of course it is,' I smiled back through gritted teeth, 'Graham?'

'Yeah it got bigger over the past few days,' Graham confirmed in an echo of his mother. I made a noise indicating I would like him to continue.

He looked like death warmed up. His skin was a slate grey. His hair was long, thinning and strewn messily across his gaunt face. He seemed to be wearing the matching respective halves of his mother's tracksuit. If you laid them down next to each other they would look like a set of bathroom tiles. He wore a stained baseball cap with the label of some industrial company adorned to it. It didn't look as though he was quite ready for dentures yet but certainly not far off; grey is never an encouraging colour for teeth. His trainers looked abnormally huge against his scrawny legs and he had managed to deposit a neat line of mud up the examination couch. Well I hoped it was mud.

'Ok when were you last well,' I pressed after another pause as Graham failed to take the prompt.

'I haven't felt well for a while.'

'Oh?' One didn't need a medical degree to see that.

'But my stomach blew up a few weeks ago and now it's massive so thought I better had go to hospital.'

'I think he needs a good shit because he rarely ever goes,' the booming voice of medical authority cackled from the corner. Her voice was deep and gravelly from years of cigarette smoking, her fingers tinged an unpleasant yellow from the tar. Her lips and philtrum, whilst occasionally revealing a set of pearly white false teeth, were wrinkled and puckered like a twitching anus delivering successive movements of verbal excrement. She looked in her 70s but had probably ridden that hard Paper Round of life before handing over the bicycle for her son to take over. I again smiled and hoped the smile wasn't denigrating to a haughty sneer. The patient cackled at her own joke triggering a violent coughing fit.

'Ok Mr McPhee, has this ever happened before?' I attempted to continue.

'Nah,' he emphasised with a shake of his head.

'Never happened before?'

'Nope.'

'Tell me about your bowels? I think there was some indication that they were a bit sluggish?' I continued glancing only briefly back towards his mother not wanting to encourage her further.

'Yeah, I try and go a couple of times a week but sometimes it is hard to push out.'

Enough, I thought, scrambling around the edges here. I know what is wrong with Mr McPhee. His dishevelled appearance, his distended abdomen but emaciated body and his slate grey appearance. He was an alcoholic in decompensated liver disease. I knew exactly what I would find when I would examine him too from top to toe; the yellow tinge of jaundice in his eyes right the way down to the lack of sensation in his feet. The swollen abdomen is the most obvious sign seen in decompensated alcoholics due to fluid collecting there; known as ascites.

'Do you drink much alcohol I asked?' I was expecting a guilty nod of affirmation, perhaps him avoiding my gaze like a discovered child. Furthermore I was expecting his mother to pipe up in the corner and tell me how much cider he was actually drinking per week; dobbing in her loved one, while standing on her pious podium of moral superiority issuing a damning judgement and casting herself as some sort of amateur alcohol abstinence practitioner. Despite all of her care and council she had been craftily hoodwinked by the devious macerations of Graham's secret hard-core boozing.

'No, not really, I don't like it.'

'You never drink alcohol?' I said surprised.

'Well I've tried it years ago.'

'Well how much would you drink in say a typical week?' I persisted.

'Nothing I suppose.'

'Nothing?'

'No.'

'He never drinks doctor,' the voice from the corner confirmed hammering the final nail in the coffin of my sole diagnosis.

'Right,' I paused, 'well that seems quite confirmatory.'

Patients often lie about how much they drink. Just the two bottles of vodka a week when it is two bottles a day. Just the odd can meaning the odd can of super strength lager, on every odd hour of the day. Most typically, the vague alcoholics often admit to a bit of boozing, but they deny the extent of the problem and absolutely that their drinking is a problem. Some alcoholics are the opposite and seem very happy to admit their condition. I had met patients when I was a medical student who seemed almost proud of the fact that they could consume enough alcohol to make a rhinoceros topple. But I had never had anyone I suspected of drinking heavily frankly refuse that they drank at all. Which meant two things; one; he was probably telling the truth and two; I had no diagnosis yet.

But there was no blood from the back passage, no weight loss, Mr McPhee had always been thin. No vomiting, no urinary symptoms, no cough no abdominal pain (but felt generally achy). He opened his bowels at least once a week. He denied smoking, intravenous drug use, needle stick injuries or precarious sexual activities with ladies of the night. There wasn't even a family history of anything in particular with his father dying of 'smoking and coal mining but mostly the coal mining'. I was seriously running out of ideas. He didn't work, didn't smoke, lived with Grotbag in the corner and spent his time playing computer games on his games console.

'So Mr McPhee is there anything else, anything at all that I've missed?' I asked rather exasperated.

'Nope.'

'Nothing?' I sounded almost desperate.

'Nope.'

'Well I suppose I'd better examine you?'

'Sure, sure.' He sat up in an expectant manner and started unzipping his striped tracksuit top in expectation. I stood up and turned toward his mother in an attempt to emphasise my intention to examine her adult son. Despite the addition of, what I hoped was, a quizzical eyebrow she sat there nonchalantly watching me.

'Could you give us a moment?' I asked.

'Oh....' She paused having apparently not considered that her 35 year old son may not want to be poked and prodded in front of his mother.

'Graham, I'll pop out for some fresh air, alright?'

'Okay.' He seemed completely indifferent to his mother's presence either way.

Graham continued to remove his various layers of sports tops and lay down on the examination couch, infirmed with his giant belly protruding in front of him like the unintended gravid consequence of a catastrophic scientific experiment.

I examined his hands and pulse quickly before jumping straight to his eyes. I looked carefully, altering his face to different angles to alter the light. He assisted me looking straight ahead intently. Jaundice[1] is normally seen first in the eyes before being apparent in the skin. I could see no evidence. Not even with the eye of faith could I detect even the slightest tint of yellow. I moved down, his breathing was normal, his heart sounded normal too. Not too perturbed by the lingering whiff of body odour, proceeded onto his large belly.

I shifted him from side to side and attempted to percuss his abdomen to detect any shifting fluid, a clinical sign known as shifting dullness[2]. It definitely seemed to be fluid in the abdomen rather than gas. I looked closer at his skin carefully inspecting for other signs of liver disease.

We were reaching the point of the consultation; the diagnosis, the verdict. Like a judge the good doctor has listened to the facts from the patient, asked appropriate questions of clarification and conducting a thorough examination of the evidence presented before him. Now the patient must listen to the decree.

---

[1] Jaundice- is the clinical sign of yellowing of a patient's skin and eyes due to high bilirubin levels in the blood. It can be due to too much bilirubin production, an inability to metabolise the bilirubin due to a defective liver or the inability to drain the bile containing bilirubin into the guts.

[2] Shifting dullness- a clinical sign involving percussing the abdomen to detect the presence of ascites. Fluid sounds dull in comparison to air in the abdomen sounding tympanic. A similar technique is used in the chest to detect pleural effusions; fluid between the lung and chest wall.

'I'll be honest Mr McPhee,' I started my explanation as I turned on the tap in the corner of the cubicle and rinsed my hands, 'I'm not really sure what is going on.'

I continued to rinse my hands as I considered the potential diagnoses. I knew the causes of abdominal distension from the famous medical school mnemonic; the seven famous 'fs': fat, faeces, foetus, fibroid, fluid and frightfully big malignancy. Well it is certainly not fat. He probably isn't pregnant and probably doesn't have uterine fibroids; I'd look forward to my guest spot on Embarrassing Bodies if he was. I didn't think he was full of shit; in the literal or figurative sense although the jury was still out on his Mother. Fluid in the abdomen is most commonly due to liver failure, which I could see no sign of, so that left frightfully big malignancy or, as it is also known; cancer. That's it. He must have cancer. Poor bastard. Still I needed to do more tests to confirm my diagnosis.

'Um,' I crooned attempting to seem erudite, 'so your tummy has blown up because there is fluid in there.'

'Fluid,' he parroted.

'Yes fluid. Often that means a trouble with the liver but I can't work out what that trouble might be. Sometimes it might be due to some other things though,' I said deliberately vaguely, 'we'll have to have a look.'

'Ok, fine,' he shrugged quite nonchalantly.

'We'll probably have to try and draw some fluid from the abdomen with a needle and analyse it under the microscope. We should also do a scan of the abdomen to see what is going on.'

'Fine,' he looked over my shoulder as his mother walked back in the room stinking of cigarettes. I repeated my plan of action to her.

'Any questions?' I asked.

'Will he be staying in?' the mother asked.

'I think that is best for now just so we can work out what's going on.'

'Where will he go from here?'

'Probably to the gastroenterology ward or to the Clinical Decisions Unit.' We said our goodbyes and I opened the door to the sight of the tea trolley. 'Just in time for a cuppa tea,' I said jovially.

Never mind that your son's got cancer at least you caught the tea trolley.

'He won't have any anyway, he's a fussy bleeder, white, five sugars for me though love,' she retorted to the healthcare assistant.

'Sure you don't fancy a cup Mr McPhee?'

'Nah. I don't like tea. Or milk.'

'Hmm,' she said with her mouthful of tea, 'he only eats chips.' I ignored her and gave her another saccharine smile before manoeuvring past the tea trolley to action my plan. I stood outside the cubicle and paused. What did she say? After a moments deliberation I waited for the tea trolley to move on.

'Sorry? What was that?' I asked seeking clarification.

'What?'

'You said something about what Graham eats?'

'He only eats chips,' she repeated innocuously.

'He only eats chips?!' I looked at Graham as he lay back on the couch grinning at my surprise to this rather absurd revelation. 'Chips and what?'

'Just chips, it's all I like,' he explained grinning inanely. 'With ketchup.' He added as though trying to convince me that this transformed it into a wholesome meal.

'Well you must eat something else?'

'Nope he did when he was a young boy but since the age of 14 he's only eaten chips.'

'Only eaten chips?' I repeated incredulously. 'Chips?' I was aware my voice was raising higher and higher with each utterance. 'So you eat no other food?' I asked deliberately seeking final clarification.

'Nope,' they echoed together.

'You can't survive on just chips. What do you drink?'

'Irn Bru mostly.'

'Chips and Irn Bru?' I paused, 'oh my giddy Aunt,' I said like a despairing old Headmistress. Doctors should be non-judgemental to all the various ways their patients decide to kill themselves but I was struggling to comprehend how anyone in their thirties could just eat chips

'Yep,' Grahams smirked. He seemed almost proud.

'But what do you get your protein from?'

'Well,' his mother decided it was high time for her to chip in (boom-boom) again.

'I did once take him to a doctor, 'cause I was worried with his fussiness, like, he gave him these milkshakes but he doesn't like milk,' she explained. 'I've tried to get him to have other things but he won't eat them. I just gave up.'

'I see.' I really didn't see. From my secluded middle class upbringing, whilst I could understand obesity, or drinking or smoking yourself to death, surviving off a diet of chips was just ludicrous.

'You know I think he's got one of them, you know, eating disorders,' she diagnosed.

I was hardly listening anymore. You can't survive with no protein. How would you make your essential amino acids? How would you have enough protein to maintain a circulating volume? He wouldn't be able to make enough albumin, he would have a decreased oncotic pressure. That would explain why he had a swollen belly. All the fats would probably give him fatty liver disease too. He might even be cirrhotic. My thoughts sprinted away in front of me.

'You've got what the children in Africa have got,' I blurted triumphantly

'Oh?'

'You know when their belly swells because they get enough food but it's just rice not protein.' I was rambling my thoughts sprinting off ahead.

'No doctor I don't eat rice just chips,' Graham replied with a confused expression.

I ignored him and, like any first year doctor, I quickly made my excuses and rushed out of the cubicle back to the haven to find a grown up. Chuck was writing his notes up and closely inspecting an X-ray of someone's abdomen on the computer.

'Hey Chuck,' I said flustered.

'Hello,' he chuckled.

'Chuck, what do you call that condition those kids from Ethiopia get with the swollen bellies?'

'Oh Kwashiorkor?'

'I've just seen a 37 year old man who I think has Kwashiorkor,' I announced. I saw the other three doctors sat busily writing their notes look over and glance up like startled lambs. They leaned in, their interest aroused, to hear the story.

Stroking...my foot

Jeremy Kyle was wittering his sanctimonious judgements. Bianca-Leigh was insisting on her fidelity despite the lie detector saying 'that was a lie'. I was watching inanely in a post-prandial daze sipping my turbo-charged coffee; three teaspoons of cheap instant, supplied courtesy of the NHS, and enough sugar and milk to make it just palatable enough to drink.

I was sat on the sofa in the Doctors' Mess with the orthopaedic senior house officer and registrar who were whooping and baiting Bianca-Leigh via the screen for her confirmed infidelity. It had been the first sit down I had had all day. I was absolutely shattered. I rubbed my temples in an effort to try and resuscitate my tired mind. There was still 4 hours of my on-call shift remaining. With a further shift tomorrow followed by three days of night shifts, the concept of being on-call was quickly losing its novelty.

My pocket wailed like a banshee. The pager demanded my attention with the characteristic bleeps of an impending emergency. The orthopods quickly checked their pagers and, just as quickly, returned to Jezza without glancing in my direction.

I had been a doctor for well over two months and I had yet to attend a 'proper' emergency. All my peers were regaling me of the many medical disasters they had attended and vividly describing their heroic, yet usually unsuccessful, role in the patient's eventual demise. No one has a chance of surviving a cardiac arrest unless they have an obvious easily fixable cause. Fact. When a doctor asks you if you want to be resuscitated in the event your heart stops, do yourself a favour and agree.

The last emergency, which I was on the cardiac arrest team for, the nursing home had sent in because the patient was un-responsive. I raced to the Resuscitation Department in A&E where the patient lay on the hospital gurney having been transferred from the ambulance stretcher. By virtue of my sprinting down the stairs I was second on the scene with the ED senior house officer and paramedic.

'What's the story?' I was mimicking word for word what I had watched George Clooney say on ER. My composure was slightly impaired by my exercise induced shortness of breath.

'This is Mr Latimer an 84 year old gentleman,' replied the paramedic, 'he was found unresponsive in his chair at the nursing home this morning. His observations are all normal but he is unresponsive to pain or loud voice.'

'I'll go and organise a CT scan for his head,' said the ED SHO indifferently yawning. The nurse on scene started getting intravenous access by inserting a cannula into his arm. The patient didn't flinch.

'Mr Latimer, this is the doctor,' I said with a significant sense of self-importance. I paused, entirely for effect, 'open your eyes.' I commanded in a deep booming voice like a faith healer.

I was as astonished as everyone else when Mr Latimer's eyes slowly opened and he turned to face me. I was pretty sure that qualified as a miracle. Maybe I'll get beatified like Mother Teresa?

Following a small discussion with the patient it turned out he found the loud screeching cackling of the health care assistants who worked in his nursing home quite irritating. So he closed his eyes; perhaps to partially attempt to block out the unwanted sensory stimuli, perhaps partially in protest. When they attempted to rouse him, such was his quest for peace, he decided to continue his protest. So they called the paramedic.

'Did you not think to open your eyes when the paramedic arrived?'

'Well I was in too deep by then,' Mr Latimer replied. 'Many of the residents are deaf and you could fire off artillery shell and they wouldn't notice. For some reason, despite my age, I seem to be cursed with decent hearing. I'm in the nursing home because my legs don't work. Those women just bicker and shout they are so loud and abrasive and I hear it all and because of my legs I'm unable to escape from them you see. I'm afraid to say doctor today I reached the end of my tether.' There goes my audience with the Pope.

With my attention diverted pleasingly from Jeremy and Bianca-Leigh the monotone switch board operator provided additional detail by droning through the pager voice amplifier 'FAST positive ETA 7 minutes'.

The health service had been putting adverts on the television for a year or so about the FAST campaign. The posters, depicting what the public should do in the event of a stroke, also adorned the walls of our Acute Medical Unit, A&E and Acute Stroke Unit. If your face suddenly drooped, your arms became weak (or lost feeling) or you were suddenly unable to speak then you were to come to A&E immediately.

Immediately is indeed the imperative part. After all, people had been having strokes for years and eventually even the stoic English gentleman made it to hospital when he realised that the reason he had lost the ability to speak and move the left side of his body for the last week might not be because he overdid it on the brandy at the quarterly golf club dinner.

What is a stroke? A stroke is when the blood supply to the brain is interrupted somehow. The term comes from a 16th century term where the sudden random attack was through to be due to the 'stroking hand of God'. Stroke describes the clinical presentation but whilst the patient's symptoms can be very similar regardless of the cause, the aetiology can be very different. Broadly speaking stokes can be due to an artery in the brain becoming blocked or due to bleeding from a vessel into the brain itself; therefore simply subdivided into haemorrhagic or ischaemic.

Strokes can be pretty catastrophic life altering events. A person can be a normal, fully functioning member of society one minute to becoming fully dependent on carers, unable to speak, unable to move, unable to understand people. I occasionally hear people utter that we, as human beings, only use 10% or 1% or however many percent of our brain capacity. This is complete rubbish.[1]

---

[1] If the brain had spare capacity it would, in theory, be able to take the vascular assaults of stroke. So how is it people can recover some function having had a stroke? Well the brain is able to re-organise itself and form new pathways in some instances, a concept known as neuronal plasticity, but often a lasting disability remains.

With regard to the ischaemic strokes or blockages in the arteries the mainstay of treatment until recently was good old Aspirin. The same stuff that was used in the form of willow leaves for millennia. But there has been some fairly recent progress with some studies showing that you have a better outcome in terms of the degree of your lasting disability if you have a treatment called thrombolysis.[1] The studies showed that the treatment, an injection, had to be given in fewer than 4 $^{1/2}$ hours of your symptoms starting for the benefit to outweigh the risks. The intricacies and minutia of this fantastically interesting and complex condition is more than enough to justify an entire speciality dealing entirely with this condition; Stroke medicine.

Unfortunately it isn't as simple as just giving everyone with a stroke the thrombolysis treatment. As I said strokes can also be due to a bleed from one of the vessels in or encircling the brain. The vessel therefore isn't blocked but leaks blood into the surrounding brain tissue putting pressure on it, starving it of oxygen and therefore mimicking what you would see if there was a clot. If you gave thrombolysis, a clot busting drug, in this situation it would be rapidly catastrophic. The bleed would get bigger and bigger squashing the brain in the skull and rapidly causing decreased consciousness and death. So how do we differentiate a bleed from a clot? We scan them. A CAT scan, CT scan or computerised axial tomography scan of the head.

So this could be it for me; a real emergency as well as my first chance to give brain saving thrombolysis treatment. I arrived just to see the paramedic wheel the patient into one the Emergency

---

[1] Thrombolysis was a treatment first used for patients having myocardial infarctions (heart attacks). They found that a bacteria called Streptococci activated a protein in the blood stream that dissolved blood clots. One clever fish one day must have thought; if thrombolysis clot busting drug worked for heart attacks when the clot stops the blood flow to an area of the heart muscle, then why couldn't it work for strokes when the clot blocks blood flow to an area of the brain?

Department cubicles. One of the ED doctors stood outside the cubicle looking disinterested in the blasé way of a battle-scarred healthcare worker who had seen it all before.

'What's the story?' I asked (cue George Clooney again). The ED doctor snorted and looked me with an expression of 'are you for real?'

'This is Mr Hargreaves, he is 42 year old, previously well male, with sudden onset, right sided weakness and right sided facial droop. Observations normal in ambulance. ECG was sinus...'

'Looks stable, onset was within 3 hours, I'll go and organise the next CT head slot,' the ED doctor said yawning, 'sorry mate I don't know your name?'

'Thomas,' I said hesitantly, 'I'm the medical FY1.'

'Parv, ED Reg,' he declared himself, 'does the Medical Reg know?'

'Not yet. She went to intensive care an hour ago and I've not seen her since.'

'Can you assess and do the NIHSS score? Don't dilly-dally just in case we need to thrombolyse.' He sauntered off in the direction of radiology presumably to speak to the radiology registrar to organise the CT scan. .

'No problem,' I replied. I had no idea what NIHSS meant or what the score was. I had a quick look at his sheet. Blood pressure was normal, temperature normal. His heart trace (ECG) looked normal. I looked up and had a quick glance at the patient lying on his back. With short, cropped, receding hair and a vast midriff he looked like Baloo from the Jungle Book. The right side of his mouth closed and drooped. It seemed devoid of muscular tone with his cheek sagged extenuating his jowls contorted into a grimacing, grumpy, Victorian gargoyle.

'Hello Mr,' I paused prompting myself from the ambulance sheet, 'Mr Hargreave my name is Dr Parsons.'

'Hullo,' he replied

'So what's been going on?'

'I can't move the right side of my body.' He spoke out of the left side of his mouth with the right corner remaining closed.

'Your right arm and right leg?'

45

'Yep.'

'How did it happen?'

'Dunno.'

'Well what were you doing at the time,' I tentatively enquired.

'Watching tele.'

'Okay, and when did it happen?'

'After me Tea'

'And when was Tea?'

'Half six-ish.'

He was being peculiarly non-forthcoming, I think if I suddenly lost the ability to move one side of my body I would be more than a little perturbed. In fact I'd be pretty desperate for someone to do something about it and really quite quickly. I wondered whether the stroke might have affected his speech or comprehension.

'Move your right arm for me,' I commanded again almost anticipating a further miracle. Nothing. The same occurred with his right leg. It would seem he did have a complete inability to move the right side of his body; what we call a dense hemiparesis.

A porter arrived standing behind me.

'Hi,' I said smiling as I continued my exam, 'CT?'

'Yep, whenever you're ready Doc.'

'You're going for your scan Mr Hargreave,' I explained, 'I'll see you when you're back.' I walked over to the phone whilst I was waiting and updated the Medical Registrar on-call.

'Hello Med Reg,' a recognisable strong female Yorkshire accent answered.

'Donna?'

'Yep.'

'It's Thomas.'

'Who?' she replied.

'The house officer?' I thought I heard her mutter an obscenity.

'Yep?' she said just failing to keep the impatience from her voice.

'I'm at the FAST call in A&E.'

'And...?'

'I was hoping I could discuss the case with you?

'Just give me the headlines will you?'

'He's got a dense right hemiplegia and right facial droop.'

'Right facial droop?'

'Yep.'

'But right hemiplegia[1]?'

'Yep.'

'Are you sure?'

'Err…,' I hesitated.

'Have you examined him?' I could tell her inference was 'you haven't examined the patient properly'.

'Yes, briefly, he is being scanned now.'

'Is he within 4 hours?'

'Yes 1 and a 1/2 hours currently.'

'Good. Go and examine him again,' she paused, 'properly.' The intonation was obvious and I felt my face flush despite being told off on the phone.

'Okay. Definitely. Absolutely,' I was like a frenetic but ineffective puppy trying to please but just being an annoying distraction.

'And do the NIHSS score. I'm stuck in HDU with someone who keeps trying to die on me and the SHO is up to his ears on AMU. I'll be down shortly. Parv, the ED Reg is down there too. Ask him if you have any dramas.'

'Donna?' I asked.

'Yep.'

'What is an NIHSS score?'

'National Institute of Health Stroke Scale. It's a fucking tick sheet to assess the stroke severity and see whether the patient can be thrombolysed. It's colour by numbers. Ask Parv. I really need to go.'

'Okay thanks bye.' She had already hung up.

'It's normal,' he said dismissively.

'Normal?'

---

[1] Hemiplegia is the complete inability to move half of your body, is one arm and one leg in comparison to paraplegia which is the inability to move ones legs. A hemiparesis is a weakness in one half but not the complete inability to move them.

'Yes totally normal, another normal scan,' the Radiology Registrar confirmed yawning.

'Definitely no bleed though?'

'Nope, normal, normal, normal,'

I had pestered the radiology registrar, what with my keenness to please Donna, midway through his reporting to get a quick decision on the scan result. I had invaded his darkened chamber of banks of computer screens of endless blurry images. Radiologists are the specialists in interpreting X-rays, CT scans, MR scans; all sorts of pictures really with all sorts of clever contrasts. These picture machines have revolutionised diagnostic medicine ever since the first ever X-ray. The radiology registrar is the most senior radiology doctor in the hospital, out of hours, who agrees to perform the scans as well as reports the images when they have been performed. They guard 'their' machines possessively. Daily battling with radiologists is, as I have probably mentioned, *de rigueur* for the most junior doctors in hospital.

So the CT scan of the brain was normal. I knew that in an embolic (clot) stroke the CT scan can be normal initially as the part of the brain affected has to be starved of oxygen for a period of time in order to be seen on the CT.

I found the NIHSS forms; essentially a tick sheet to grade the severity of strokes. You have to examine the patient to assess different parts of the brain including sensation, higher function, visual field losses, speech and limb power. He had a complete inability to move the right side of his body. He also denied being able to feel anything on that side including his face. It was as though someone had joined a vertical line down the whole of his body with the complete loss of all function on the right side. A total right hemiparesis and hemi sensory loss. I worked out the score and looked at the exclusion criteria for thrombolysis and I was pretty sure we were a go. Finally I would get to thrombolyse a stroke and hopefully fix Mr Hargreaves. Time to ask the medial registrar to come down and rubber stamp my medical prowess.

'Hi Donna,' I said in an attempt to get her attention. I had called her down to ED. She walked straight past me ignoring my salutation and picked up the phone, looked at her pager and entered the number of the person who was obviously trying to contact her.

'Med Reg,' she said when someone picked up the phone. 'I'm in the Emergency Department already...I know...I know...I've come down to see him! I......,' she paused intentionally for effect, 'know!' delivered through gritted teeth. 'I am going to see him now alright!'?' she said in a raised voice before slamming the phone down. She turned to me.

'Fucking nurses,' she said by way of explanation, 'right, are we thrombolysing or not?'

'He meets the criteria,' I said.

'Does he want it?'

'He doesn't seem to care,' I explained, 'about anything.' Donna took a packet of chewing gum out of her pocket and popped a piece in her mouth. Without offering it to anyone else she replaced the packet. She grabbed the tendon hammer which I had recently used.

'Let's go and see him.'

The NHS hospital standard tendon hammer seems to be uniform in every hospital. A white plastic stick with a metal disc encircled with a rubber washer just in case you miss the patella tendon and whack poor old Granny in the shins. If you do manage to hit the patella tendon you activate a nerve impulse which is sent to the spinal cord which stimulates the unopposed contraction of the quadriceps and the lower leg jerks.

The other end of the white stick shaft of the hammer is a sharpened point. It was commonly used for eliciting something called the plantar reflex or Babinski sign first discovered by the French neurologist Joseph Babinski in the 19 century. This clinical test is used to distinguish damage to the spinal cord or brain tracts from damage to the peripheral nerves or lower motor neurons. Both are required to move your legs. The reflex is elicited by dragging a blunt instrument over the outside edge of the sole of the foot. If there is damage to the upper motor neurons (the brain or spinal cord) the big toe extends up toward the head whilst if no damage is present the normal response is that the toes curl over. Why not try it yourself; endless hours of fun with loved ones in the comfort of your own home.

I'm not sure if this sharpened point at the end of the hammer was specially designed for eliciting the plantar reflex but I can see no other purpose for it. I seem to remember a wizened old neurologist, who came down from his ivory tower (or headache clinic- they spend 98% of their time in one or the other) and forbid us from using it for this purpose. Apparently it is too sharp and doesn't reliably elicit this important sign but instead elicits a withdrawal response due to pain. A key or a pen lid is preferable. I remember someone asking this old erudite Professor of Neurology:

'Prof, I understand why we look for the Babinski sign but why does it actually occur? I mean why if the lesion is upper motor neuron does the toe curl up and vice versa?'

The professor removed his horn-rimmed glasses and polished them slowly on his handkerchief. 'No idea, if you find out let me know.'

'How are you getting on Mr Hargreaves? Any change?' Donna asked. She looked at him up and down without saying anything. I thought I saw her briefly smirk.

'No still the same,' he blurted through the corner of his mouth

'Try and move this leg.' The patient's face strained with effort as though his leg was pinned by a ton weight which he was unfortunately incapable of moving.

'Ok,' Donna reassured giving him permission to stop trying, 'and the arm?'

Nothing. It lay lifeless next to his torso.

'Can you feel me touching you Sir?' Donnas asked making sweeping movements up and down his arm and leg with her hands to crudely test his sensation.

'No.'

'Just going to take your shoes off Sir.'

The patient accepted with a grunt of consent as Donna removed his shoes to be greeted by an odious waft. His socks smelt like they doubled as sleeping bags for decomposing mice. Donna, unruffled, pulled off his socks. She grabbed the sharp end of the tendon hammer and jammed it into the heel of his foot. The foot, that foot, so limp and lifeless only moments ago, jumped up in the air with its attached leg and body in painful recoil as the patient gasped with the shock.

'Bloody hell!' I exclaimed somewhat unprofessionally in front of the patient.

Donna smirked, 'I think you'll be fine Sir. No need for any clot busting medications.'

I followed her back to the central nurse's station. She sat at one of the computers. I was speechless as I mulled over what I had just witnessed.

'What is his hospital number?' Donna asked bluntly.

I read it out. She tapped in the patient's details into the entry bar on the electronic patient record. There were little columns on the top of the screen so you could view previous attendances. Categories included were icons like patient details, clinic letters, discharge summaries, pathology and radiology. You click on one and a submenu scrolls down to see all the different blood tests or radiological investigations or clinic reviews, essentially everything ever done on that patient in that hospital trust. But only for that trust. If the patient had previously been to a different hospital you would be usually unable to access anything done their, at your hospital. In fact most trusts, to my knowledge, seem to use completely different software systems to access the huge amounts of medical data generated every year. As soon as you work out how to use one, you move jobs and have to figure out a completely different system.

The government has been trying to join up these fragmented systems. The benefit is obviously the prevention of duplication, the ability to quickly see patient's medical history when they didn't know it or were too incapacitated to relay it, as well as to communicate between different specialist teams. Also the potential for research, if we get a handle on all this data, would be vast and of huge benefit to the British public. So far, after several years, all our glorious politicians have managed to pull out the bag is a few wasted billion pounds and....well...that's it. Currently the whole project is in a state of abandonment following years and years of delays and excuses. The computer system, I believe was called Lorenzo. One could certainly conclude that Lorenzo isn't a computer system at all but a fat balding man from Essex who has spent the entire NHS computer budget on handmade suits, bottles of Dom Perignon, Cuban cigars and his giant yacht which is currently moored in Montego bay with half the Playboy mansion whilst our able politicians scratch their heads and wonder where all the money has gone.

It is quite ridiculous when you consider that sometimes these trusts are located within 10 miles of each other so if a patient calls an ambulance it is often to the whim of the ambulance controller where you end up. You might order a patient a bucket load of tests unbeknown to you that some identical poor prick like me ordered the same ones last week only a stone's throw away. Of course you could ask the patient, but half the time they haven't the slightest clue what the test is for, never mind the result.

Let's not forget that most doctors seem to suffer with the most terrible OCD and will only believe something if it is emblazoned in text, ordered by their own hot little hand and present and signed right before their very eyes. One way around this conundrum is to phone up the other hospital and get them to fax you a copy. This is how I commonly spend my days. There is a reason why the rest of the English speaking world abandoned fax machines in the 1980s[1].

Donna found the patient's details and clicked on the radiology tab showing us all radiology examinations Mr Hargreaves had

---

[1] How to get patient's old results NHS style: Usually you phone up the hospital and have to listen to 5 minutes of automated messages from the switch board about how one shouldn't come to their hospital if you have diarrhoea and vomiting. When you finally get to speak to the switchboard operator you then have to wait another 10 minutes for the doctor you're trying to get hold of, just to answer their pager. Finally they have to print off the piece of information and fax it to my fax machine but not before I have sent them a test fax so they can be sure I am actually a doctor not someone trying to get hold of their wife's sexual health screen results to prove my suspicions between her and Mr Dedicoat who lives down the street at number 47. When something inevitably breaks down in this sequence and you have to conduct the entire charade again you just eventually lose the will to continue and repeat the test at your trust. A cosmic waste of resources.

previously had at this trust. The column dropped down the page like a trap door on a hangman's platform. He had had over 400 radiological investigations. Everything was there, from ultrasound scans to MRIs to CTs to chest X-rays to knee X-rays to foot X-rays to hand X-rays to face X-rays. He had had over 12 CT heads from what I could count. He had attended more outpatient clinics than I had in all my years of medical training. He had been to A&E on at least 42 occasions in the last couple years with a fantastical array of complaints. I wouldn't have been surprised if he had even claimed pregnancy.

All the radiological tests have a report typed up from the radiologists, I scrolled through them all, most of which had been done under the premise of a stroke; everyone seemed to be normal. He seemed to have been in last month for a weeklong stay with a dense hemiplegia affecting the right side. No one recovers from something so debilitating so quickly only to get it again 5 minutes later.

'Looks like he's the latest member of the Munch bunch,' Donna commented. 'Make sure you write a discharge summary giving the discharge diagnosis as Munchausen's Syndrome. If he is still there you can tell him he can go and you will refer him to psychological services.'

'Still there?' I questioned.

'They usually scarper when they have been busted,' Donna explained.

The term Munchausen's condition is derived from Baron Karl Friedrich von Munchausen an 18th century German nobleman who reportedly told the most fantastically ridiculously impossible tales about himself. It was first described by Richard Asher in the 1950s in the British Medical Journal in patients who present with self-harm:

> 'Here is described a common syndrome which most doctors have seen, but about which little has been written. Like the famous Baron von Munchausen, the persons affected have always travelled widely; and their stories, like those attributed to him, are both dramatic and untruthful. Accordingly the syndrome is respectfully dedicated to the Baron, and named after him.'

You may ask, like I did when I first heard the condition, why anyone creates an illness for themselves, learns about its symptoms and signs and how it is managed enough to be able to trick exceptionally intelligent doctors, like me, so as to go to hospital repeatedly? Well they say it is because they long for the care and empathy, respect, comfort, attention, interest and investigation that being ill affords you. Thy often have other co-existing psychiatric conditions and being a patient fills a void for them.

Just by way of explanation, so you don't point accusing fingers at husbands around the country, it is quite distinct from hypochondriasis. Here people actually believe they have something wrong and often over-exaggerate the severity of their problems such as my sore throat must be throat cancer, my cough must be tuberculosis. The Munch-bunch (an affectionate term usually used by doctors who are commonly fooled by them), by contrast, are quite aware they are exaggerating or just plain story telling.

Despite this, patients with Munchhausen's often have had appendixes removed or gall bladder surgery or invasive biopsies, scans, or scopes. In fact millions of pounds has been spent on time, inpatient care, invasive procedures and desperate treatments to try and diagnose this crafty cluster who know full well that if they are busted they can wander down the road and play the same game at the next hospital by virtue of the fact that governments make it quite impossible for hospitals to effectively communicate with each other.

An even more incredible subset of this bizarre condition is those suffering from Munchausen syndrome by proxy. Here, instead of fabricating illness in themselves, the perpetrator will induce illness in others. This can be in the elderly, whom they care for, or even their own young children. The victim almost always is unable to declare for themselves what is occurring. By doing this the perpetrator gains attention and empathy, not as a patient but as a distressed relative. Munchausen's Syndrome by-proxy has gained considerable notoriety as it has been considered previously as the cause of cot-death or sudden infant death syndrome. It is a murky business indeed and often requires covert surveillance when suspected.

I quickly wrote as detailed discharge summary as I could, as Donna had requested, and printed it out in order to give to the patient. I took a moment to consider what I would tell the patient. I thought it best not to be too judgmental. My main aim was to get him to accept psychological help. I had no idea whether he would show up for the referral or even whether psychological therapies were effective in Munchausen's syndrome.

I decided to take one of the Emergency Department nurses with me for support for the patient but also as a witness for the conversation that I anticipated might be difficult.

'Hi,' I said tentatively to one of the staff nurses whom writing names on the whiteboard. 'Can I borrow you for a moment for a chaperone?'

'Yep,' she said not looking at me but continuing writing.

'I'm Thomas the medical house officer.'

'Who is it for?'

'Mr Hargreaves, cubicle 8.'

'What has happened with him?'

'We are sending him home,' I confirmed.

'I thought he was FAST positive?'

'He is making it up,' She turned and stopped writing.

'Reeeaallllllyyyy?' she said sensationally, 'wow, let's go and see him now.' I filled her in on the story and scan results and his many attendances to hospital with nothing wrong with him.

The curtain of the cubicle was drawn when we approached. I pulled it back to find the empty couch. The monitoring leads dangled off the end of the bed having been disconnected. The cardiac monitor attached to the wall would normally have alarmed when the leads were not connected to the patient's skin but the monitor had been switched off.

I looked at the nurse.

'He's gone.'

I'm afraid you'll be leaving us now

'Hi it's Tom,' I wearily answered my pager.

I glanced at my watch. It was nearly midnight; still nine and a half hours to go. Nine and a half hours of prescribing paracetamol, sleeping tablets and warfarin. Nine and a half hours of reviewing demented patients who had fallen out of bed. Nine and a half hours of replacing cannulas and prescribing intravenous fluids.

You may have guessed, from my tone, that I was feeling a trifle disillusioned with my work. The honeymoon period of becoming a doctor, strutting around the hospital and feeling all important when someone bleeped me had well and truly gone. I had swiftly come to realise that the work of a junior doctor was long, relentless, badly paid, and, in the most part, intellectually lacklustre. I felt like one could train a chimpanzee to do 95% of my day-to-day tedium. Whether on-call (more like beck and call) or on my base ward of CDU; it was the same tedious chasing, sorting and phoning with the end goal being, not to make the patient better, but to get them out of hospital; a similar but not tantamount end point. I rarely felt I made even the slightest smidgeon of difference.

'It's Zoe,' a female voice said. I must have zoned out slightly. I paused, prompting her to continue; 'The night reg.'

'Sorry Zoe,' my tired brain leapt into life, 'running a little empty at the moment. How are you?'

'How are the wards?'

'Well, you know,' I paused not knowing whether it was prudent to disclose my abject boredom, 'same, same. Full of old ladies waiting to be discharged to a care home.' Hopefully I didn't sound too mutinous.

'Are you busy?'

'Steady.'

'Can you possibly come down to AMU? We are getting smashed. It would be great if you could clerk a few patients. It's nearly midnight and we still have at least 10 to be seen before the post take ward round; some were transferred from A&E several hours ago and are still waiting.'

'Of course,' I replied, 'happy to be of some assistance.' And I meant it.

Walking through the double doors of the AMU was like walking through the gates of Hades without the fire but with slightly more wailing; mostly emanating from cubicle 4 for some reason. I cautiously made my way to the central rectangle of solace narrowly avoiding a nurse speeding towards the sluice with a full sick bowl and getting run over by a full commode heading in the same direction. The department was perpetually being labelled, day after day, as 'the busiest I had seen it' but this really was the busiest I had seen it. Worse still, considering the late hour, it showed no signs of abating. Zoe appeared from behind a cubicle wearing rubber gloves carrying a collection of blood bottles.

'Great, you're here, thank you so much for coming down.' She was broken off by another loud wail from behind the curtain of cubicle 4. I glanced in the direction poised to leap in and assist. 'Young girl; fifth presentation in as many months with severe abdominal pain, had every investigation you could think of but no one can find the reason. Waiting 'gyne' outpatients,' she explained.

'I see,' I commented, 'well I'm happy to help.' Although I wasn't quite sure how much help I could be amongst this terminal state of total chaos. We walked into the central solace.

'Right I need to go to A&E to start BIPAP[1] on lady, Zainab is here clerking,' Zoe gestured in the doctor's direction, who continued to write like her hand was on fire, with her gloved hand still carrying

---

[1] BIPAP- Bilevel Positive Airway Pressure is a form of Non-invasive ventilation which is essentially a giant mask that is strapped to the face to assist in the oxygenation of the blood and the removal of carbon dioxide which, if left to accumulate, can make the patient quite acidotic and sleepy. Commonly used for the treatment of COPD; an almost exclusively smoking related disease

full lab bottles of blood. Zainab was a Foundation Year 2 Doctor (FY2), so a year more experienced than me. 'Nadia is already in A&E and there are about 6 here in the department that need clerking and a further 6 or so in A&E that currently we don't have room for.'

'Right,' I said. I was pleased to get stuck in. All hands to the pump.

'If you could see the chap in cubicle 3, he has chest pain, no ECG changes, first trop[1] was normal, will need second trop in 12 hours, so around now. If you could take that and then ask him if he doesn't mind going home, even at this late hour.' She shook the bottles in her hand, 'assuming the second trop is normal.'

The ECG or electrocardiogram, or EKG if you're American and/or can't spell, is a process of recording the electrical activity of the heart over a period of time. This spits out several wiggly lines on a 12 inch pink piece of paper. Interpreting ECGs is something that all medical students learn but some, usually surgeons, tend to forget rather quickly. Hence the joke: 'What does an orthopaedic surgeon hold that is pink, hard and 12 inches long?' Or for those with a research bent: 'What do you call two orthopaedic surgeons reading an ECG? A double blind study.'

When a patient has chest pain, by looking at a particular segment of this electrical activity, called the ST segment, one can often tell whether one of the coronary arteries supplying the heart muscle is severely blocked, compromising the blood supply to the heart and so requires to be opened with a stent as soon as possible.

I sat down in the rectangle and reviewed the patients clerking documents and medical history. The patients name was Henry George and he was 50 years old. He was obese, had diabetes, high blood pressure and high cholesterol and had presented at 2pm that afternoon to the Emergency Department with central crushing chest

---

[1] Troponin- Troponin is a type of protein involved in muscle contraction. It is found in skeletal muscles as well as the heart muscle. There are specific heart muscle types that can be detected in the blood when there has been heart muscle damage. The detection of this has revolutionised the diagnosis of heart attacks.

pain that had started around mid-day. I glanced up towards the direction of cubicle 3, hoping to catch sight of the man, only to see the curtain drawn. The A&E doctors had taken a blood test which had been in the normal range. The blood test, called troponin, looked at the breakdown product of heart muscle so one could infer, when it is raised, that the heart muscle was damaged in some way. This is usually, but not exclusively, due to a lack of blood supply to the heart muscle secondary to a blocked coronary artery. However the level of troponin in the blood takes time to rise which is why a further blood test had to be taken 12 hours later. I stood up grabbed the notes and made my way towards the cubicle doing my best to ignore the wailing emanating from next door.

'Knock, knock,' I said loudly outside the closed curtain. I heard no response so I poked my head around. A large, heavy set man's eyes flicked towards me. He lay on the hospital bed topless. There was a glistening sheen of sweat trickling from his close cut balding head. His skin was a cadaverous pale grey. An empty sick bowel perched precariously on his sizeable gut.

'Hello Mr George. My name is Tom, one of the doctors. How are you feeling?' I asked.

'Pretty grim Doc. The pain has come back pretty bad,' he clenched his hand in a fist and raised it to the level of his heart.

'Describe it?'

'Like a vice gripping me.'

'Ok,' I paused, collecting my thoughts. 'How long did you have it before you came to hospital?'

'Couple of hours.'

'What happened then?'

'They gave me some morphine in the A&E and the pain went.'

'How bad is the pain now?'

'Worse than when I came in.'

'For how long?'

'An hour or so I guess. I spoke to the nurse who was going to try and get you to prescribe some more morphine.'

'Sorry about the delay Mr George,' I said, 'it's a bit manic around here at the moment.'

'Tell me about it Doc.' He glanced in the direction of the interchangeable sobbing and screaming still occurring in the cubicle next door.

'Have you ever had pains in your chest before, excluding today?'

'A few times Doc, not quite as bad as this. I thought it was just trapped wind.'

'Still smoking?'

'Afraid so.'

I glanced up at the monitor which was supposed to display a continuous readout of the patient's heart rate and rhythm. A yellow light flashed and a flat line trace showed indicating that the patient was either in cardiac arrest or that the monitor wasn't plugging in. The loud ping intermittently emanating from the monitor, unnoticeably adding to the cacophony of noise in the department, coupled with the quite evident fact that the patient was still speaking to me led me to the conclusion that the monitor leads were not attached to the patient. I picked up the three wires dangling from the machine.

'Sorry Doc, I had to disconnect them to go to the lav to be sick.'

'No problem,' I smiled. I reconnected the leads and immediately saw how fast the heart was beating. A further glance showed what seemed to be quite obvious ST segment elevation[1]. 'Shit,' I muttered just audibly.

'Doc can I have something for the pain?'

'Of course Mr George I will just see to that. We might need to repeat a full ECG too.' I tried to sound calm. I didn't want to alarm the patient further but I felt the flames of fear licking my inside. He

---

[1] ST Elevation- The ST segment on an ECG is the interval between depolarisation (the electricity flowing through the heart so contracting the heart muscle) and repolarisation (the heart cells returning to a resting state ready for the next flow of electricity). When the heart muscle is acutely and severely damaged this interferes with the electrical balance of the heart resulting in the ST segment of the ECG elevating. This is commonly due to a severe heart attack.

looked sick. 'Yes the heart trace,' I added inanely looking into thin air and doing little to settle the patient.

I popped out from behind the curtain my thinking distorted by panic; if he was having an ST elevation myocardial infarction he was essentially having a serious heart attack. We don't manage serious heart attacks in this little hospital.[1] So this meant I was dealing with an emergency. My first proper emergency and despite all my years of training and life support courses, despite all my in-depth knowledge of the pathophysiology and natural history of coronary artery disease and despite all my self confidence in my own ability I was going to do what every junior doctor does. I was going to find a nurse. And the first nurse I could find. She was a young pretty brunette who was hanging a drip on an elderly lady found on the floor of her bungalow.

'Are you looking after cubicle 3?'

'No it's Rachel looking after cubicle 3,' she replied racing past me to do another job.

'Where is Rachel?' I implored following her.

'Not sure, on her break I think.'

'Great,' I replied throwing my hands up in the air struggling to keep the sarcasm and panic out of my voice, 'is anyone covering her?'

'Not me,' she almost sang.

'Can I help love?' A rather rotund female healthcare assistant in her 30s with short pinked cropped hair and a nose stud waddled out of a cubicle having overheard our conversation and probably sensed my fear. She was known affectionately in the department as 'Coops' and was carrying soiled sheets in her large plastic gloves. She dumped her bundle in a plastic bin liner and peeled off her gloves. 'Cubicle 3 is it?'

---

[1] ST Elevation heart attacks or ST elevation myocardial infarction or STEMI was previously managed with thrombolysis (exactly how stroke is currently managed). It was show though that if a catheter could be put into the heart and the blocked artery unblocked, firstly by inflating a balloon and later by inserting a stent, patient outcome was much better.

'Yes please, he isn't very well Coops,' I added, 'I need a repeat ECG.'

'Can you not do ECGs yourself?' she asked.

'I can never get a clean trace and I always put the leads on the wrong way round.'

'Well let's get you sorted then love.'

We walked toward the cubicle together and I remember feeling an overwhelming sense of relief that I had bagged some help when a piercing siren of 'bings' and 'bongs' cut through the background noise of the department. It seemed to be originating from behind the cubicle. I could feel everyone's heads swivelling towards me. I stood motionless, my mouth opening and shutting like a morose fish. The healthcare assistant swept the curtain aside and I glanced at Mr George fearing what I already knew to be the case. The department sister raced towards us but I remained, fixed in position.

'He's in VT,' the sister shouted, 'get the crash trolley, call cardiac arrest.' I heard my own rote learning resonate again in my head; "VT or ventricular tachycardia is a type of regular fast heart beat that arises from improper electrical activity in the bottom chambers of the heart," yet still I remain transfixed.

'Tom, Tom!' Coops shouted, 'start chest compressions.' The directness of the request seemed to bridge the gap between my brain and body. With a few skips I was immediately at the side of the patient where the bed had been lowered flat. I started performing chest compressions. The theme tune to 'Nelly the Elephant' reverberating through me with each compression of cardio-pulmonary resuscitation like I was in a bizarre Carry-On film. Whilst I had never performed CPR on a real person, I had performed it endless times on a resuscitation manikin (commonly called Resusci-Annes) and had sung to myself the theme tune of this timeless cartoon, at the behest of the Resuscitation Officers, as the tempo was exactly the same as one should aim to provide whilst performing CPR to allow for good cardiac filling. Now it just seemed frankly inappropriate considering the lifeless man who was ebbing away in front of my very eyes.

Before I knew it I was being asked to cease temporarily in order for pads to be stuck to the man's chest and connected to a box which lay on top of a red trolley at the patient's side.

'Stop compressions,' a voice shouted, 'stand clear,' it said again. I glanced up to see Zoe standing at the foot of the bed. Zainab was stood next to the red crash trolley with her finger on the defibrillator.

'Shocking,' she said clearly, 'stand clear.' She pressed the button delivering 150J of electricity into the patient who visibly jolted with the shock. I walked forward a pace to start CPR again.

'Wait,' Zoe's voice commanded. The heart rhythm and normalised with the complexes narrowing and patient stirred.

'Hello Mr George,' said Zoe loudly. The patient stirred and looked around quizzically. 'What happened Tom?' she added. 'I left you alone for 5 minutes.' I stood there feeling like the puppy that had pissed in the pantry. I opened my mouth to try and explain and shut it again. Guilt washed over me. I wasn't sure what I felt worse about; not getting help sooner, being completely ineffectual and useless and totally reliant on a healthcare assistant who had a fraction of my education and training.

'Err,' I mumbled.

'Tom I need you to get on the phone get Mr George transferred as an emergency for a stent,' Zoe replied, 'when you're done with that speak to critical care for an escort. We need to get the patient transferred to Resus.'

'Yes, of course,' I was spurred into action and spun around. I paused briefly and spun back again. I thought I should probably at least wish my first emergency well on his way; 'I'm afraid you'll be leaving us now Mr George. There is nothing more we can do here. We'll be sorry to see you go though.'

He looked at me aghast, eyes as widened to the size of dinner plates.

'I'm going to die?' he blurted astonished.

I looked at him a little confused before I realised; 'I mean to go to another hospital. To get the stent to mend your heart attack.'

I glanced at Zoe who rolled her eyes at me.

Surgery

The practice of medicine is a thinker's art the practice of surgery a plumber's.

Martin H. Fischer

To Infinity....and beyond

'Thomas you'll be starting on nights tonight so once you've finished the computer training go home and rest. You can do the on-line training modules whenever you get a moment,' the surgical rota coordinator said.

I actually felt thankful that someone had at least noticed. What job tells you when you turn up for your first day, at 8am, that you had actually turned up for work 12 hours early but, whilst your here, we have some stuff we need to go through with you before you come back and work all night?

It was the first day of my next rotation as a Foundation Year 1 doctor. I was now the surgical house officer on a colorectal surgical firm. I had enjoyed surgery at medical school. I had learned about all the surgical conditions and what operations are required to fix them. I had learnt the complications patients have after surgery. I was even considering whether a career in surgery was for me.

Whilst at medical school I had visions of my time as a surgical house officer; scrubbing in to assist with complex intestinal surgery. Having a bash at an appendix or two. Wrong again. My time in medicine had taught me that I am a junior doctor; an administrative assistant with a medical degree. I had absolutely no doubt that the chances of me performing any surgery, whatsoever, were slim. Anorexic even. In fact the absolute opposite of the patients that inhabited the re-enforced floor of our ward; as a regional bariatric centre. So what variety did I anticipate to my role as a surgical house officer? Well I might request from the same radiologists a slightly different type of scan on a slightly different type of patient who was in hospital for a slightly different reason but the remainder was the same delightful repertoire of junior doctors up and down the country; phlebotomy, cannulas, discharge summaries and chasing. And getting 'educated' that I wasn't doing any of these particularly effectively.

I left the induction early, without requiring prompting from the surgical coordinator who undoubtedly had forgot. Not living far from the hospital, I went home and tried to sleep. Due to the diligent incompetence of medical staffing I had no forewarning that I would be on-call all night and I had, the night before, decided to go to bed early so I would be on top form for my first day in the new role. I consequently struggled to fall asleep again to properly rest for being up all night. I tried all my usual tricks; watching Loose Women and reading Biochemistry textbooks. In a fit of exasperation I had to turn to my e-portfolio; our on-line training log. It must have been late afternoon when, half way through a 'reflection', I must have managed to drop off. I awoke to the low battery noise of my lap-top, somewhat disorientated with it dark outside. If nothing else the e-portfolio is, at least, an effective hypnotic. I climbed out of bed with a hideous headache and jumped in the shower to get ready for my first day/night on-call as a surgical house officer.

I walked into the Surgical Assessment Unit that night with my surgical blue scrubs and a spring in my step. I felt optimistic about the next four months. Even if I was doing the same old crap jobs; I was a surgeon now. I was told that handover, the vital transfer of patient information that occurred every evening and every morning with the changing shifts, occurred in the surgical on-call office. Glancing left and right as I walked through the ward, any hope of a break from the unrelenting volume of patients seen on my previous Medical jobs did not look like it was going to happen tonight, if at all. Patients lay on gurneys at the entrance of the ward and seemed to queue along the side wall where an exasperated nurse was doing her best. Several were vomiting into those grey reconstituted paper bowls. Relatives stood close by with grim faces. I quickly skipped by into the handover room and shut the door. I sat down on a plastic chair alone seemingly the first to arrive. I waited patiently hoping someone would come and tell me what to do. I knew the surgical house officer on-call mostly covered the ward inpatients whilst the surgical senior house officer clerked the new admissions referred from the GPs or A&E. The surgical registrar usually did the emergency operations until midnight.

A tall broad blonde guy about my age, but twice the size, walked into the room 15 minutes later.

'Are you the surgical house officer?'

'Yes, I'm Tom.'

'Hi mate, I'm the night SHO on-call.'

'Hi,' I answered. 'I'm glad someone has shown up as I'm not entirely sure what I'm to do,' I smiled.

'Right well outside is bedlam. There are 15 patients to clerk and a further 3 in A&E. Some have been waiting more than 6 hours. The day team are still scrubbed in theatre finishing off a Hartmann's[1].' He pulled out his mobile phone and appeared to be checking something whilst he continued speaking. 'The night Reg and I are going to try and bash into some of these admissions. Have you been around the wards yet?'

'No,' I said. He looked pissed off. I didn't know whether he had realised I had only been in work for 15 minutes.

'Right well can you first go down to A&E and clerk in those waiting.'

'Sure,' I said with false confidence.

'Just call me if you're worried or you think someone needs an operation and either me or Alex will come and review them all when you're done.'

'Okay.' It didn't feel okay. I hadn't the first idea who Alex was for starters. I hadn't even been to A&E here. 'What about the wards?' I asked.

'Yeah if they bleep tell them just urgent stuff, you'll get time later to do the scut.'

I wasn't sure what scut was. I didn't know where my bleep was, what this chap's bleep number was so I could contact him if I needed him. I didn't even know his name. I didn't know where the day

---

[1] Hartmann's procedure is the surgical removal of the rectum and sigmoid colon. The anorectal stump is sewn over and the colon is brought out as a stoma through the skin. A bag is used to collect the poo which comes out of the abdomen. It is commonly used as an emergency operation where joining the bowel back together so one can poo out of their bottom again is too high risk. It was first described by French surgeon Henri Albert Hartmann in the 1920s.

house officer was who I was supposed to get a handover from. I was frankly clueless.

'Any dramas?'

I hesitated. 'No, no problem.'

With that he walked out.

I took off my jumper and left it on the chair. I pulled my stethoscope and a pen from my bag and set off to find A&E.

'Hi,' I said to the nurse in charge. She was chewing on her pen whilst staring at the computer showing how many patients were in the department and, more importantly, how long they had been waiting for. It looked like she was trying to solve an impenetrable Sudoku puzzle. A&E looked to be in an even worse state than the surgical assessment unit. Paramedics were queuing outside the door with patients on trolleys. Staff were racing around the department. I was beginning to think that the demand for the NHS constantly just exceeded resources. The sister either didn't hear me or was just too involved with fretting over the number of departmental breeches.

'Hi,' I repeated louder. She looked up.

'Hey,' she said.

'I'm here to clerk surgical patients.'

'Where have you been, we've been bleeping for the past 2 hours.'

'I don't know I only started at 8.'

'Well cubicle 5 first. Mr Ball, Enjoy that one,' she replied smirking.

'Where do I find the notes?'

'Racks behind,' she directed with her head, her eyes remained transfixed on the screen. I heard her pick up the phone to plead with the manager for more beds.

'Hello Sir,' I said walking in the cubicle. 'Tom is my name, one of the surgical doctors.' I glanced at the Emergency Department referral information; Mr Ball, 53 years old, 'foreign object in rectum'.

So the first person I am going to see as a surgical house officer is a middle aged man who has something stuck up his bum. How clichéd.

The patient was lying on the hospital trolley on his side with his back facing towards me.

'Hello,' he replied trying to spin around.

'So Sir. What's bought you to hospital today?' I asked. I decided to try and sound as innocent as possible as I manoeuvred around the bed to speak to him face to face. He was an average looking middle aged man. A little overweight with a slight paunch and thin greying hair with a matching thick grey stubble.

'Don't you know?'

'I have an idea. Just hope you can fill in the spaces,' I replied. Poor choice of words in retrospect.

'Well I have something up my arse.'

'Right,' I replied passively a little taken back by his candour. Nothing followed and a slightly awkward silence began.

'What do you have in your bottom Sir?'

'A toy man.'

'Right and when did you.....' I paused and rephrased the question; 'how long has the toy man been in your rectum?'

'I dunno, bloody ages, since early this afternoon.'

'And would it be fair to say you slipped and fell on this toy man?' I was hoping I was cutting him some slack and saving him some blushes.

'No, I stuck it up there myself.'

'Right.' I was struck momentarily speechless again by his frankness. 'Right,' I repeated. 'Okay.' I gathered my thoughts.

'And have you any stomach ache?'

'A little, but not especially. No more than anyone else who has a piece of plastic stuck up his arsehole,' he said a little irritably. I wasn't sure what the benchmark level of abdominal cramps was for someone who had a toy man inserted in his rectum so I thought I'd let it pass. My aim was to elicit any features that he had perforated his bowel by inserting this toy soldier.

'Any fevers?'

'No.'

'Can I examine you?' I asked. He rolled over and adopted a foetal position ready. 'Can I just examine your stomach first?' He rolled back I gave a cursory prod of his stomach which felt soft and normal

69

enough. I certainly couldn't feel any evidence of the offending foreign object through his skin. 'And can I have a look down below?' He grunted his consent and re-adopted the foetal position. He lower his tracksuit bottoms shuffling his bottom in my face from left to right to lower them further. I lowered myself onto one knee like I was conducting the world's most peculiar proposal, and was met with a giant wad of bum roll.

'What's the toilet roll for?' I asked.

'There has been some bleeding.'

'Bleeding?'

'Yeah,' he hesitated, 'when I realised I couldn't get the plastic man out with my hand, as it had gone too far up, I tried to get it with a pair of pliers.'

'Pliers!?'

'Yeah. I didn't manage to get hold of the toy but I think I tore something, as it bled like stink.'

'Right,' I paused, 'right'. I tried to maintain my composure as I put on a pair of rubber gloves. Inside I was thinking, firstly, why anyone would decide to turn himself into a Russian doll. Secondly I cannot think of any problem which could be successfully solved by self-inserting a pair of pliers in one's rectum. 'I'm going to remove some of this loo roll Sir,' I declared.

'Okay Doc.'

I carefully pealed back the layers and layers of packed bog roll. It wasn't long before I came across some strike-through of blood. As I continued to peel the layers, like soiled puff pastry, the toilet roll became increasingly sodden with fresh red blood. I had already filled two grey reconstituted cardboard sick bowls by the time I reached the end of the line. There looked to be a plug of blood sodden roll inserted into his anus which was continuously oozing red venous blood.

'Did you put some loo roll up your bum?

'Yep.'

'I'm going to take it out to have a look.'

'Okay Doc.'

I grasped the sodden ends of the saturated plug and gently eased it out of his anus to be greeted by a deluge of shit stained claret depositing itself onto the crotch of my scrub trousers. Nice. Blood continued to pour. I started to feel slightly apprehensive. There was, quite literally, shit loads of it.

'Everything alright Sir?' I asked more for my reassurance than for his,

'Yep.'

I grabbed an incontinence pad off the shelf behind me in the cubicle and rammed it into his arse crevice applying a decent amount of pressure. I had absolutely no idea whatsoever how to proceed. In fact I was somewhat nervous of this chap losing so much blood from his bum. Heavy bleeding tends to have a somewhat deleterious effect on the cardiovascular system. Time to phone a friend.

'It's still bleeding quite heavily Sir,' I helpfully explained exactly what he knew already. 'I am going to ask the team the best way forward. Have you had an X-ray yet?' I asked glancing at the ED plan for an abdominal X-ray.

'Just before you came Doc. The other doctor who saw me a couple of hours before you asked for it.' The patient remained in the foetal position

'Perfect, I'll take a look at that too. A nurse is going to come in and just check your pulse and blood pressure again too.' My nice reassuring voice hopefully calmed the patient at least. I walked out the cubicle dispensing of my blood stained gloves. The scrub trousers would have to wait although I was beginning to sense the slow ooze through the thin scrub trousers into my boxer shorts. Overall the whole situation was far from ideal. I could imagine the laddish tones of the surgical senior house officer I had met upstairs: 'Yeah.... so Tom managed to see one patient who bleed out from an arse wound and all Tom could manage was a heavy bought of menstruation.'

I walked back to the centre desk as surreptitiously as possible and picked up the phone. Having no idea what the surgical SHO or registrar's bleep number was I phoned switchboard and asked to be put through to the SHO. Whilst waiting I logged into the system to review blood results and saw that this little episode of bleeding had made him, reassuringly, only slightly anaemic although I bet things had progressed since the blood tests were taken three hours ago. I stopped a nurse who was walking past with a commode and asked them to pass on a message to the nurse looking after the patient to repeat his observations. She sulkily agreed. Her facial expression suggesting she wanted to say 'do I look like I have nothing to do currently dickhead? Why can't you do it yourself?'

'The SHO isn't answering his bleep,' the lady on switchboard spoke back to me, 'do you want me to try the Registrar?'

'Yes please.' I rehearsed my story and made sure I had all the facts to hand. Registrars usually had little patience with an incompetent referral from a junior doctor. I logged into the system to view the X-ray whilst I was waiting.

'Just connecting now,' the switchboard operator confirmed.

'Hi Alex, surgical reg.'

'Hi it's Tom, the surgical house officer.'

'Hi.'

'I don't think we've met.'

'No. Are you down in A&E?'

'Yeah.'

'How is it going? How many are down there?'

'Not sure but I've seen one and I was wondering if I could ask your advice,' I could hear him quietly sigh.

'Sure but be quick, I'm just about to scrub.'

'Okay middle aged man with a toy soldier self-inserted in his rectum. He tried to self-extract with a pair of pliers and looks to have done some damage as there is heavy bleeding.'

'Pliers?'

'Yeah.'

'Different.'

'Hmm.'

'Ok well have you had a look?'

'Yes but I couldn't really see much. There was a lot of blood.'

'Where is the blood coming from?'

'Not sure, inside somewhere. It seemed to have been maintained initially by a plug of toilet roll he had shoved up there.'

'Okay well you need to have a look. Soak some gauze with adrenaline from the anaphylaxis kit and shove it up his arse. Is he haemodynamically stable?'

'He is talking and seems well, I'm just getting the nurse to repeat his observations. Bloods taken 3 hours ago showed a haemoglobin of 11.[1]'

'Okay, if he isn't stable call me back. Is the foreign body still up there or did he mange to get it out with the pliers?'

'Still there.'

'X-ray?'

'Just loading now.' I glanced at the screen. The toy soldier didn't look like your classic small beefeater toy soldier standing to attention but a fairly sizeable figurine with a globular head and midriff complete with batteries.

'Um,' I hesitated, 'you better have a look at the X-ray.'

'Hang on. What's the guy's hospital number?' I read it out to him. I could hear talking in the background as he typed on the computer.

'What the.......' he paused, 'well it is going to have to come out. If the bleeding stops then stick your finger up there with loads of lube and see if you can get it out. What goes up must come down.' Newtonian physics, it seemed, even applied to self-gratification with a toy soldier.

'Okay,' I said wearily, 'what if it doesn't come out?'

'We'll try under anaesthetic and if that doesn't work....well...bad times for him.'

'Okay.'

'Let me know when you're done and I'll come down as soon as I can.'

'Sister I need some adrenaline,' I said to the nurse in charge. I had asked the nurse looking after him who had responded by looking at me blankly. She looked up from the monitor for a moment.

'Why?'

'The guy in cubicle five. He is bleeding pretty heavily.'

'Bleeding?'

'Yeah.'

---

[1] A normal range for haemoglobin for a man is 13-17g/dl.

'What are you doing with the adrenaline?' She was obviously worried I was trying to inject the poor bugger with it.

'Soak a gauze in it and shoving it up his bum,' I responded. 'Can I just take the anaphylaxis auto-injectors from the crash trolley?'

'No don't do that, we might need them in an emergency,' she replied. Interesting logic considering I need them now to prevent an emergency. 'Hang on I'll get you one from pharmacy.'

I was partially reassured that Mr Ball's observations were in normal parameters. Twenty minutes later having taken the adrenaline from the crash trolley (I just neglected to tell sister; he would have bled to death waiting for pharmacy) I shoved a wad of adrenaline soaked gauze in his cavity in the hope of stemming the flow. I walked out of the cubicle to update my notes when I ran into an irate middle-aged women.

'Is he in there?'

'Who Ma'am?'

'My bloody husband, Warren.'

'Warren?'

'Yes Warren Ball.'

'Yes just here ma'am,' I pointed to the cubicle I had just exited. This is going to be interesting. 'Can I check he is all set for visitors? Is it Mrs Ball?'

'Yes, yes if you could please.'

I walked back through the cubicle and knelt down next to the patient, this time to his front side rather than rear.

'Mr Ball, your wife is outside, do you want to see her?'

'Not really Doc no.'

'Okay what do you want me to tell her?'

'Whatever you want Doc. I just don't want to see her.'

'That's fine, I can tell her we are involved in a medical procedure but what if she asks me why you are here and what is wrong with you?'

'It's fine.'

'So I can tell her?'

'Yep.'

'Everything?'

74

'Yes.' He looked at me despairingly like a man who had accepted his judgement. 'She's used to it,' he added. I walked out to be met with his wife.

'Mrs Ball,' I addressed his wife. She now had a teenage girl stood next to her. I hoped it wasn't his daughter.

'Can I go in and see him?'

'No,' I hesitated, 'he is just undergoing a procedure.'

'Has he done it again?'

'Done what again?' I replied as innocently as I could.

'Shoved something up his arse!'

'Um,' I hesitated again.

'Oh my God. Doctor, I have no idea what is wrong with him. This is the third time he has gone to hospital. I swear he never used to be like this. I just don't understand why he does it.' She stopped her tirade temporarily to inhale.

'It was a toy soldier this time apparently,' I added. 'Is that the usual?'

'Oh no doctor, he will stick anything up there. Last time it was one of those big cans of furniture polish. He has probably decided to put one of my grandson's toys up there.'

'Right,' I said in faux understanding. Is this a child protection issue[1]?

'Oh God doctor I am so embarrassed.'

'Well I better go and see how he is getting on. Please excuse me.'

'Mr Ball, let's have a look and see if we have stemmed the bleeding.' I said walking back in the cubicle.

'Ok Doc.' I walked behind him and lifted up the blanket. I put on a fresh pair of gloves and removed the adrenaline packing. A trickle of blood leaked but otherwise it seemed to have done the job. 'How is it?'

'Looks a lot better Mr Ball. I'm going to see if I can remove the...,' I hesitated and stopped my sentence.

---

[1] If a doctor thinks a child is at risk of harm then one is duty bound to raise it.

'Great,' he replied. I wasn't sure what he meant by this having inserted the toy, presumably, for gratification. Was he being sarcastic or not? I wasn't sure which I preferred.

I liberally covered my index and middle finger of my right hand with lubricant gel and slowly inserted them into Mr Ball's back passage. He responded with a disconcerting guttural groan. Again I wasn't sure whether the derivation of this was pleasure or pain or which I preferred. I continued to advance my fingers until I could touch, what felt like, the tip of the toy's feet. The groans had now regressed to shrieks which were now definitely due to pain. I poked around for a moment before realising I was getting nowhere.

'Ok Mr Ball, I'm coming out.' Again a regrettable choice of phrase in retrospect.

'Any luck Doc?' he enquired breathing heavily.

'Sorry Mr Ball, it is just too far up.'

'What now?'

'I will speak to my Registrar but you might need an operation.'

'Oh', he said, 'oh dear.'

'I'm just going to pop back in the adrenaline soaked gauze to make sure there is no more bleeding,' I said. I reinserted the gauze and felt an overwhelming desire to escape. I felt suddenly hideously claustrophobic and in need of some, much deserved, fresh air. 'Back in a jiffy,' I said grabbing the notes. I was relieved to see the mother and daughter no longer waiting outside so I wouldn't have to fend any further requests.

I was writing my notes at the desk when I felt a hefty hand land on my shoulder.

'Tom is it?' I glanced around to see a tall muscular chap who looked to have been cloned from the surgical SHO. I immediately guessed he was Alex the surgical registrar on call. 'Alex,' he affirmed. 'Sorry I've been a while, let's have a look at your chap then. Is that his X-ray?' Not unless there are two patients with battery operated toys up their arse today. 'Any luck with getting it out?' Alex asked.

'No, too far up, I could feel it with the tip of my finger though.'

'I think we might need to book him for a GA[1], I'll consent for laparotomy and operative removal too,' Alex said glancing again at the X-ray.

'You think he'll need an operation to get it out?'

'Well we can try and get it out via his anus when he is sedated under anaesthetic and give loads of muscle relaxant. Failing that we will have to get it from inside which will mean he'll get a stoma.'

'Shit,' I said.

'Don't worry, I'll book and consent him,' Alex said, 'can you nip around the wards and try and find the day house officer, if she's still here, to get handover from.'

'Sure.'

'Thanks for your help.'

'No problem.'

It was 2am when my pager sounded.

I had managed to rescue it from the day officer, a pleasant girl called Aoife who looked like she was close to breakdown on the wards. She was initially reluctant to leave despite it being well beyond her contracted hours. She said she had not got anywhere near completing her list of jobs. I reassured her I would pick up where she left off and had been working through them since my trip to the A&E. The ward nurses were ensuring my list maintained an insurmountable size.

'Hi it's Tom; surgical house officer.'

'Tom, it's Alex, can you come down to the Emergency Theatre?'

'Of course.'

'Quick as you can.'

I hung up and raced down the stairs to find Alex waiting for me by the entrance.

'Show me your hands?' I did as I was instructed, 'Excellent, follow me.'

---

[1] GA: General anaesthetic. It is the noble job of the anaesthetist classically involving one little syringe of clear stuff followed by one big syringe of white stuff and a bumper magazine of Sudoku puzzles.

We walked through the double doors of main theatres and turned left into Theatre 1; the designated out of hours emergency theatre.

'Ah the feminine fingered cavalry have arrived,' said a man through his facemask. He was sat at the head of an anesthetised patient and so presumably was the anaesthetist. The patient was on their side facing me and, despite the breathing tube hanging from his mouth, I immediately recognised him as Mr Ball. On the far side I recognised the hulking form of the surgical SHO whose gloved right hand was covered in poo and blood.

'So we need someone with smaller hands,' explained Alex. 'Both Hugo and I have somewhat hefty ham-hocks.' It would seem he was referring to the equally enormous SHO as Hugo. I looked down at my hands having never previously thought of them being small. I felt a little emasculated.

'So what do you need me to do?'

'Ever seen All Creatures Great and Small son?' came the voice from the anaesthetist. He let out a guffaw of glee.

'Just put on a gown and gloves and see if you can have another go. Both Hugo and I have tried but our hands are too big. If we don't manage to get it out through his arsehole I'm going to have to bring in the consultant who was rather keen for us to get it out this way, however possible,' explained Alex.

'Fine,' I said. I had often wiled away a boring journal club[1] meeting day-dreaming of a future time where an emergency medical situation would arise which required my expert assistance. It is probably not surprising that this was not what I had envisaged.

Only a few moments later, the mask hiding my facial expression, I had my hand inside Mr Ball's capacious rectum.

---

[1] Journal club is a lunchtime meeting held in the hospital. Usually a poor junior doctor gets told, by their consultant, to present a clinical paper related to their consultant's speciality which they are supposed to critically appraise the strengths and weaknesses of. They invariably do this poorly giving opportunity for widespread education by embarrassment. If your hospital is not deeply in debt lunch is occasionally provided otherwise you also have to endure a tedious presentation from a drug rep.

'It is much farther up than before,' I commented.

'That's what she said?' the anaesthetist commented rather expectantly. No one seemed to be laughing but he seemed quite pleased with his own repartee.

'Yes that is probably our fault,' said Hugo. He was stood by Alex behind me. My fingertips were again just touching the feet of the toy. I had managed to pincer the feet between my index and middle fingers but the toy kept on coming loose every time I tried to extract it. I provided a running commentary of each failed attempt much to the glee of the anaesthetist.

'Alex you're are going to have to make a decision. His anaesthetic is lightening. Are you calling in your boss and going for laparotomy or what?' the anaesthetist said to Alex.

'Tom are you any closer?'

'Nearly,' I said through concentration. I was now on my knees, wearing this poor bloke like a puppet. My index finger and middle finger again had a firm grip of the feet. Suddenly the patient started coughed, through his lightening anaesthetic, on his endotracheal tube. The toy seemed to momentarily descend with the transient increase in intra-abdominal pressure from the cough. I gripped it tightly and pulled.

'I have it,' I shouted excitedly.

'Ok pull it out gently, you don't want to restart that bleeding from the torn mucosa,' Alex said calmly. I gently eased my hand out of his anus, rotating the toy to 'birth' the legs. Slowly I continued to extract it using my other had to stretch his anus open. Finally I pulled clear the toy and cast it aloft like a trophy spraying shit and blood as I did it.

'Well done young man,' the anaesthetist said, 'a career defining moment if ever I have seen one.'

'Is that,' Alex paused, 'a Buzz Lightyear?' He took the small version of the character out of my hands and deployed the figurine's wings.

'I think it might be,' Hugo said.

We all looked at each other and a silence descended over the emergency operating theatre.

'To infinity....and beyond,' the anaesthetist said followed by a roar of laughter.

I've done something I'm not happy with

We were sat in the surgical junior doctor's office updating the patient list following the morning ward round when a rummaging could be heard at the door. The office, a windowless, airless dungeon that stank of wet coats, coffee and farts, was probably once a sizable store cupboard sandwiched between the two main general surgical wards. It was accessed by a key code lock. The scrabbling continued with the key code entered several times, probably incorrectly, until the intruder finally gave up and a loud knock resonated. I got up to open the door. A thin, tanned, handsome, dark-haired chap I recognised as Paul, a Senior Cardiothoracic Registrar, poked his head around the door.

'Could one of you come and assist in theatre this afternoon?' said Paul. He had the forthright ability of a consultant to make a question seem like an order. Without glancing to look at my colleagues on the colorectal firm I volunteered:

'I will,' I failed not to sound too eager, 'I mean if no one else wants to.'

'Fine by me,' Claire, my fellow colorectal house officer said. 'We are pretty light on patients at the moment and I am happy to hold the fort.'

'I don't care who comes really, sort it out amongst yourself,' Paul said impatiently. 'Just make sure you are in theatre four by one-thirty pm.' With that, he removed his head from around the door and was off.

'Are you sure you don't mind?' I asked Claire.

'God no,' Claire replied, her gaze not shifting from the patient list open on the computer, 'I detest assisting in theatre. Eight hours of inadequate retractor holding and sexism. I'd rather set myself on fire thanks. Besides I had to cover the thoracic wards one weekend and that guy was a complete wanker.'

'Right,' I murmured, 'thanks.'

At precisely 1325pm I was stood outside the entrance to the surgical theatres, like a lemon, pushing the 'attention' buzzer which, like every other 'attention' buzzer in the National Health Service, was either not registering with anyone (a phenomenon called alarm fatigue) or was being deliberately ignored. Despite repeated swiping of my identification card the light would flash red and the double swing doors remained resolutely closed. I was obviously far too insignificant and junior to consider giving access privileges to such an esteemed place as the operating suite. It would seem the first challenge of becoming a surgeon was, quite literally and metaphorically, to get someone to open the door for you. Luckily I didn't have to wait more than a couple of minutes before a porter (whose card worked; obviously of more importance than me) appeared behind me with a bed carrying an elderly lady who was obviously first up to have some frightful undertaking performed on her person. I tailgated in behind the bemused bed-wheeler who glanced back at me contemptuously. Inside there was an unnamed reception desk guarding the entrance to the veritable Aladdin's cave of corridors and warrens filled with scrubbed individuals wearing clogs and jazzy theatre caps carrying bizarre pieces of operating equipment.

I saw a sign pointing the direction of 'Theatres 1-4' and sauntered in the direction as inconspicuously as possible despite feeling a total imposter. I turned a corner to see a sign on the wall emblazoned 'Theatre 4- Thoracic Surgery'. In front was a red line painted on the floor with a further sign: 'Do not pass unless wearing theatre scrubs.' I halted at this command and tried to solve the equation of meeting Paul outside Theatre 4 but not wearing the appropriate dress. I considered that waiting a stone's throw from Theatre 4 was an acceptable compromise. Fifteen minutes later I saw Paul, with a gaggle of others wearing blue scrubs, approach theatre 4 from the opposite direction.

'Err Paul,' I hollered from behind my appointed barrier. 'Paul,' I shouted. It was almost as bad as if I had followed my pleas for attention with a 'coo-wee'. He looked up, shook his head and audibly swore.

'What are you doing there you moron. Go and get changed. You can't operate in your chinos.'

'Ok,' I said turning around instinctively to the command. I turned back. 'Err,' I hesitated, 'where?'

'The changing room?' Paul raised his voice at the end as though asking a question.

'Where is that?'

'Christ do you want me to dress you too?'

'No. Just furnish me with the necessities,' I mumbled somewhat frustrated. He grabbed me by the arm walked me around the corner where he pointed the sign for the male changing room.

'There. Hurry up. The first case is already getting anesthetised.'

'Thanks,' I said a little too acerbically.

The changing room was not dissimilar to one you might find in your local leisure centre. Walls of lockers lined each wall with a further central bank. Stacks of hospital laundered scrubs lay in disarray on shelves on the far wall. Although there were different shelves for different sized trousers and tops this system had seemed to have been abandoned for a more chaotic format. I quickly approximated my size and changed. With a quick glance down I realised that the scrub trousers were far too short reaching, just about, to my mid shin. I hesitated whether to gamble with a further change but, not wanting to anger Paul further, I resolved that they would have to do. All the lockers seemed to require keys to unlock; which I did not possess, so I just left my clothes and shoes in a pile on top of the locker bank. There was an assortment of clogs littering the floor all of which seemed to have been made for people with smaller feet than my Grandmother and none of which matched. I shoved my feet into the largest odd pair I could find which were still too small and curiously stained with what I hoped was an iodine based sterilising agent but rather suspected was organic. I pulled a disposable scrub cap from the box on the way out the door and walked with speed to Theatre 4. I walked into the scrub room where I met Paul furiously watching his hands. He glanced at me and immediately let out a howl of delight.

'Who do you think you are Tom Sawyer?' Paul said roaring in laughter.

'No, Tom Parsons,' I mumbled confused. I had never read much Mark Twain.

'Love the half-mast look. Has someone died?' He pointed at my scrub trousers and continued laughing at his own joke. I felt my cheeks redden with embarrassment.

'Couldn't find the right size,' I mumbled.

'Have you got two left clogs on?' I glanced at my feet and swore under my breath. 'We are going to have to keep a close eye on you. You can't even dress yourself never mind operate.' My cheeks burned red.

'Come with me lad I've got a spare pair in my locker.' A voice came from behind me with a thick Indian accent. I felt a hand on my shoulder. 'Paul, my son, you are a nasty bastard,' he commented without significant rebuke.

'Sorry Mr Mishra,' Paul said sounding as though he wasn't very sorry and this was a reoccurring theme.

I followed the tall Indian man out of the scrub room and back to the locker room. I felt too embarrassed after Paul's humiliating dressing-down to even utter a word.

'What is your name?'

'Tom,' I replied meekly.

'Babu Mishra,' he said holding out his hand. He opened his locker with a key produced from his scrubs pocket and pulled out a pair of old stained clogs.

'Thank you Mr Mishra,' I said kicking off my odd pair of too small, left clogs and inserting my feet into the other ones.

'Let us get you scrubbed up so you can do the operation with Paul. We are doing a right thoracotomy and upper lobectomy today for early lung cancer and followed by that a median sternotomy and excision of a thymoma.' I felt like the little boy who having soiled his pants in a public place had to be taken aside by his Dad for a quick change.

'Do you know what a thymoma is Tom?'

'A benign tumour of the thymus,' I answered almost sulkily.

'Well that is true in that a thymoma doesn't metastasise but it is very locally invasive and, as it sits around the heart and great vessels it is 'tiger territory', as you shall see.'

We returned to the scrub room; a smallish room with a large sink covering the whole of one wall with shelves on the opposite wall and a metal bench. Opened on the bench were two sterile scrub gown sets.

'The most important thing Tom, my son, is that if you notice you have touched anything unsterile, except the patient, when scrubbed up is that you tell myself or Paul. There is no shame as we all often have to change gloves or gowns in an operation. But you mustn't ignore it,' instructed Mr Mishra.

'I understand,' I said.

'Now watch Paul scrub,' Mr Mishra commanded walking into the operating theatre in only his theatre blues and sitting down at a computer in the corner. I watched as Paul scrubbed. He cleaned his hands over and over again, using a scrubbing brush to clean his fingers and then his elbows to extract more brown iodine based soap from the dispenser so as not to contaminate his hands again. I watched him spin around so he was in front of the scrub gown set. He dried each hand with a sterile cloth sat on top of the scrub gown. He then picked up the gown from the inside and shook it out ensuring the gown touched nothing. For the final performance Paul put on his gloves with him inserting his hand followed by some bizarre flick in order to not touch the outside of the glove I surmised.

'Your turn sunshine,' said Paul all gowned and sterile. I dutifully stepped up to the sink and began imitating what I had seen. 'What size gloves are you?'

'Six and a half.'

'Start again,' Paul said sternly. 'You've forgotten to put on your facemask.'

'Shit.' I stepped away from the sink and secured the facemask before starting the ritual cleaning again. I followed all the steps, struggled to get my gown on without touching the outside and then inserted my gloves in a more traditional fashion. I glanced at Paul who seemed satisfied.

'Cross your arms and stay there whilst we get things set up.'

I watched, riveted, as the patient was wheeled out by the anaesthetist and ODP (operating department practitioner) already with a breathing tube hanging out of his mouth attached to the ventilator.

Mr Mishra went through a checklist as the theatre staff positioned the patient on the operating table.

'Everyone this is Tom, my houseman, who will be assisting Paul,' Mr Mishra introduced me.

'Tom Sawyer,' snorted Paul through his mask as he hung sterile drapes from the patient to ensure a sterile field.

'Hi Tom,' said a female voice behind a facemask as she sorted out the huge racks of surgical equipment.

'Right Tom step forward, said Paul from the far side of the operating table. Skip in there next to Maureen,' I presumed Maureen was the scrub nurse who had greeted me. I did as I was told holding my hands up to ensure they didn't touch anything. I was standing opposite Paul with the patient between us. To my left was Maureen, with the anaesthetist at the patient's head end partially obscured by a sterile drape.

'Happy to start Doc?' Paul asked. The face of the anaesthetist appeared around the sterile drapes.

'Very happy, thanks.'

'Mr Mishra, Sir, are you happy for me to start,' asked Paul. He emphasised the 'Sir' like a Sergeant Major.

'Carry on my son,' said Mr Mishra not looking up from the computer screen, a pair of reading glasses perched precariously on his nose.

'Knife,' instructed Paul. A metal tray appeared with a scalpel sat in it. I looked at it and then glanced at Paul. 'Pick it up then.' I saw his eyes meet mine, the rest of our facial expressions obscured by the scrub masks. I picked up the knife in my right hand.

'Good,' he commented his voice heavily laced with sarcasm, 'now cut the skin in a crescent, from here to here.' He trace the outline of the incision he wanted me to make with his finger.

I sank the blade of the knife into the skin and followed the motion. 'Nice,' Paul complimented. It felt good. 'Blade back ma'am,' he added. The metal kidney dish appeared and I placed the scalpel back in the dish. 'Cautery,' he commanded. A yellow implement appeared in his hand. 'Have you used cautery before?'

'No,' I responded, not looking up from the incision I had made and the blood leaking from the wound.

'Really easy yellow button to cut, blue button to cauterise.' You'll have to press the pedals too which should be near your left foot. Your other left foot,' he added chuckling no doubt making reference to my recent faux pas. 'Now depress the button and put your foot on the pedal and touch that small bleeder there,' he said pointing toward an oozing skin vessel leaking blood from my recent incision. I did exactly what I was told and heard a buzzing and cracking. A slight smell of burning flesh entered the air accompanied with a small plume of smoke. The vessel stopped bleeding. 'Get the others too,' commanded Paul. I did as I was told to leave a clean, non- bleeding wound. 'Now for the subcutaneous fat. Use the cutting button and I'll pull the wound apart and just touch the cautery in the plains of the fat and the wound will open up,' Paul said putting the tension on the skin on either side of the wound so opening up the wound. I touched the cautery and retraced my incision with the blade. 'Slow down,' he instructed. I watched as the fat sizzled and split apart. 'Stop when you get to muscle.'

'How will I know?' I asked.

'You'll know.' Sure enough I reached the healthy carnelian red of intercostal muscle.

'Here it is.'

'Touch the muscle with the cautery,' Paul said pointing with his finger. I did as he said and touched the intercostal muscle with the tool. The muscle twitched violently in response to the electrical stimulation. 'Neat eh?'

'Yes.'

'Ok, cutting button, cut alongside here,' Paul directed. 'We try not to cut through the muscle tissue but between the muscle layers.' I seemed to be struggling to get through. Paul grabbed the electrocautery and ran it across a green scourer attached to the sterile field similar to the type one would use to scrub burnt pans. The coating of charred flesh attached to the electrocautery blade came away. Paul handed me back the device. I continued carefully depressing the pedal and simultaneously pressing the button; applying the device to where Paul pointed.

'Lung down?' he asked.

'Yep, lung is down,' said a voice from behind the drapes. I glanced up at Paul. He must have sensed my quizzical expression.

'Good idea to deflate the lung before you barge in wielding your cautery like a glow stick at a gay disco,' I heard Paul say as I continued to tease the muscle layers apart. Suddenly the device reached a hard substance. 'Don't try and burn through there you plank, you're on a rib.'

'What now?' Despite the occasional barbed insult and homophobic insinuation from Paul I was absolutely enthralled and, at that moment, I wouldn't have swapped my position for all the tea in China.

'Rib cracker please Maureen,' Paul said. He snatched the electrocautery out of my hand leaving the nurse holding the metal contraption. 'I'll just quickly tidy up this dog's dinner you have made.' Paul quickly cut around the ribs with the electrocautery before snatching what appeared to be a giant set of garden secateurs and securing it around the rib. He let go. 'Grab it and squeeze,' he instructed. I did as was told and nothing happened. 'Squeeze you fairy!' He repeated loudly.

I pressed my hands together with all my might and was rewarded with the hideous splintering sound of breaking bone.

'Why do we need to do that?' I asked.

'It heals faster if we break it deliberately than if we break it accidentally.'

'We have to break it?' I asked.

'Well I'm going to struggle to get the lobe out otherwise,' Paul said in a manner that was keen to point out how ridiculous my questions was. 'Retractors please.' The scrub nurse passed over what looked like a freakish mediaeval torture implement; two metal blades were attached to a ratchet with a crank to increase the distance between them. It didn't take a cardiothoracic surgeon to know what was coming next. Paul inserted one blade abutting one rib and the other abutting the rib next to it and started cranking up the ratchet so the distance between the two blades increased. The hole of the cavity increased and I could see the pink lung pulsating with each beat of the heart. A slight ferrous aroma mixed with the smell of uncooked

88

meat filled my nostrils through the mask. Paul continued to crank up the rib retractor until I heard another bone cracking sound.

'Ah fuck,' muttered Paul, 'broke a rib anyway. Swabs please,' he said holding out his outstretched hand. The scrub nurse seemed almost telepathic having already got ready the large woven pads. Paul placed them around the wound. 'To protect the skin,' he commented anticipating my question, 'So now you have done your first thoracotomy.'

'Awesome,' I said.

'Right swap places now Sawyer. Do not touch anything when you come around,' he commanded. He raised his gloved hands and held them to his midriff in a purposeful fashion, to avoid desterilising himself, before walking all the way around the anesthetised patient lying on the table. I did the same, disentangling myself from the electrocautery cables with the help of one of the ODPs[1].

Paul proceeded to isolate the right lung's upper lobe. He worked at a fast rhythmic pace asking for implements and holding his hand out where they were delicately placed. I stood as still as possible, trying to not even breathe and followed his commands closely. He carefully tied off the attached arteries and veins and removed the huge hunk of tissue through the open wound.

'Done,' he said irrevocably. The lobe of the lung which concealed the tumour was slopped into an awaiting kidney dish and removed. 'Right swap, you can close.'

'Close?'

'Yep unless you want to leave him with a big hole in the side of his chest?' He raised his hands again towards his chest and stepped over the cables and we swapped sides. 'First thing is to close the ribs.' He removed the retractors and realigned the ribs. 'Like this.' He took a needle driver pre-loaded with a special type of suture, took

---

[1] ODPs: Operating Department Practitioners are trained healthcare professionals that have specialist knowledge of all the operating department equipment. They also assist the anaesthetist with difficult Sudoku puzzles.

a large bite between the ribs, pulled and I watched the ribs appose. 'Come on, I'm not doing them all.'

A needle driver appeared in my hand and I tried to follow Pauls lead. I had managed one suture in the time it took Paul to do the rest.

'Lung up,' he instructed. The anaesthetist seemed to awake from his slumber and performed some jiggery-pokery at the head end. The lung, minus a lobe reflated in the chest cavity.

Suddenly a different needle driver and suture was offered into my open hand, without me asking for it, as we continued to close the wound.

'Faster you flid,' Paul helpfully commented. 'Hands away,' he said as I tried to use my left hand to guide the needle. I continued to try and work as fast and accurately as possible, saying nothing and not rising to the bait.

'Right you are doing the rest,' Paul said with just the skin to close. 'And if I don't think you are sewing fast enough I will twat your hands with this retractor.'

'Ok,' I laughed. Despite his constant critiquing I was enjoying myself. In a way it seemed like I was serving a rite of passage. Suddenly Paul, who held a retractor in each hand brought whacked me on my left hand.

'Faster,' he said. I glanced up at him and our eyes met. Despite the masks I could see, from the sparkle in his eyes that he was smiling. We held each other's gaze for a moment before I returned to closing the skin, weaving the needle in and out of the edges of the wound.

'Faster, no hands,' Paul said hitting me again on my left hand.

'That is a trifle distracting,' I said almost pleadingly.

'So is a large bleed when you are trying to sew up the vessel.' I took his point and sped up, working the needle as fast as I could I closed with a final flourish I learnt on a surgical skills course as a medical student.

'Good,' said Paul. I knew it was all the praise I would get. But it seemed more than sufficient. 'All done Sir,' he said loudly.

'Very good,' replied Mr Mishra from the computer, 'how was the young maestro Paul? Good enough for the second case?'

'It looks like he has two left hands to go with his two left feet Mr Mishra.' An audible chuckle came from the computer.

'The thymus my son,' Mr Mishra said taking a slurp of the coffee I had just made him, 'is a gland located right in the centre of the chest.' He pointed to his sternum. 'It has a role in the immune system in children and teenagers and then shrinks. When a tumour originates in the gland's ruminants it doesn't metastasise but don't ever let anyone tell you it is a benign tumour. It invades locally into the great vessels around the heart and it can be a son-of-a-bitch to get out. You need to dissect the whole thing too; the complete capsule, or you find yourself having to do the god-damn operation again.'

'And that is what the next patient has?' I asked.

'Yes. So we do a median sternotomy [1]and hopefully a complete thymectomy.'

Following the last patient being transferred to recovery we were in an office opposite the theatre reviewing the next case's chest CT. Mr Mishra was responding to my questions whilst Paul was typing up the last patient's operation note.

'We had better hurry up,' Paul said to me, 'we are running behind. I'll go see whether the patient has arrived yet.'

Fifteen minutes later I was stood opposite Paul whilst he cut through the anesthetised patient's sternum with a saw. A moment later, once the retractors were in place I, on Paul's request, ratcheted them open to see the patient's beating heart. The lungs expanded and deflated with each puff of the ventilator he was attached to via the endo-tracheal tube.

'Mr Mishra, I'm in,' said Paul loudly glancing over his shoulder. The cardiothoracic surgeon got up from the computer and walked behind Paul. Without touching his sterile Registrar he peered into the open chest cavity. I looked upon the obvious fleshy mass too. It seemed to be gripping and invading the centre of the patient's chest.

'See what you can do my son,' he said.

---

[1] An electric saw is used to cut through the middle of the breast plate. The chest is then opened giving good access to the heart.

Paul, now with loupes (magnified glasses strapped to his head and protruding from his face like miniature binoculars) was carefully dissecting away the mass from the adjoining great arteries. I stood opposite him with a suction catheter, occasionally clearing away any point bleeding so he continue his delicate dissection. It was obviously tough going and progress was irritatingly slow as Paul would frequently indicate by enlightening my inadequacies as an assistant;

'Not there, get that sucker out of my grill,' he muttered at me attempting to use my initiative in sucking up some blood in his field of work. This was followed by; 'Are you going to suck that blood up or are we waiting for it to evaporate.' And 'You couldn't assist me in holding my coat whilst I went for a shit, never mind in complex cardiac surgery.'

'This thing is pretty stuck down Mr Mishra.' Paul's voice jolted me back to life. I wasn't sure if I had been day dreaming or sleeping standing up. I would be surprised if it was the latter; I thought only horses could do that. I still had the suction catheter in my hand. I glanced at Paul who didn't seemed to have noticed my nap/ lapse of concentration. I looked at the clock on the wall; it was now half past 6 in the evening. Mr Mishra's face appeared over Paul's shoulder again.

'I have managed to dissect away the lower pole but, considering the time, I've hardly got anywhere.'

'I just don't think this is worth it Paul,' Mr Mishra said,' it is too big and locally invasive. It's too dangerous. I think the patient needs to go for radiotherapy or chemo or something first before we try again.'

'You want me to close?'

'I think so,' Mr Mishra confirmed, 'we are not getting anywhere.' He glanced at me and I nodded as though I was giving my agreement and permission.

'Well shall I try and de-bulk as much as I can first?'

'Hmm,' murmured Mr Mishra.

'Might as well, we have come this far?'

'Ok my son, remove as much as you can.' Mr Mishra went and sat back down at the computer where he had spent the majority of the afternoon.

'Knife,' said Paul. A scalpel appeared in a metal dish. He picked it up in his right hand and began hacking away at the mass in the centre of this patient's chest, carving off pieces of tissue like beef off the bone. He moved the scalpel to the right of the gripping mass and irritably hacked away.

'What the fuck,' Paul said. The right side of the chest around the right lung began to fill up with blood. Automatically I tried to suck up the blood with the suction catheter which quickly was unable to cope with the demand. Paul shoved a swab down into the patient's chest towards his right shoulder. He pulled it away again to see another gush of blood and the chest cavity fill again. There was a brief pause and our eyes again met across the patient.

'Mr Mishra, I've done something I'm not happy with.' Mr Mishra glanced up from his computer before springing to his feet. He appeared again at Paul's shoulder.

'There is a lot of blood,' Paul said showing him. The anaesthetist popped her head around the drape?

'Problem?' she asked.

'Yep,' Paul confirmed, 'Heavy blood loss and still actively bleeding.'

'Ok,' she replied calmly. Bags of fluid were quickly replaced on the drip stand as I heard the first alarmed gong from the monitor warning us of low blood pressure. I glanced into the chest cavity and saw the heart, despite being partially hidden by a swab, beating faster to try and compensate for the blood loss.

'I'm going to scrub,' said Mr Mishra. He disappeared.

'Pack it,' commanded Paul, presumably to me. Swabs were thrust into my hand by the scrub nurse which I ploughed into the crevice just under the patient's right collarbone. Mr Mishra appeared without mask and with his gown hanging loose at the back. He smoothed the crinkles on his gloves, from their rapid application, by pushing on his finger webs.

'Let me see,' Mr Mishra said.

I removed the packs to see the blood pool again rapidly.

'Running into trouble here,' said the anaesthetist from behind the drapes with just a hint of desperation. No one answered her.

'Where the fuck is it coming from,' asked Mr Mishra rhetorically. Paul suddenly appeared at my side having walked around the table to make way for the boss.

'Let me in here mate,' he said forcibly. I shuffled down so I was stood around the patient's left hip. I had been subbed to spectate, and happily so. I had no idea how Paul felt or Mr Mishra as the consultant and responsible surgeon, but I could feel my own heart fluttering in apprehension.

'Swab on a stick please[1],' Mr Mishra said. The machine was now beeping regularly warning us of the patient's terminal blood pressure which was intermittently un-recordable. A long metal clip with a piece of rolled up gauze clasped at the end appeared in Mr Mishra's hand. He tilted his head to look inside the thorax, towards the patient's right shoulder. Paul adjusted the overhead light illuminating the area and creating a sheen on the pooled blood.

'Suction,' commanded Mr Mishra. Paul sucked up all the blood whilst Mr Mishra probed the area with his swabbed stick. I could hear all manner of frantic activity occurring behind the sterile drape that hung in front of us, separating the patient's head and torso, as the anaesthetist busily tried to prevent the patient haemorrhaging to death.

'I can't see a fucking….,' Mr Mishra's sentence trailed, 'Give me another swab on a stick.' He prodded into the crevice whilst Paul continued to suck up the blood being pumped out.

'There,' exclaimed Mr Mishra. He put pressure on the bleeding point with his swab on a stick.

'Subclavian vein,' said Paul, 'You want me to do it?'

'You want to do it?' asked Mr Mishra.

---

[1] A swab on a stick is a metal clip which has a rolled up gauze mounted on it.

'How are you getting on?' asked the anaesthetist with more than a mild sense of urgency. 'I currently have a blood pressure of 60 systolic. I noticed blood bags had replaced the bags of fluid.

'Give me a suture on a long needle holder,' Mr Mishra asked seemingly making the decision. He released the pressure on the lacerated vein with a consequent gush of blood. I watched his hand shaking probably at least partially due to trying to manipulate the long needle holder deep under the patient's collarbone. He released the pressure supplied by the swab on the stick and I saw the blood gush from the lacerated vein quickly obscuring Mr Mishra's view.

'Fuck it,' he grimaced re-applying the swab on a stick. 'Paul, I need you to hold pressure. Tom get in there with the suction.' I gripped the suction catheter and by partially mounting the patient I managed to reach the tip close to the area.

'Two swabs on sticks,' commanded Paul to the scrub nurse.

'Let go of the left swab Paul,' directed Mr Mishra. The lacerated vein began to gush again as Mr Mishra took a bit of it with the mounted needle and suture. 'Suck Tom suck!' he commanded. I wiggled my suction catheter as he grabbed the needle having apposed the two walls of the vein. He tied off the vessel with swift hand ties. The bleeding seemed to stop. I sucked up all the remaining blood whilst Mr Mishra performed more ties, effectively closing off the vessel.

'I need to go and have a heart attack,' he said his hands visually shaking. I glanced at Paul who looked discernibly white.

'Do you have control,' the anaesthetist asked popping her head from around the curtain.

'Yes I think so,' said Mr Mishra.

'Thank God for that,' she commented, 'I didn't think he had much longer.'

Dicking and Turfing

'Hello is that the RSO?' said the voice over the phone.

'This is the RSO,' I responded. It felt good. The RSO is the Responsible Surgical Officer; a rather grandiose title for the person who accepts and clerks all the surgical admissions to hospital. If anyone wants to admit a patient under the care of the surgeons in my hospital, for that day, they have to have permission from me. Me!? House officers are not usually trusted with this role and, considering I spent 30 minutes trapped in the store cupboard last week before being rescued by a bemused healthcare assistant; I can see why. The RSO rota is usually populated with senior house officers (SHOs); that is doctors with at least 1 years' experience since qualification from Medical School. Foundation Year 2 doctors were therefore the most junior of junior doctors on the rota. I had earned myself a 'field promotion' based solely on the circumstance that one of the SHOs had resigned to go and work in Australia and there was a gap in the rota that had to be filled. The trust also had no money to hire a locum. Still I wasn't dwelling on this; I was the RSO and I had been promoted.

I arrived to the Surgical Admissions Unit early and saw the swarm of junior doctors and medical students loosely circulating around the consultant conducting his post take rounds and seeing the patients admitted overnight. I opted to tactfully avoid the hive of ineffective activity on the basis that one of the masses of medical students could draw the patient's cubicle curtains just as effectively as I could. Instead I opted to sit in the surgical admissions office, drink coffee and wait for the first punter. It was just after 9 when my pager went off. I dialled the number back immediately, keen to get started.

'Hi, it's Brijesh, one of the A&E SHOs.'

'What can I help you with Brijesh?' As if I had an arsenal of expertise I could offer.

'I'd like to admit a patient under you if I may?'

'Shoot,' I said grabbing a piece of paper to write down the details.

'Okay, 19 year old girl with abdominal pain, name of Jemma Carrington. She has had some supra-pubic and right iliac fossa pain now for,' he hesitated, 'a while, and I think it is appendicitis. No past medical history.' He paused again, as if considering what else to tell me. 'Really,' he added vaguely, 'apart from a previous admission with abdominal pain; no cause found. No medications.' On the face of it this seemed like a reasonable enough request. But, being the RSO, I had been forewarned to have a highly attuned sense of smell in discerning bullshit referrals.

The general surgical consultant on-call today, who would be reviewing (a process called post-taking) all of my admissions was Richard Buckley. Mr Buckley was known, behind his back, by all the junior doctors, nursing staff, healthcare assistants, porters, domestics and the chap who fixed the printer as simply: Dick. Whilst Dick is an acceptable shortened form of Richard, my fellow colleagues tended to emphasise the consonants so as to, and let us be under no illusion, pronounce the name pejoratively. We would never be rude enough, nor brave enough, to address this pillar of surgery as Dick in person. That he insisted that his consultant colleagues referred to him as Richard and to everyone else he was known as Mr Buckley, made Dick an even better moniker.

Mr Buckley was a bit of a tyrant. He was short, rotund, supremely arrogant and impressively rude. He offended people with reckless abandonment and was so short tempered that even other surgeons avoided him. He was permanently between secretaries as they kept resigning due to his beastly nature. He hated being anywhere but in the operating theatre. Ward rounds, particularly after a large take of patients, made him impossibly short tempered and he demanded that they were conducted quicker than your babysitter's boyfriend when the car pulls up. The rounds must therefore be run with the speed and precision of a war effort where the only two options, in terms of patient management, were that the patient should be discharged or operated on (and then discharged).

We suspected this was to enable Dick to get back to his private practice as quickly as possible in order to pay for his large Bentley sat in the consultant's car park. How could such a loathsome person be allowed to continue to practice? Well allegedly he was an excellent surgeon with excellent outcomes. Consequently, and despite his loathsome manner, his private practice was reportedly like him; corpulent.

It was a couple of weeks prior when a rather wistful, preoccupied FY2 doctor with floppy hair and skinny chinos was undergoing his first shift as the surgical senior house officer on call. The consultant on-call was again Dick. Being perhaps a little low in confidence, or just merely ambivalent, he had admitted everyone referred to him without so much as a cross question. Luckily the Surgical Registrar had got wind, knew that Dick was on, and had managed to skip up from theatre and discharge, or refer on, the vast majority of patients who he knew wouldn't require operative management. It would seem one or two had escaped however.

'Well that is all very interesting,' Dick said following the FY2's stuttering presentation of the patient's history, 'but why are they under me?' Dick liked to start off slow, like a steam engine leaving the station. It would seem this floppy haired chap had admitted an elderly lady with suspected bowel obstruction who was quite obviously just constipated.

'Well because they had abdominal pain...,' the naïve RSO replied almost as if Dick had asked a moronic question or failed to grasp the concept of emergency surgical admissions to hospital.

'So what,' Dick would reply bluntly, 'I've got stomach pain. But I need a big shit which I'm going to take on your head young man if you don't give me a sound reason why this lady is under my care.'

A warning glare by Dick would quickly extinguish any giggles that wold emanate from medical students at the back of the post take ward round.

'So the next patient....,' the FY2 would say tactfully trying to avoid this patient and continue with the ward round.

'Well hang on a minute Princess,' Dick had a penchant for using female terms of endearment to male junior doctors when he got riled up. We thought it was perhaps a tribute to Dr Cox, from the TV show Scrubs, although I doubt Dick had ever watched an episode,' we haven't finished with this patient. Now,' he paused and fixed the bemused SHO with a malevolent glare, 'why is she under my care?'

Silence ensued. We awkwardly shuffled and looked down at our feet like the floppy haired FY2.

'Ok, if you can't answer that question, what does her X-ray show?' he would ask pointing at the patient's X-ray on the screen of CoW^2 which I had just loaded.

'Err,' the young house officer, now with dry mouth and sweaty palms would shift from one foot to the other with palpable nervousness, 'just some dilated bowel loops.'

'No,' Dick snarled, 'it is normal. So can you tell me how this patient with obstruction has a normal abdominal film?'

'Early obstruction?' said the FY2 quickly glancing furtively at the rest of the post take ward as though begging for some sly assistance.

'Do you even know what bowel obstruction is?' Dick asked rhetorically as though inferring he definitely didn't know what a bowel obstruction was. 'What are the blood test results?'

'Oh, they haemolysed so I need to retake them,' said the FY2 somewhat dismissively. I saw the Registrar standing to my left wince. No doubt he would be getting both barrels from Dick later for not having a grip of the surgical take. At least Dick was decent enough to disembowel his senior trainees in private.

'You mean you have no blood test results yet?'

'Not yet. No,' the SHO answered inconsequentially.

'When did this patient arrive?'

'Last night.'

'What time?' asked Dick quietly.

'About 11pm,' the FY2 replied glancing at his clerking sheet.

'It is now 815am so this lady, who you admitted for bowel obstruction, a life threatening condition, has been here for over 9 hours without any blood tests?'

'I suppose so yes.'

'You suppose?' Dick growled. The flash to bang was quick. Dick's face would grow redder and redder. 'Can I have a word?' The question was undoubtedly rhetorical.

'Yes of course,' mumbled the SHO as if this was going to be a pleasant pastoral chat with coffee.

'In here,' Dick would gesture into the relatives' room. In the unsuspecting junior doctor went following by an incandescent Dick.

The door slammed shut behind them. The relatives' room had windows, with curtains, which adjoined the ward. The curtains were swiftly drawn by Dick resulting in the remainder of the ward round, including the Registrar, bustling each other out of the way to get a peek through the gaps of the curtains. Dick was apoplectic and had gone a deep shade of crimson, his neck veins were bulging as he screamed at the junior doctor. Projectiles of spittle flew from Dick's mouth and hit the curtains, the occasional speck seeking a way through to hit the window, much to our bemusement. The swear words were audible through the closed door peppering and reverberating around the ward.

A nurse walked past and whistled; 'my, my, what language. Is that Dick in there again?'

We nodded stern faced.

A few minutes later a white, shaky and dazed RSO exited looking slightly teary and as if he had been ridden around the room, by Dick, like a Blackpool Donkey. Dick followed him out:

'Is there any danger getting through this ward round before Christmas?' he asked. No one answered and we got on with the remainder of the ward round where this SHO, at least thrice got a thorough mauling from old Dick and spent all afternoon and evening on the phone to every Tom (but not Dick) and Harry begging them to take over patients that he had been 'stupid' enough to admit with 'nothing surgically wrong with them'.

I had been recounting this tale at the bar the following week to a chap I played rugby with at University. He worked for Dick last year as a SHO before starting Core Surgical training. He had been on the receiving end of a 'dicking' in the relative room ('dicking' is the term used for a systematic bollocking from Mr Buckley, also known as a 'buckaroo') for screwing up a discharge summary. Dick during his tirade had told him: 'The only gifted thing that has every come out of your mouth is your boyfriend's cock.' Inspirational stuff and certainly now considered an uncommon pedagogic technique. Now getting 'dicked' or receiving a 'dicking' or being 'buckaroo'd' had entered the junior doctor's lexicon, not only for our hospital but also the region. Previous recipients wore it as a badge of honour and would proudly recount the moment they got 'Dicked'.

What made Dick so angry was that anyone could be so audacious to refer him a patient who did not require an operation. To refer a patient is the act of transferring responsibility of a patient's clinical care from one consultant to another. Whilst I have never seen, nor heard, of any rules that ratifies this process, it is commonly held that the patient, once referred, must also be formally 'accepted' by the team referred to. This usually always goes on without the patient's knowledge but medicine is a team discipline and referring patients to other consultants, who have a particular specialist knowledge about a certain facet of your patient's management, is working as a team and good for the patient.

In most circumstances it is not usually the consultant who refers or accepts the patient but the junior doctors working for that consultant. Sometimes this will be at the consultant's behest. Sometimes not. Usually this transfer of care is achieved by a simple phone call from the referring junior doctor to the accepting junior doctor. Even the GPs join in when they want to send in their patients for an emergency admission. Usually this seamless transfer of care is for the benefit of the patient.

Occasionally though it is not seamless nor to the benefit of the patient. Whilst these are real people with tangible problems, in the process of referring and accepting patients and so transferring their responsibility and care, you are also transferring another commodity; work. Dick's work, as he saw it, was to operate (preferably for lots of money in the private sector) and then discharge his patients when the operation was performed successfully. A patient who was transferred under his care who did not need an operation he effectively saw as a 'turf'.

Turfing is the art of finagling your patient to another team or, even hospital, by carefully manipulating the patient's history so that the transfer appears appropriate. This falsity is achieved by subtly extenuating certain aspects of the patient's complex history whilst conveniently ignoring other imperative features. It is a way of making patients not your problem; a way of lightening your workload or shifting your responsibilities. Who, having chosen to enter a caring profession and taken the Hippocratic Oath, could be so compassionless? Who could possibly condone such an odious and selfish practice? Well, probably the majority of doctors. Not just junior doctors either but GPs and consultants too. Furthermore, I suspect it is probably becoming more, rather than less, frequent.

There are actually a small minority of doctors who probably have not entered the profession to care for patients. Being constitutionally too lazy or selfish they would rather spend their time in the Doctors' Mess watching chat shows and eating toast than rolling up their sleeves and mucking in. I'm sure these are a small sect perhaps only confined to orthopaedics. Some even seek acclaim in the burdening of other hospital disciplines. Boundless satisfaction is gleaned from offloading your patient to some unsuspecting bugger who is too busy or too naïve to recognise your malign intentions. Meanwhile equal pleasure is received from putting up a verbal wall to teams who try and get you to take over their patient, even if their reasons are entirely in the patient's best interests. The travesty can quickly descend into an odious and tedious game of medical top trumps.

Turfing can be performed at any aspect of the patient journey and involve any department though, particularly for inpatients, the traffic seems to be mostly one way; from surgery to medicine. Whether it is the 89 year old with a three page spread of co-morbidities that someone has performed a heroic bowel resection on which, despite initial surgical 'success' has, unsurprisingly, gone hideously, resulting in a somewhat protracted inpatient stay. This leaves the patient in an unsolvable limbo; neither capable of getting better nor unwell enough to expire. The plan in that case will almost undoubtedly be: transfer the crumbling wreck to medicine for 'rehab and discharge planning' which effectively means palliation and death from a hospital acquired infection.

Take the 65 year old lady who has come in with a fractured hip. The A&E SHO calls orthopaedics to refer the patient. But wait....she has a history of smoking related chronic obstructive airways disease? Better bounce the patient to medicine and instead offer 'advice as required'. Forget that the broken hip was the reason they came to hospital in the first place and they gave up smoking ten years ago.

Psychiatry shit their trousers even with the most mundane of medical problems and don't even bother to refer, sending their mentally fragile in the back of an ambulance with a note to A&E as soon as they have so much as a sore throat.

But the worse turfers of them all have to be A&E. To be fair to the Emergency Department they are regularly crippled with huge demands on their services. Consequently they often have to quickly decide, with little information, whether the patient is too unwell to safely go home and therefore needs to be admitted. Trouble is patients don't tip up to A&E and say; 'I have a gastroenterological problem and I require a pipe up my bum' or 'I have a surgical problem and I require an appendicetomy'. They tip up with symptoms and signs which require interpretation and confirmation. Due to the Department of Health stipulations that patients must be seen and managed in four hours or the trust faces serious financial penalties, time is short in ED and the turf is commonly used to bounce patients through the system and increase 'flow'; a rather colonic management term. GPs are in a similar situation often with even less time so are also not adverse to the odd turf.

In many respects turfing is just a symptom of ever rising demand coupled with a slow sustained squeeze on funding. Everyone is just a little bit too overworked. Clinics are full, waiting lists are packed and that is just the elective work. In the acute setting more and more ambulances queue up outside the front door bringing more and more patients with more and more problems that, as we keep getting better, become more and more complex and have to be solved quicker and quicker. Like some macabre merry-go-round spinning faster and faster to the fairground music playing louder and louder.

It has got to the point where admitting patients under your team has now become a bit like having your in-laws over for Christmas. Whilst husbands and wives up and down the country know that they will have to take their turn some time, each year they are quite happy to debate with each other, at length, unbeknownst to their respective pairs of parents, that this year can't possibly be their turn. Moreover they are jolly keen to try and dispose of their poor old relatives before they have even had a chance to get their slippers out of their overnight bag or got stuck into the Eggnog.

'Well, what goes with it being appendicitis?' I asked, 'Could be one of a number of things,' I added before reeling off the potential diagnoses. The trouble is, if I accepted the turf, and the young girl turned out to have a urinary tract infection, period pains, constipation or had caught a dose of the Clap, none of which required an operation to fix, I would be in hot water with Dick if I couldn't get her turfed on to another specialty.

'Listen mate,' Brijesh said down the phone. The old A&E trick of calling the referring team's doctors as 'mate'. A bit of camaraderie thrown in to try and create the illusion that we are all in this together. But Brijesh won't be receiving the Dicking when this girl has period pain not appendicitis. 'Listen mate,' he continued, 'I'll be honest, it could be appendicitis, it could be any other cause of suprapubic and iliac fossa pain. But I picked up her notes on 3 hours and 49 minutes so I have 10 minutes to find a team to refer her to or she breaches and the bosses are already going ape-shit because we are on red alert again. Basically, I'm doing a pregnancy test now to rule out an ectopic, if it's negative, can she come to you?'

It was an emotive appeal. I felt for the guy. He sounded genuine and had made it difficult for me to flatly refuse him.

'Can't you admit her to your observation ward to see if things settle?' I asked in a final last ditch effort.

'No can do mate,' replied Brijesh. 'There is no protocol for appendicitis in the Observations Ward (a dumping ground in A&E to put people who don't need to be admitted to hospital but will obviously take more than four hours to sort out). Plus she has had a big slug of morphine and the nurses get a bit twitchy to sending her to Obs.'

I sighed heavily and hesitated before relenting: 'Ok, send her up.'

'Thanks mate, I owe you.'

It was an hour or two later before the patient got up to the Surgical Assessment Unit and I finally got hold of her notes and opened up the A&E clerking documentation on 19 year old Jemma Carrington. As I turned over the pages of hand written scrawl it became quite clear my 'mate' Brijesh had shafted me. Looks like he had tried to refer poor Jemma to every team in the hospital before me. He had originally thought the patient had a urinary tract infection and referred her to Medicine who had declined to accept the patient on the basis that the urine dip [1]showed nothing, the patient had no fever in keeping with an infection and the medics suggested it was probably a gynaecological problem and to contact the gynaecology team. Brijesh dutifully phoned the gynaecology registrar on-call who had declined to accept the patient until a surgical problem had been ruled out. My 'pal' Brijesh had also declined to mention that the patient had had, not one attendance, but multiple admissions with the abdominal pain, numerous normal scans and a good track history for self-discharging when previous doctors had attempted to explain to her that her pain had no pathological basis. Someone had even previously stuck a laparoscope through her belly button to have a look around. Furthermore Jemma was already under the care of the gynaecologists but refused to attend any outpatient appointments. Dick was going to have my balls for breakfast.

'Jenna? Jenna?' I asked poking my head around the curtain. An overweight girl with bleached blond hair and jet black visible roots lay on the bed dozing with her head tucked into the pillow. She startled to my call. She had a piercings in her eyebrow and lower lip and her eyes were blackened with dark eye shadow.

'Yep,' she replied stirring a little too theatrically. She briefly flicking her hazel eyes to meet mine before flicking them away and readjusting her sizeable frame in the bed to sit up a little. She crossed her legs in the bed and sat in the middle.

How are you?' I asked walking in behind the curtains of the cubicle.

'Better thanks.'

---

[1] A urine dip, or urinalysis is a highly sophisticated rapid diagnostic test which involves dipping a stick with lots of colours on it into a patient's wee and matching the colours up on the panel on the side of the bottle. Colour blindness can further decrease the test accuracy. For diagnosing a urinary infection, if the dipstick is negative it definitely doesn't mean you don't have a urinary tract infection.

'Great,' I commented. A plastic chair was adjacent to her bed which I pulled out and sat on. 'So you had some pain in your tummy again?'

'Yep,' she said rolling her eyes. She struggled to keep any eye contact when we spoke and seem to mostly flick them over my head as though looking at an interesting hat I was wearing. She nibbled on the ring in her lower lip.

'Is it better now?'

'Yep.'

It felt like I was trying to cajole a dog into bath tub. 'So what happened?' I asked. Jemma looked past me again briefly but didn't respond. I too remained silent trying to fix her eyes in some sort of mute duel. Nearly a minute must have gone by but, despite a thick atmosphere of awkwardness developing between us I remained resolute.

'Listen all I wanted was for some more painkillers,' she finally broke. 'I took my prescription in to get some but the pharmacist said I was out of repeats so I would have to see the GP,' she paused to briefly nibble on the ring in her bottom lip again. 'The GP didn't really listen and when I told him I had pain in my abdomen he sent me to A&E saying I had an appendicitis. I told him I get the pain regularly and I just manage them with pain killers but he still said I had to come to hospital.'

'And now A&E have sent you here,' I pre-empted.

'They were originally going to send me to gynaecology ward,' she added finally allowing her large hazel eyes to rest on me. 'They seemed in a bit of a rush too.'

'So I gather,' I added as non-judgementally as I could, 'how is the pain now?'

'Better.'

'Is the pain still there?'

'A little I guess.'

'Where do you get the pain?' I asked, 'point to it.' She pointed to the bottom of her abdomen just above where the transition to her thigh. 'So that is where your appendix is,' I added, 'and that is why A&E have sent you to see us, the surgical team.'

'Do you think I have appendicitis?' she asked with a hint of contemptuousness.

'Appendicitis comes on over a short period of time the pain and doesn't come and go. You've had this pain for some time judging by your medical record.'

'And no one can find the cause and now they seem to feel reluctant to give me pain killers too,' she muttered staring at her crossed legs. 'So can I go now?'

'Why do you keep having to take prescription pain killers Jenna?' I asked boldly ignoring her. 'You're 19 years old. You should not be reliant on morphine based pain killers.'

She shrugged still looking down at her legs.

'How long have you been taking them?

'Nearly three years,' she muttered.

'Did something happen three years ago that started this?'

She briefly glanced up as though imploring me to stop. I could see the tears welling in her hazel eyes, the jet black make up running. It was then that my bleep sounded interrupting us.

'Sorry,' I said, 'go on.' She paused for a while before her head flicked up and mouth opened again as if about to tell me something. My bleep rang out again.

'Go ahead,' she said, 'answer it.' I glanced down at the number. It was A&E no doubt trying to refer another patient.

'I'll be back okay?' I added. I left Jemma in the cubicle, answered the pager. It was another referral from A&E, and then one of the ward patients who was post-op started vomiting everywhere and before I knew it I caught up in the maelstrom of the day.

'I have a couple for you to discharge,' I said to James the Surgical Registrar. It was lunchtime and he had popped up from operating in the emergency theatre to see how I was getting on. 'First is Jemma Carrington. She's a...'

'You'll have a job,' he interrupted.

'Have a job what?'

'Sending her home,' he added taking a big bite from his tuna mayo sandwich. 'I've just taken her appendix out.'

'What?' I said incredulously, 'the big girl with the blonde hair?'

107

'Yep that's the one. Just did a lap appendicectomy on her.'

'But she's had that lower abdominal pain for ages, several admissions?' I questioned quizzically, 'she has had a previous laparoscopy!'

'Had she?' replied James ambivalently. 'When I popped up between cases at about 1030 she was tender in the right iliac fossa despite having had a slug of morphine. I said it could be appendicitis but best not to dick about and just crack on and whip it out.'

'Whip it out?' I replied incredulously.

'Steel-to-heal Tom, you'll learn,' he smiled before taking another huge bite of sandwich.

'Well did she have appendicitis? How did the appendix look inter-operatively?'

'Probably not, but she won't have it again,' he smiled, 'besides, good one for my logbook. My Annual Review of Clinical Practice is coming up.'

'You know that she just wanted painkillers from her GP who turfed her to A&E, who turfed her to us.'

'Serves them right for shovelling their shit then,' he commented nonchalantly. 'Who's next?'

Legs man

My cheap alarm clock brayed the white noise of a detuned and unrecognisable radio station. I awoke with a start, sat bolt upright and felt immediately as though my head had been used all evening as a stage to audition for the musical 'Stomp'. I strongly considered, as I hit the snooze button and buried my head in the pillow, whether I was having a sub-arachnoid haemorrhage[1]. As my tongue felt like a nightclub carpet, I reassured myself that my penetrating headache was probably due to the cocktails at last night's Doctors' Mess party. Flitted flashbacks of the night pierced through my partial amnesia as I sunk my head deeper into the pillow. I remembered the disappointment of watching that delightful young student nurse who worked in the day surgery unit, who I had been buying drinks for all night, leaving the bar with 'Cockney John'; the surgical theatres porter. I had drowned my disappointment with a round of Sambuca and a conciliatory solo kebab. The aforementioned processed dog meat was now playing havoc with my guts and there was an aroma permeating and pervading my bedroom like a portable lavatory on the final day of Glastonbury.

The Doctors' Mess is a welcome anachronism. A throwback to a time where junior doctors or 'house officers' lived in the hospital that they worked largely due to the punishing and frequent on-call schedule. The focus, for the doctor, was probably the small bedroom where they would try and snatch a few hours of sleep in between their punishing shifts. But, talking with the old and bold, retrospectively they say that the Mess was so much more than a plastic mattress on a rickety wooden bed in a small room with a leaky window. The Mess was the doctor's living room and dining

---

[1] Subarachnoid haemorrhage is bleed on the brain from vessels which lie under the arachnoid layer. They are usually due to a deformed blood vessel. Patients classically present as though they have been hit around the back of the head with a shovel

room. It was where they socialised and blew off steam about their bosses and the arduous nature of the job. It was a font of support, of friendship and even, in some cases, love. And the doctors shared a sense of belonging for which the Mess provided a physical location for. Not to mention being a useful hive mind of medical knowledge before the concept of continuous professional development [1]even existed.

But that was then and this is now. Since the introduction of the European Working Time Directive doctors are mere shift workers commuting to work like the rest of society. The hospital accommodation that served the Mess now either lies dormant, houses temporary doctors or has been annexed to serve as a recluse for information technology bods to hide from fixing my printer.

There is no Mess canteen, now doctors pay for their lunch at Costa-lot coffee like everyone else. The hospital bar has long been closed with the socialising venue transferred to some overly-priced trendy pub in the nearest pleasant town-centre which is usually nowhere near the hospital itself. In the new hospitals largely built by private companies and then leased back, at incredible expense, to the taxpayer the Doctors' Mess has been completely done away with. I have even seen it replaced by a homogenous, horribly horizontal and plastic multidisciplinary restroom which makes bitching about the nurses (and vice versa) incredibly challenging.

But in many of the older hospitals, despite the management's best efforts, a dreary room persists albeit cleaved from the accommodation and relegated to the basement at the back of the hospital sandwiched between the morgue and equipment library. Whilst the contents of this vestige are variable they usually contain a pool table with one semi-functioning cue and a couple of missing balls, a couple of dilapidated leather sofas and a widescreen TV

---

[1] Continuous professional development or CPD is the process of tracking and documenting the skills, knowledge and experience that you gain both formally and informally as you work, beyond your initial training. You have to achieve so many hours per year to maintain your registration with the General Medical Council.

hopefully, but not commonly, with a paid up satellite subscription. A kitchen with a toaster, some mouldy white bread and some instant coffee completes the extravagance. But the Doctors' Mess lingers on.

Before any Daily Mail types get too agitated about these jumped up junior doctors who refuse to work weekends, constantly want more money and who now demand some 'doctors' restroom' akin to a first class departures lounge with champagne bars, neck massages and widescreen sports on the tax payer, the Doctors' Messes are usually funded by the doctors themselves. Often 10 pounds a month is removed from their salary and put into a central account which will pay for a few loaves of bread, a few newspapers and a new pool cue every once in a while.

Where no physical room exists the doctors' are forced to organise a virtual mess with the collected funds spent exclusively on parties. These quarterly mess parties, organised by the 'mess committee' are often at a local swanky pub in the nice part of town where all the doctors aspire, but can't afford to, live. They almost always involve some money left behind the bar which is usually abused by the medical students and nurses before the doctors even finish their shift.

Due to a process of outright nepotism I had been 'elected', in a manner similar to Kim Jong Un, as mess president for the year. My appointment to high officer was rigorous and fair; I went for a beer with the outgoing president who I had played rugby with at university who asked me if I would take over the mantle. Last night was my inaugural mess party and despite a rather lacklustre effort of advertising the event, once again, the lure of a sizeable amount of money behind the (swanky wine) bar contributed from the, now heavily depleted, Mess accounts had been enough to attract a menagerie of healthcare professionals.

Having struggled out of bed, despite numerous hits of the snooze button, and made my way into work by bicycle (just to dehydrate myself a little further) my hangover was reaching its zenith by the time of the ward round. I had levelled with Claire my fellow General Surgical FY1, that I was a veritable shit state and liable to be neither use nor ornament today. I further begged that, what with her showing some self-restraint the previous evening, whether I could proceed to a prompt escape following completion of the ward round and a few simple jobs for a carb heavy breakfast and a doze in the Doctors' Mess in front of 'Cash in the Attic'. Claire kindly agreed. I was busy updating the patient list when the knock rang out on the junior doctors' office.

'Ah Tom, just the man,' Sudeep, one of the General Surgical Registrars said, 'Mr Kelly is wanting a house officer to assist in theatre, some big bowel resection. I'm in clinic but Khalid is down there.' Khalid was the senior General Surgical Registrar. I glanced at Claire pleadingly.

'Tom will want to go Sudeep, he is a budding surgeon,' Claire smiled at me deviously looking straight into my bloodshot eyes.

'Err but,' I stuttered.

'Super-job Tom,' Sudeep interrupted slapping me hard on the shoulder in a jocular fashion. 'You had best head down, Claire and I can whip around the inmates before I go to clinic.' I glanced back at Claire who continued to smile. Sudeep entered the office and ushered me outside into the corridor closing the door behind me. I heard, as I headed to the lifts down to main theatres, the roar of his laughter as Claire informed him of her stich up. Bastards.

Following a quick stop for an unpleasant bowel motion I presented myself to Theatre 12, one of the general surgical theatres, in my scrubs and new clogs (after last time I invested in some new rubber Crocs with the air holes). I put on a facemask outside and immediately was forced to smell my own fetid breath tinged with kebab meat and acetate. I entered the double doors and saw two surgeons scrubbed and gowned either side of a draped anesthetised patient.

'Ah Tom, excellent, you made it,' a muffled Mr Kelly said although, with the scrub masks, I was unable to fix where the voice originated from. I elected only to smile in retort and then realised that I too was wearing one. 'Paula could you show Tom where the coffee room is, I understand there was a big Mess party last night and I want to be sure he is adequately caffeinated prior to the next big case.' Mr Kelly continued without even a reply, 'Tom follow the lovely Paula whilst we finish off this hernia.' This time a pair of eyes flicked on me from the far side of the table identifying Mr Kelly.

A hugely obese form, barely contained by her overly sized scrubs, lurched from the far side of the operating theatre towards me and pulled off her mask, smiled warmly, introduced herself as Paula the theatre manager and led me through to the theatres coffee room.

'Hi Tom,' greeted Mr Kelly loudly walking into the coffee room now de-scrubbed. 'How are you? Good night was it?'

'Err,' I muttered again not sure of the correct response.

'Coffee Mr Kelly?' interrupted Khalid, 'Tom?' He added glancing at me. I had never once spoken to Khalid but he seemed to know my name. An ominous sign.

'Yep, Julie Andrews please.' Mr Kelly answered, presumably for both of us.

'Julie Andrews?' I asked.

'White nun Doc. You know, white no sugar. I believe they call it a play on words, stop me if I'm losing you?' he grinned at me teasingly. 'You know as opposed to a Whoopi?'

'Whoopi?'

'Black nun, Whoopi Goldberg. For Christ's sake Tom I hope you wake up soon, we've got a big case next and I need a good Legs man. They all said upstairs that you were the fellow for the job?'

'Oh,' I felt as though I had disappointed him already. I had absolutely no idea what he was talking about.

Mr Kelly was a portly consultant in his 40s. He was a standard surgeon; a little obsessive, arrogant and insanely busy but he was jocular and always tried to teach you something on the occasion that you saw him. He addressed all of his juniors, as 'doc'; a seemingly pejorative term on account that they weren't, like him, a surgeon[1] which also had the advantage of not having to remember any of their names. He was, according to my e-portfolio, my educational supervisor although our introductory meeting consisted of me

---

[1] Doctors are physicians whilst surgeons lose the courtesy title doctor and return to 'mister or miss' when they pass their membership exams for the Royal College of Surgeons; a throwback to the barber surgeons of the middle ages who were not considered as 'doctors'.

accosting him in the sandwich queue. He asked me whether I had any problems, whether anyone was bullying me and whether I was hating being a junior doctor. I, of course, answered 'no' to all.

'So what type of surgeon do you want to be Doc?' I had heard that Mr Kelly often light-heartedly asked this question as though to suggest that the only medical specialty worth doing was a surgical one.

'Not sure,' I replied.

'But you do want to be a surgeon?"

'I think so.'

'Well you should talk it over with your educational supervisor,' he asked.

'You're my educational supervisor,' I added quietly.

He laughed. 'Well we better talk it over then,' he glanced at Khalid as though seeking approval for his jesting. Khalid continued to fixate on the computer screen. 'Well we should probably have another meeting. Let's do it at the end of the list and we can do the e-portfolio bits and bobs.

'That would be good,' I lied seeing any chance of me escaping home for a warm bath and to sleep off my hangover now completely evaporated.

'Doc, the next one is a big case; an A-P resection. Do you know what that is?' Mr Kelly asked.

'It is an abdominoperineal resection for bowel cancer that is low in the rectum so requires the removal of the rectum and the anus, the bottom sewing up and a permanent colostomy.

'He knows a thing or too this lad doesn't he Khalid?' Khalid grinned as he placed down our cups of coffee in front of us and sat at a computer terminal in the corner of the room writing up the previous operation notes. 'So that is why we need a legs man,' added Mr Kelly.

'A legs man?' I asked.

'Yep the legs man. Don't worry Doc, we've all been the legs man haven't we Khalid?'

'We certainly have Mr Kelly,' replied Khalid again still typing on the computer.

There was a brief pause in the surgical banter onslaught as Mr Kelly checked his emails on his mobile phone. I considered my current state of wellbeing and concluded that the sloppy poo I had done in the male changing room had made me feel a little brighter.

'Patient is under,' the hefty theatre sister said appearing at the door of the coffee room.

'Action time then chaps,' said Mr Kelly putting down his coffee. We walked into the scrub room where Paula had laid out three gowns.

'What size gloves are you Tom,' she asked.

'Six and a half please,' I answered.

'You've scrubbed up before haven't you Doc?' asked Mr Kelly.

'Yes a few times.'

All gowned up we entered the operating theatre. The patient, an elderly chap, was lying on the theatre table anesthetised on a ventilator. The nurses and operating department practitioners were busy manoeuvring him into position. The bottom end of the operating theatre table had been removed and the gentleman's legs placed in stirrups as though he was about to undergo a smear test.

'Right doc get your finger up there and see if you can feel the cancer.'

'Up his bum?'

'Well you're going to struggle to feel it from his mouth,' Mr Kelly chuckled.

'I inserted my gloved finger in the anesthetised man and felt immediately as though I was violating him. Since becoming a surgical house officer barely a day would go by without me getting a patient to roll onto their left hand side, slip down their underpants pull up their knees and then be penetrated by my gloved digit. Half the time I had no idea why I was even doing it but the surgeons believe that a PR should by the final flourish performed at the end of every abdominal examination. When questioned why this was necessary the standard retort was 'if you don't put your finger in it, you put your foot in it'. Before doctors where classified as Foundation Year 1 doctors they were referred to as pre-registration house officers or PRHOs.

'Why do I have to put my finger in their bum?' you would ask the registrar.

'You are the PRHO[1], what did you think it stood for?'

Of course I would always ask consent from the patient, not to do so would be assault, but the patients rarely ever refused. I will always remember the first time I was asked to perform this intimate task. I was a medical student working nights shadowing the medical house officer on-call. The house officer was worried a confused nonagenarian was having a gastrointestinal bleed so trundled me off to take a repeat blood test. She was continuing to drop her haemoglobin levels despite repeated transfusions and the house officer, on advice of the medical registrar had suggested I pop up a finger to see if there was any melena[2]. By the time I reached the patient it was gone 2am and I foundered in the dark to reach her cubicle at the end of the ward of eight patients. I turned on the reading light, after pressing the multitude of switches over the bed and awoke the patient. I purposefully and meticulously explained who I was, checked the details on the elderly patient's wristband and explained what I had to do.

'Whatever you think?' the elderly lady croaked. As I rolled her into position, placed on my left hand glove and covered by index finger in lube. I shuffled down her large incontinence pad and spread aside her buttocks to see some external haemorrhoids. I closed my eyes, questioned my career choices and inserted my finger into the warm cavity only to hear the now apparently lucid voice of the 92 year old: 'I thought you wanted to check my bum-hole doctor, not the other one?'

---

[1] PRHO is an old term for a first year doctor standing for 'pre-registration house officer'

[2] Melena is a dark tarry poo that is due to bleeding from the stomach or small bowel that is altered by digestive chemicals and normal intestinal bacteria. I understand it is also a very unfortunate name for a baby girl.

As I inserted my finger into the patient's anus who lay anesthetised on the operating table at the behest of Mr Kelly a swell of nausea reappeared in my gut.

'Can you feel it Doc?'

'Not really, maybe just at the fingertip?'

'Just at the fingertip? What have you got hands like an Oompa Loompa?'

'I don't think so raising my gloved hand complete with shit covered finger in the air.'

'Put your hand down Doc, you'll get it in my eye,' requested Mr Kelly without a hint of amusement, 'Khalid, get in there.' I stepped back to allow Khalid to insert his finger which he seemed to do with a final 180 degree flick; almost like a final flourish.

'Well?'

'He's right, it's quite far up.'

'For God's sake, right, let me have ago, trust me to have a team with hands smaller than my mother,' muttered Mr Kelly.

We all stood back behind the patient's exposed anus and watched as Mr Kelly took his turn between the legs to insert his digit.

'You're all right. Good job Tom. You might have saved this man's anus,' he commented. It was most certainly the most peculiar compliment I had ever received.

'Right Khalid, switch fire we can give this man an open anterior resection, join him back together and give him a loop.[1]'

---

[1] An A-P resection is for a low bowel cancer which involves or verges on the anal canal- the first part of the bottom (working from the bottom up). Here the anus and lower part of the rectum (the next part of the bottom- working up) are removed, the anus is sewn up and the patient has a permanent colostomy where the end of the colon, which was attached to the rectum, is brought out to the skin. An anterior resection results in the rectum being removed and the bit above (the sigmoid colon typically) is joined to the anus so the bowel is in continuity and the patient can poo normally. Often a loop of bowel is brought out higher up (often a bit of small bowel) to rest the colon and allow the joined together bowel to rest and heal without having poo running through it.

117

'Sounds good Mr Kelly, replied Khalid calmly, 'Ladies, Gents,' Khalid said addressing the theatre staff and the anaesthetist who was already tucking into a Sudoku puzzle. 'We are going for anterior resection and primary anastomosis with loop.'

I stood in between the patient's legs literally inches away from the patient's saved anus with a ringside seat of Khalid opening up the patient from just below the sternum to below the belly button; an incision known as a laparotomy. It wasn't long before the abdominal cavity was breached and the smell of human entrails wafted into the air precipitating a further bout of nausea in me. I let out a belch and felt the acidic taste of stomach contents in the back of my throat.

Khalid and Mr Kelly worked in precision, isolating the bowel and cutting down deep into the pelvis to mobilise the section containing the cancer. Mr Kelly occasionally murmured to Khalid who worked silently and meticulously. I was asked to hold retractors holding open the incision as wide as possible to assist until my arm ached.

'How's the arm Doc?'

'Not too bad Mr Kelly,' I lied.

'You're doing a good job Tom, having adequate access to what you need to see is an important part of surgery and I know Khalid is grateful for your excellent retraction aren't you Khalid?' Khalid stopped and glanced in my direction.

'Very much so,' he said holding my eye contact briefly before focussing again on dissecting deep into the patient's pelvis.

'Christ the bowel prep isn't very good is it?' Mr Kelly commented. I was jolted back to life. 'He hasn't taken his bowel prep has he?' Mr Kelly asked Khalid almost accusingly as if Khalid was responsible for his entire pre-operative work-up.

'No, it would seem not Mr Kelly,' murmured Khalid obsequiously.

'Right doc,' said Mr Kelly handing his dissecting scissors back to the scrub nurse. 'You can release your retractor Doc,' he added. I glanced at the clock as I massaged my aching forearm over the scrub gown. My arm had been pulling back on the metal implement for over 2 and a half hours.

'Ladies I need the big syringe and some warm water please to the doctor between the legs,' ordered Mr Kelly. A large bladder washout syringe with a litre kidney dish of warm water appeared to my left hand side held by a scrub nurse. 'Right doc, I need you to fill up the 100ml syringe with warm water, pop the spout up his bum and fire up the water,' instructed Mr Kelly. I did as requested.

'Again Tom,' ordered Mr Kelly. 'Ladies another full kidney dish full of warm water to Khalid please.'

I turned to fill up the 100ml syringe again from the warm water when Khalid poured a litre of warm water into the patients opened rectal stump. The warm water heavily caked in warm shit flooded out of the patient's anus and poured straight onto my new clogs. I had cleverly opted for the clogs with air vents in the top to ensure that one's feet don't get too sweaty and I felt the warm brown water seep into my socks. Following the liquid deluge large dollops of sloppy poo dropped onto my scrub trousers, feet and floor.

'Is there a lot of shit their Doc?' asked Mr Kelly grinning loudly.

I visibly bulked to Mr Kelly's amusement. 'Come on Doc, as I said, we have all been the legs man,' he added, 'now I need you to keep going with the syringe.' I did as I was requested and Khalid continued to work deep in the pelvis resected the cancerous section of bowel. Mr Kelly stood back almost overseeing it.

Khalid finally extracted a large portion of bowel tissue putting it in a waiting receptacle.

'Ladies, I think we are ready for the bum gun,' declared Mr Kelly. There was a murmur of whisperings from the scrub nurses and the odd giggle:

'The bum gun,' they whispered, 'get the bum gun.'

'Right Doc time for you to be relieved as the legs man,' said Mr Kelly as Khalid appeared at my shoulder. I large plastic device shaped like a Stormtrooper's laser appeared in Khalid's hand. Mounted on the front was a circular metal disc.

'Insert the bum gun!' Mr Kelly mock ordered. I stood just behind Khalid as he shoved the device up the patients arse, twisted a few nobs and with a few clicks the staples had been deployed and the patient had been joined back together.

'Right Doc, whilst Khalid closes, can you open up the resected colon and clean it down in the sluice ready for pathologists? You might want to change your trousers next.'

I bustled through a side door of the theatre into a dissection room and tore off my scrub gown. I changed my gloves and, still with my scrub mask on to hopefully attenuate the smell, I readied myself at the sink. My mouth watered in anticipation of the vomiting. Cutting through the bowel tissue to open up the inner lumen still flecked with shit was the final straw and I gagged leaning into the sink to vomit loudly. Naturally I forgot I was still wearing my scrub mask and the vomit sprayed outwards covering the scrub top, the sample of resected bowel, the sink, the floor, everywhere. I paused, removed my facemask, and considered strongly that this was an all-time career low. Whilst reflected on this, with some deep breathing and feminine moans, I vomited again having opened the flood gates to the deluge. I managed to compose myself, finish the job, clean the surfaces down, rinse my sick off the bowel cancer specimen and place the resected tissue in a labelled waiting receptacle for it to be sent to the pathologists for analysis. I walked back into main theatres to watch Khalid fire in the remaining abdominal staple.

'My, my, Tom,' Mr Kelly said eying me up and down with my shitty shoes, shitty trousers, vomit flecked scrub top and red face, 'no fun being the legs man eh?'

It was 715pm when we walked down the corridor back to Mr Kelly's office. I tried to suggest that we could move the educational meeting to another time but Mr Kelly seemed resolute:

'No Tom, you did me a favour by saving that man's bum hole so only fair that I repay it by giving you some pastoral care.' We walked along side by side. 'I'm just going to phone the kids to wish them good night.'

I walked alongside him as he said good night to his kids gaining a peculiar and slightly uncomfortable insight into Mr Kelly's home life. When we got to his office I sat down next to his desk and we quickly jumped through the educational hoops. Was I enjoying my job? What did I think I was doing well? What did I think I could improve on? How many workplace based assessments should I do?

The talk was perfunctory and clipped with the sole aim being to satisfy the requirement that the meeting had to take place and this was to be evidenced on the e-portfolio. The majority of the time was waiting for the e-portfolio to load rather than anything else. It was in one of these awkward waits that Mr Kelly turned to me:

'You may think you want to be a surgeon but let me tell you; I rarely see my kids and my wife is infuriated that she never sees me. I have hardly any friends as I spend all my time at work. Furthermore my previous mistakes haunt me and I don't sleep well at night.' A horrible silence penetrated the room as we both returned our gaze to the loading e-portfolio.

Perhaps the meeting was not as token as I had thought. Whilst I sat there wishing more than anything to go home, brush my teeth and take off my rancid smelling socks, I had come to two important decisions: 1) I was never going to go out on a school night and 2) I was going to strongly consider if being a surgeon was right for me.

Chloe

Chloe had eyes of chartreuse green flecked with hazel and viridian which slowly flicked towards me as I entered the room. Her skin, which had briefly returned to its natural colour of velvety molten caramel was now sallow and waxen. Her mother sat on the same hard plastic chair now adjacent to the bed in omnipresent vigil. She was joined this time by a smattering of assorted family. All looked up attentively as I came in. Chloe had inoperable breast cancer. Chloe was 17.

Last year Chloe had been cataclysmically excised from her life as a normal school-girl studying for her GCSEs and thrust headfirst into a fight for survival played out on the battlefields of the oncology day unit. She was currently losing, heavily, and the oncologists and surgeons had seemingly waved the white flag. Chloe continued to fight on alone.

Two days ago she had been forced to come back to hospital. The cancer had spread to her lungs and, due to the accumulating fluid in the chest cavity, she was having extreme difficulty just breathing. For some bizarre reason she ended up in the hands of the thoracic surgeons on a manic Friday afternoon. They had inserted a large pleural drain to remove the fluid with a plan of trying to get her transferred to a medical ward for palliative care input over the weekend, if the bed situation improved.

I was the Foundation Year 1 doctor looking after the surgical wards overnight for that week. I met Chloe when the ward nurse, looking after her overnight, asked me to prescribe some painkillers for the enormous hosepipe of a drain that was uncomfortably hanging out of her thoracic cavity.

I walked into her side room and, despite familiarising myself with her medical notes, I was still taken aback by how young and helpless she looked. She was lying in bed with clenched teeth trying not to breathe so her inflamed pleura didn't catch on the drain. The irony of going from not being able to breathe to not wanting to breathe all in the space of one afternoon. A fashion magazine lay open but disregarded on her lap. Her mother sat by the end of the bed and glanced up as I came in.

'Hello,' I greeted.

'Hey,' Chloe managed to whisper.

'I'm Tom. I've been asked to prescribe some painkillers for you?'

'Thank God,' her mother interjected. It didn't seem to be said snidely or with anger or contempt but with desperation, inexorable fear and the unremitting exhaustion borne from the callous circumstance of a mother forced to watch her daughter slowly ebb away.

'Have you been waiting long?'

'Not too long thank you doctor,' Chloe replied stoically raising a half smile, 'I feel much better after the drain, it just hurts every time I breathe in or out.'

'That can happen I'm afraid,' I added. 'Do you have any allergies?'

'No.'

'Super.' I picked up her drug chart and made several additions. 'I have written you up for several regular pain medications, some morphine now and some extra pain medications that if you need, you can ask for and the nurse will give to you.'

'Thank you doctor,' Chloe replied.

'Thank you,' her mother echoed. I glanced at the drain which was collecting the blood stained fluid leaking out of her thoracic cavity. Over 2 litres had drained already.

'So what's the plan?' I asked.

'I think we are waiting transfer to another ward,' the mother said wearily, 'now the surgeons have put in this drain.'

'Well if you need anything more, just ask the nurses and they can bleep me. I have a few other jobs to attend to, if you'll excuse me?' I said. 'If I get time I'll pop back and see how you're doing.'

'Thank you Doctor,' they both echoed.

It was 2am by the time I came back. I glanced through the door. By the dimly lit light emitted from the corner lamp I could see the curled figure of Chloe asleep in the bed. Her mother, still sat on the hard plastic chair, had moved it closer to the side of the bed and was holding her hand gently stroking the palm. I elected not to disturb them and continued with the hum-drum of night time surgical ward cover.

'How is the girl in side room B on Ward 26?' I asked the SHO at hand over the next day.

'Been struggling a bit today. No medical beds to transfer and no one has tried to get palliative care input over the weekend. The drain has slowed a lot but her breathing is much worse. The medical registrar came but he was getting smashed down in A&E with admissions so he just made sure she was not for resuscitation and wrote her up for a syringe driver[1] if required'.

'Really?' I asked.

'Yep.'

That was all that was said on Chloe and we proceeded with handover. I had struggled to sleep during the day today which I had put down to the swift inversion of circadian rhythm required of switching from day shifts to night. This did leave me time to mull and dwell over Chloe's iniquitous predicament and the futility of life.

It was shortly after 11pm when I made it up-to Ward 26; the thoracic surgery ward. I spent some time reviewing all of Chloe's medical notes and glanced at her admission CT scan which showed the aggressive widespread metastases ravaging her lungs.

Chloe's eyes of chartreuse green flecked with hazel and viridian slowly flicked towards me again as I entered her side room. She lay prostrate in the hospital bed with the head raised at 45 degrees. A special non-rebreathe mask delivered high flow oxygen as she fought for each breath. It was quite obvious that Chloe was dying. I noticed the neglected fashion magazine had now fallen to the floor where it lay in-between myself, in the doorway, and the occupied bed. I took a step reached down and picked up the magazine. Her mother still

---

[1]A syringe driver is a large syringe usually containing a sedative and morphine based pain killer often used to ease symptoms when patients are dying.

sitting on the same hard plastic chair adjacent to her daughter surrounded by a smattering of assorted family and friends saw me.

'Chloe loves fashion,' she explained. 'She has done some catalogue work, as a model but she dreams of being on the catwalk. Don't you princess?' Chloe's eyes flicked back to her mother but she didn't answer. All effort seemed to have been diverted to making her chest rise and fall with each breath.

'How are you getting on Chloe?' I asked.

She slowly raised her thumb keeping her arm by her side.

'Might I have a word with you doctor?' her mother asked. Gesturing towards the door.

'Of course.' We stepped outside the room together into the dimly lit darkness of the ward corridor. Another member of family followed the mother outside. I opened my bleep which had been going off at a fairly constant steady rate and pulled out the battery to ensure that it would just be the gentle snores of the other asleep patients on the ward that would provide the background noise to our conversation.

'This is my sister,' explained Chloe's mother.

'Hello I'm Tom. I am the ward doctor overnight.' Neither lady volunteered their names. In anticipation of the topic of discussion, that I was sure we were about to have, I stupidly forgot to ask.

'Well it was just an update really doctor,' Chloe's mum volunteered after a brief pause. 'She has really got worse over the past day or so, I mean she wasn't too bad after that drain but today she has really struggled.'

'Has anyone come to speak with you?' I asked.

'Not really. Someone did come but they kept on getting paged and interrupted and they never came back,' the mother replied.

'Oh,' I paused, 'I am sorry for that.' I hesitated again.

'Is there any news on when she will get moved to the other ward for more specialist help? Her breathing is bad now.' I looked at them both with their imploring eyes and swallowed hard. I felt pissed off. This is not the job of the on-call night doctor nor one of the most junior doctors in the hospital. All patients at the weekend should be at least seen by the surgical registrar and they had obviously skipped over Chloe this morning and purposefully decided that they didn't need to have the conversation I was about to have with Chloe's family. I felt an overwhelming urge not to duck responsibility but to do the right thing.

'Her breathing is bad but I don't think we will be moving Chloe,' I stated. They both looked at me but said nothing. Their features showed neither shock or indignation or anger. Almost acceptance. I let my words sink in. 'I think Chloe is dying.' I added softly. Chloe's mother looked at her sister. The tears began streaming down her face. They hugged. I stood next to them and said nothing although every urge was for me to fill the uncomfortable silence, the lump in my throat prohibited it. I heard the soft sobs emanating from the hugging sisters adding to the background staccato of snoring.

'I knew it,' said Chloe's mother after a while. 'I knew when she came to hospital this time that...' she failed to complete her sentence.

'Do you think she is comfortable?' I asked. 'Is there anything more we can do?'

'No doctor, I mean yes, I do think she is comfortable. The syringe is helping.' I hadn't been asked by the nursing staff about setting up the syringe driver. They had obviously anticipated the inevitable even though the surgical registrar had elected not to.

'When the heart stops and it is due to an illness like cancer we usually don't try and re-start the heart with powerful drugs and compressions on the chest, do you agree with this?' I asked as sensitively as I could.

'Yes absolutely, as does Chloe,' her mother said resolutely.

'I think that is a wise decision,' I added. Several minutes seemed to pass with no one saying anything.

'Dry your eyes,' I finally said walking a foot to the nearest sink, pulling a hand towel from the dispenser, 'and we can go in and see her,' I added handing over the coarse recycled paper.

I opened the door and allowed the mother and sister to pass before entering the room myself. Chloe lay in the bed where we left her, rapidly breathing in and out. Except for the gushing sound of high flow oxygen the room was deathly silent; as though waiting in anticipation. The remaining roughly outlined members of family sat and looked on; all conversation seemingly exhausted. I knelt down next to her so I was only a few feet from her.

'Hey,' I said touching her hand. Her eyes flicked open, the deep green flashing awake. 'Are you in pain?' I asked. She shook her head.

'Do you know what is happening to you?' I asked.

Chloe looked at me straight and nodded. She raised a half smile, summoned all her effort and mouthed through the oxygen mask; 'I know.' I felt the warm tears forming in the corners of my eyes and the hard lump in my throat reappear. Soft sobs emanated again from the opposite corner of the room. I hoped the dimly lit room would at least not betray me. I stood up and touched her hand again.

'Anything you need......,' I let my sentence fade away.

'Thank you doctor,' the room murmured. And with that, I left.

I briefly outlined the conversation I had had with the nursing staff and made sure they did not interfere in this cataclysmic but special time for the family by taking endless sets of blood pressure and oxygen saturation measurements. I then phoned the surgical registrar but was forced to relay Chloe's situation through a theatre runner; him being scrubbed in for an appendicectomy. The runner relayed back his tacit approval with little interest. I finally reinserted the batteries in my bleep only to be greeted by a cacophony of noise.

'Where have you been?' said the voice on the end of the phone, 'we have been bleeping for ages.'

'Sorry,' I replied, 'with a patient.'

'We have some fluids for you to prescribe and two cannulas, can you come now.'

'Sure, I'll be right there,' I replied wearily.

At 6am I popped my head around the door of Chloe's side room with a cup of tea which I handed to her Mum. She remained by Chloe's side still holding her daughter's hand; another full night without any sleep. Chloe was now in a coma with only irregular agonal gasps as she clung onto the vestiges of life. I explained my shift was shortly ending and again asked if I could help with anything. The mother again thanked me and said that neither Chloe nor she needed anything. It was the last time I would see them. She died that morning.

Foundation Year 2

General Practice

'It cannot be too often or too forcibly brought home to us that the hope of the profession is with the men who do its daily work in general practice.'

Sir William Osler

GP Land

General practice; how I've longed for your warm embrace. I am sick of being a ward dogsbody. Being dragged along interminable ward rounds. Bed after bed, ward after ward, day after day. Always the same routine: race around finding the patient's notes, swear at the computer when the X-ray fails to load, the swift pull of the patient's curtain, the cursory glance at the observations chart and attempting to decipher handwriting in the notes whilst you add to the record in your own unique hieroglyphics. I was sick of finding empty phlebotomy request bags on the ward with 'patient being washed' scrawled across the top of the form. I was sick of writing discharge summaries. I was sick of putting in cannulas. I was sick of requesting scans. I was sick of 'chasing' them. I was sick of never being able to get on a computer that worked. I was sick of most of the work of junior doctor being on a computer. I was sick of requesting consults on patients where I had no idea what question I was asking or why I wanted some esoteric specialist to see the patient.

What am I hoping for from general practice? I am hoping to be a doctor not a part-administrative assistant, part-secretary, part-scribe, part-errand boy. I was hoping to have a direct influence on my patient's health rather than just a face that they see writing in their notes in the morning before popping back later and failing to insert a cannula in them. I was hoping to be treated with just a modicum of respect rather than being ignored or belittled.

So first day of general practice and I awoke early to allow myself the appropriate amount of time to strongly consider my GP attire. I was grateful I was no longer constrained by the hospital 'evidence based' infection control policies; bare below the elbows; no watch, no ties, no white coats, no rings (except a wedding ring because that, by the grace of God, is impervious to infection). This leaves you with the chino and open shirt with sleeves rolled up combination making you look like you're popping off, after the ward round, to spend the afternoon punting. My clothing was now only limited by the patient's perception of what a GP should wear, or even, would wear. I had had a think and made the bold step of buying a new woolly pulley. It was royal blue, and a tank-top rather than long sleeve. I remember analysing myself in the mirror wearing it. I looked like primary care personified. Sadly the clothing budget didn't stretch too much further and I had to resurrect my old cords which were slightly too tight and had an odd stain in the crotch region that I'm quite sure is sadly innocent. Topped off with a pair of 10 year old scuffed Chelsea boots and a tweed jacket with elbow pads, I absolutely was finding it hard to get over myself. The tweed jacket I had originally bought from Oxfam for a stag party. We went dressed as farmers to rather rural North Wales. For some reason the reception of 20 pissed males wearing various assortments of ridiculous farming related garments was not as cordial as one might expect. Perhaps it was the blow up inflatable sheep with a tomato ketchup bottle inserted into its factory manufactured plastic anal canal that tipped the edge and forced our rather ragged, bloody retreat. At least I imagined it being bloody, come to think of it, it could well have been ketchup.

My perceptions of a male GP harked back to my own old, now retired, GP: Dr Edwards that I used to visit as a boy with my bloody knees and snotty nose. He wore waistcoats in colours favoured by manic patients and would check his pocket watch if my mother droned on for too long. He wore a bow tie which, on a Friday, was often polka-dot. His look was crowned with a pair of off-the-peg reading glasses perched precariously on the tip of his nose and a perfectly trimmed moustache. He would peer down his nose, from behind his mahogany desk, to inspect my various ailments without ever moving an inch towards me. With a flourish of a pen the prescription was written and I was out the door before I had barely had the chance to sit down. With a final glance in the mirror I had concluded that, although I hadn't quite reached the magnificence of old Dr Edwards those many years ago, I was ready.

I parked up my old green jalopy in what looked like a Mercedes Benz show room masquerading as a staff car park. I was confident my fourteen year old Skoda Fabia estate 1.3 would hold her own and not embarrass me. If not I'll just reverse into a few of the competition. What with her detachable wing mirrors (they were secured in position with duct tape) and her many dents (several reversing incidents usually involving shopping trolleys or my housemate's car), I was proud of the fact that I had never cleaned her. As I regularly told my friends, when they were unlucky enough to be offered a lift, that they will never get a ride in such a dirty girl ever again.

'Hold onto your hats fellas,' I would say whilst I listlessly ascended her to cruising speed, 'you're about to be driven to the moon and back.' This wasn't a lie either; I am relatively sure, what with her impressive six figure mileage, that she had literally been to the moon at least once

I parked up and walked in through the front door to meet the receptionist Glenys. I had spoken to her before when discussing my impending rotation. I was attempting to get hold of the senior partner. She had performed her duties as GP receptionist admirably and been completely obstructive. Still, now I was an accepted member of the club.

'Good morning Dr Parsons,' she said in her melodious Irish tones remembering me from our telephone conversation. 'Would you care for a cup of tea doctor?'

'That would be wonderful Glenys,' I replied with a smile whilst trying not to focus on her hirsutism.

'All the doctors are in the coffee room. Go ahead, I'll bring it through for you.'

I sauntered into the meeting room.

'Hi I'm Tom, the new FY2 doctor,' I declared whilst quickly scanned the room. There were at least half a dozen sat around a large coffee table reading post and drinking coffee. I quickly noticed that I was the only idiot wearing tweed. The men were all in shirts with the majority wearing ties. Some complemented this with a suit jacket. The women wore skirts and cardigans with the occasional trouser suits. Everyone looked up from their mail on my entrance and I felt immediately self-conscious. It was like I was at my first day at a new school when I was quickly designated the nickname of 'Fatty tommy no-friends'. Hopefully a wedgey, a kick in the balls and having my lunchbox thrown on the roof wasn't on the cards today. I do have a theory that most doctors were bullied at school, especially the old guard. The privately educated specky lot; all lifetime members of 'The Wets, Weirdos and Fatties Brigade'; the games teacher's worse nightmare. Removed of their tuck money before ten to nine and forced to retreat to their hiding place between the reference books and non-fiction section in the library where they remained through their school years. There they would become highly educated before being delicately plucked by likeminded individuals for a career in neurosurgery.

A chap stood up at the back. He had a thick head of black hair that looked suspiciously manicured. It wasn't....no surely not....I think it might have been a wig. He adjusted what looked to be NHS issue glasses as dense as jam jar bottoms, did up the bottom button only of his tweed jacket to hide his rather sizable gut and made way towards me with an outstretched hand adorned with signet ring. I was delighted to find I had modelled my primary care dress code on the one GP who has a dead racoon living on his head.

'Ah yes you must be Tom, I'm Dr Clive Love the senior partner here I'm delighted to meet you.' I took his outstretched hand and tried not to look at his Barnet. 'And this is Angela Thompson, Kay Rapley and Dave Simons the other partners and this is Kevin our visiting CPN[1] and Margaret, one of our practice nurses.'

'Pleased to meet you all,' I responded forcing my gaze to meet theirs. Their warm greeting smiles reassured me I would be able to keep my lunch money today.

Clive ushered me out the staff room to the formica'ed facility next door where Glenys was hopefully knocking up my cuppa.

'Now you know where the kitchen is don't you Tom?'

'Yes thanks I've had a good snoop round, I wanted to see if there was anything I could steal,' I said smiling. Dr Love's head quibbled and his chins wobbled slightly. An awkward silence ensued between

---

[1] Community Psychiatric Nurse: Drafted in to manage the large volume of mental health presentations in primary care. A good 30% of all patients' presentations to their GP have a mental health component.

us. Surely he didn't think I was being serious? I blushed and rubbed the side of my nose as we walked out of the kitchen.

'Right then, ahem,' he said clearing his throat and terminating the silence. 'Well let me show you where you will be working Thomas. Do follow me.'

I followed him down the corridor walking away from the waiting room. We walked past several consulting rooms with the practice GP's and nurse's name emblazoned on them. 'Here we are Thomas,' he said arriving to a final door at the end of the corridor. He opened the door. I struggled to hide my disappointment as I cast my eyes around the condensed little space. It was half the size of somewhere someone would normally use to keep their boiler in. The examination couch was rammed up against the wall opposite a small desk with a computer perilously perched upon it. A sink, a bookcase, a cupboard, a metal set of drawers of clinical equipment and an assortment of small bins with different colour bin bags similar to hospital. I could never work out what waste went in which bin. There was just about enough room for 2 chairs haphazardly placed in the middle of the room for patients to plonk themselves down on. There was, for little old me, a large comfy leather executive office chair which could spin around 360 degrees and had a rather impressive assortment of ergonomic features. It looked a trifle too comfortable as though there might be the very real danger of drifting off into a micro-nap during a patient's particularly tedious soliloquies.

'Now the complementary therapists use this room on Thursday so you will be sitting in with me every Thursday. Other foundation doctors have found this highly useful and I dare say you will too,' said Clive. So my input here is so inadequate that every Thursday they would rather invite a quack to rub margarine into people's feet in order to reorganise the 'spirits and humours that are disjointed within'. Heaven forbid I would tread on the reflexologist's toes, although, undoubtedly, she would have some essence of dog piss massaged into a significant pressure point to relieve the inflicted malady even if I did.

'Ok, sounds good,' I lied.

'So I'll let you settle and drink your tea and then we have a few computer induction modules for you to go through.' What a little treat. 'Tomorrow is Thursday so we will do a clinic together and also your induction meeting to organise your personal development plan for the next four months.' Clive seemed to have swallowed the entire lexicon of medical education pedagogy and was now regurgitating it in bit size chunks on my lap.

'Sounds great Dr Love.' Never in the history of medicine had anyone suited that name less. He walked out wobbled his chin slightly and replied;

'Call me Clive.'

I opened my leather satchel I had slung on my back and removed 1x Oxford Handbook of General Practice, 1x Oxford Handbook of Clinical Medicine, 1x Stethoscope, 1x fundoscope/otoscope set donated by a kind drug rep along with a number of assorted pens) and placed them on my small desk. I felt a rush of self-importance.

I surveyed the room again. It would seem my allied health professionals, whoever they were, hadn't left a trace of their existence; no trephining equipment, candlewax or Ouija boards. I was almost disappointed. I wanted to test whether I could pick the correct colour-coded bins before doing the induction module on waste management.

I took off my tweed and realised that despite being August and the height of summer it was cold drizzly weather outside. The radiator seemed to be located under and behind the large examination couch. I attempted to move the examination couch. I had so far, in my short medical career, managed to duck out of attending an NHS Manuel Handling course. I grabbed at the couch and attempted to heave it to allow access to the radiator. The bed didn't move but an acute spasm erupted in my lower back as though I had been kicked by a Grand National Winner. The couch, it seemed, was actually made out of railway girders. There was a gap down the side of the couch so I attempted the superior approach but lost my balance leaving me upside down with my head jammed against the cold painted metal of the bed and the radiator with my legs akimbo waving in the air. A new angle of attack was required; the all fours approach. I tunnelled under the couch and played with knob which helpfully had no markings and no indication on which way to turn it.

I continued to fiddle attempting to grade temperature change by pressing my hand hoping for warmth. First day in General Practice and I was already starring in my own version of a Carry on Film; on all fours with a knob in my hand. Where is Matron when you need her?

'Sorry Dr Parsons,' an interrupting female voice startled me. My head slammed up into the girder. I don't know how sick the patients were at this practice but I had concussion, lumbago and hypothermia already this morning.

I manoeuvring myself around like a Challenger tank attempting a 3 point turn in a Tesco car park with my head bowed to avoid a further blow. I managed to orientate myself to the voiced assailant and arose from under the couch rubbing my cranium and straightening my crooked back.

'Thought you might need this Dr Parsons,' the voice rang out again in a northern twang as I continued to spin my main turret to face the enemy. She was probably of similar age to me and reminded me of the new blonde Carol Vorderman replacement on Countdown. She carried an electric fan heater in one hand and the steaming cup of tea Glenys promised me in the other.

'Thank you,' I said as I ungraciously staggered off my knees.

'We have been having some problems with the central heating in this part of the building. There is also no insulation in the walls here. We called the engineers out last week. I think all they did was put up some carbon monoxide stickers, declared everything fixed, charged an astronomic amount and then buggered off. To be honest I doubt that even if they did know what they were doing it would have made much difference. All the other partners have always called this room The Fridge'.

'Super,' I said sarcastically.

'They always just give it to the foundation doctor. And the complementary therapist,' she added. A silence ensued.

'Well I'm Tom, I'm the new Foundation doctor.' I dusted my hands off and offering her one. Not sure why I had to introduce myself as a Foundation doctor when she had just mentioned that I was one.

'Grace.' She took my hand, noticed that I had transferred some dust to hers. She unconsciously wiped her hand innocently on her jumper leaving a paw-print over her left breast. I felt my cheeks redden. The awkward eternity of silence restarted.

'Err have you worked here long?' I asked.

'Just a few months, I graduated last August in Biochemistry. I didn't really want to do a PhD.'

'Marvellous,' I paused, 'well sorry, no,' I hesitated, 'it's not marvellous that you've not found a job, but marvellous about your degree and stuff.'

She smiled sympathetically.

'I was thinking of applying for medicine,' she added, 'so that is why I took a job here.'

'Clive last time let me sit in some sessions with the foundation doctor. He said I could learn more from them as he went to medical school eons ago.'

'I see. Well I am always happy to put off a future doctor,' I smiled.

'Great, I'll look forward to it.' She returned my smile, put the tea and heater on the desk and walked off.

I plugged the fan heater in and positioned it under my desk. I thought whether it would be more caring to share the heat with the patients and moved the fan heater so it blew out the side of the desk. I thought again and pointed it at my feet.

So I had my room and I had made it slightly more environmentally habitable with the warmth beginning to penetrate my frozen feet. Next I suppose was computer access. Perhaps if I knocked through the online induction quickly I could see some patients this afternoon, or even better, go home. I turned it on and heard the familiar sound as it booted up. I tried the password I had been furnished by Glenys which of course didn't work. I picked up the phone and read off the handset 'Reception; 1', 'Dr Clive Love; 2' and so on. I pressed one.

'Glenys,' I paused, 'hi it's Tom.'

'Hullo Dr Parsons....is everything okay there?'

'Yeah I can't get onto the computer.'

'Have you tried the password?'

'Yep'

'It's case sensitive you know?'

'Yes I know.'

'What's it saying?'

'It's says I don't have access privileges.'

'Bugger,' she said under her breath, 'Barbara,' she shouted, 'Barbara,' again at increased volume, 'BARRRBBBARRAA.' Perhaps Barbara worked from home.

'What?' I heard a voice yell back.

'I thought you set up Tom's computer?'

'Who?' Charming.

'Dr Parsons you know the new young doctor?'

'Hang on.'

'We'll try and do it from down here Dr Parsons I'll ring you back in a second.'

I arranged my pens and books around my desk and spied the bookshelf in the corner. Perhaps that bookcase would provide a good home for my endless, still cellophane wrapped, copies of the British Medical Journal that I continue to convince myself I will eventually read. Or maybe Kumar and Clarke's Clinical Medicine, the bible of medical textbooks; everybody owns it, nobody has read it. Perhaps even a hefty rheumatology tome. It would have to be for show only, not for genuine storage of reference material. Besides, due to the rather unfortunate proximity of the patient couch it was effectively impossible for anyone except a contortionist to remove a book from there without pre-emptively dislocating your own wrist.

I got up from my self-built igloo in the middle of the arctic tundra and assessed the books already sitting on the shelf. 'An Atlas of Human Anatomy' was so old it looked like it might have explanatory arrows pointing to the Gallbladder with inscriptions depicting where to put the leeches. I picked out 'Modern Surgical Practice' and found the published date to be 1954. I hastily returned it to the shelf. There was the ubiquitous dermatology photo book, a textbook on paediatrics and some sort of medical ethics book that looked like it originated from the Boer War.

Then I saw it, bile reared in my throat and I emitted an audible snarl; 'A Practical Guide to Reflexology'. I picked it out holding the slim volume using a thumb and forefinger only like I was handling nuclear waste. I read the quoted reviews on the back. 'Ideal for the budding complementary therapist' and 'a thoroughly absorbent practical guide.' Good, I thought, I'll put that to the test next time the upstairs lavatory runs out of bog roll. My brewing arrogant medical cynicism was interrupted by the phone ringing.

'Hello?'

'Dr Parsons, it's Glenys, you're up and running.....'

Computer induction modules here I come.

Ideas, Concerns and Expectations

I caught Clive Love in a mild daze when I barged through the door of his consultation room for our first Thursday session and my second day as a Foundation doctor in General Practice. He physically startled in a slapstick comedy fashion.

'Morning Dr Love,' I greeted heartily.

'Ah yes Tom,' he paused, 'good morning,' he added, 'good morning, good morning,' he continued inanely. He picked up some hospital letters off the desk and shuffled them aimlessly seeming to exhibit the illusion of preoccupation and interruption. 'Yes' he paused, 'Right… well. How today will work is that you will see the patients and I will sit in and make sure you are coping with the IT and everything and, all going well, we can give you your own list tomorrow. Sound okay?'

'Great,' I responded. I dumped my bag next to the desk and stood next to the GP hesitantly. He picked up the papers he had been shuffling and put them down in exactly the same place. He then fiddled about with his email allowing me to continue my uneasy loiter.

'Pull a chair over,' he ordered releasing me from my toilsome limbo.

I dragged one of the patient's chairs across the carpet dutifully and sat to the left of Dr Love's desk.

'So we have a little bit of time before the first patient arrives. So what do you think you want to get out of the next four months of your Foundation programme placement in General Practice?'

I thought for a second and tried to come up with something useful. 'I suppose practice at delivering management plans to patients and making diagnoses. I mean, we don't get much chance to make diagnoses and management plans in hospital medicine as we are often tied up doing the ward work,' I rambled.

'Right well today we can work on making the diagnosis and getting the patient to accept the diagnosis and management plan. In order to do this you need to elicit their what?' he asked.

'Um,' I hesitated.

'Ideas, concerns and expectations?' He droned doctrinally.

'Ah yes of course.'

'I know the medical school probably drum this into you like it's the 11th commandment but it is important,' he lectured. 'The patients out there, as we speak, will have an idea what they think is wrong with them. They will be rehearsing what they are going to say to you. They will have an agenda. In order to be able to help them you need to understand their agenda and marry it up with yours. Does that make sense?'

'Yes,' I tried to enthuse.

'For you it could be a simple cough,' he continued, 'however they might think they have cancer. But they might not volunteer that information, maybe because they are scared or don't want to look a fool in front of you. When you 'fob' them off with some Paracetamol without understanding their concerns they are much less likely to accept your diagnosis. If you can understand their concerns and address them by reassuring them that you definitely don't think their cough is cancer they will go away happy and reassured.'

'What if they do end up having cancer?' I asked.

'Which is why you must safety net your consultations. If one's cough hasn't settled down in a month or so, come back and we can review you.'

'Understood.'

'Now expectations; the patient will expect you, as the doctor to manage him in a certain way. He might want something that his friend had which worked well for a cough. He might be convinced it is a pneumonia and want antibiotics. So you can see that if you understand the patient's ideas, concerns and expectations together you can address them, reassure them and manage them appropriately. Now it may well be that they expect something which you, the doctor, can't provide or are unwilling to provide. That is where diplomacy comes in. This takes some time to master.'

'Hmm,' I murmured.

'So here lies to the first two lessons of General Practice. Elicit the ideas concerns and expectations of the patient and always safety net your consultation and document in the clinical notes that you have.'

'Got it.'

'Now if you would be so kind as to pull a chair up I will show you again how the computers work.'

'And then you press F8 to call in the next patient,' Clive said.

'F8?'

'Yes so look on your appointment screen, and double click, and then F8, so your first patient is Miss Clementine Westbrook-Smith.'

'Bit of a mouthful,' I added. 'And you can see her demographics there?' I asked pointing at the screen.

'Yes she's a 13 month old little lass, by the looks of it.'

'13 months?' I said. I hadn't seen a child as a doctor. Ever. To be honest the thought of doing so filled me with trepidation.

'Yes, now to check her past medical history; click here. So 6 week baby check was fine, a consultation for colic, some difficulties breast feeding, a few viral infections, some vaccinations and that's about it.'

'Okay?' I glanced at him, 'should I call her in?'

'Have you had much experience with kids?'

'Not really,' I mumbled.

'Have you done any paediatrics as a doctor?'

'Not yet, I've got A&E to come though.'

'Well listen why don't I see this patient and we can use it as a template to work on?' Dr Love asked. I was unwilling to relinquish the reins just yet. Surely children are just like little adults?

'I am willing to give it a shot,' I said stubbornly.

'Are you sure?'

'Well I might not know what is going on but...,' I let my sentence trail away.

'Well I'll sit just next to you at the desk and lend a hand if required. And, let's not forget it will be their ideas, concerns and expectations not the child's we have to elicit as the child is,' he paused, 'well a child,' he guffawed.

'Sure. Shall I call them in?' 'How do I...' I gestured towards the Tannoy system on the desk.

'Ah, yes, so click this and you can call them through by speaking into this here.'

'Just say the name?'

'Well yes, usually helps,' he snorted. I picked up the phone and pressed the speaker button transmitting his voice to the bustling waiting area.

'Miss Smith err Westbrook please,' I hesitated.

'You might want to say where you want them to go.'

'Shit,' I swore pressing the transmit button.

'Hopefully you haven't just said shit to the waiting room.'

'Room, err, what room is this,' my finger still on the button.

'Seven,' Clive added, 'you are still broadcasting.'

'Shit,' I flustered again probably to the waiting room, 'room number seven please.'

'Right well that could have gone better,' Clive sighed. 'My fault we should have done a dummy run. You might need to go and find them,' he half suggested half ordered.

'Right, yes.' I hopped up and leapt out the door to go and rescue the parents of this nipper who, if they had been following my instruction, might well be queuing up outside one of the traps in the gentleman's lavatory looking for 'shit room number seven'.

I found the couple with the baby in a car seat just outside the clinic door. I opened the door to allow the couple to walk into the consultation room and apologised profusely being sure to mention that it was my first day and I was still learning the ropes. Mr Westbrook-Smith; a middle aged fit looking balding man was carrying the baby. Mrs Westbrook-Smith brought up the rear. She was demure and seemed to be lacking in confidence. She was a bespectacled, thin but pretty lady with delicate features. She seemed younger than her husband.

'Please come in, come in,' I greeted them warmly trying to recover my serenity. I smiled and ushered everyone into the room and offered them all to sit down.

I sat down, crossed my legs and smiled. I let my arms fall gently into my lap and clasped my hands together. I looked up and saw Clive perform the exact same mannerisms. I immediately placed my hands on the desk.

'Well I suppose we had better make some introductions,' Clive said. 'My name is Dr Clive Love, I'm the senior partner at this practice. This is Tom he is a junior doctor who is getting to grips with General Practice and today is his first clinic so sorry for the mix up with finding the room.'

'Hi, yes I'm Oliver,' he replied commandingly, 'Oliver Westbrook-Smith, and this is my wife Amanda.' She raised a greeting hand like a Native American. 'I'm involved in a lot of training myself with my company so I appreciate the importance of birthing the next season's calves so-to-speak, he said nodding in my direction.' I tried to not let my face register this bizarre metaphor.

'Right,' Clive hesitated, 'good. Well. Ok, well, if you could address Tom here with everything and I'll try and keep schtum and then if he struggles I'll chip in.' Everyone paused, I glanced over at Clive as though waiting for a starter pistol to fire; 'take it away maestro.'

'How can I help?' I asked.

'Well it's our daughter,' the husband took the reins, 'I think, well,' he glanced at his wife, 'well we think she is having some sort of seizure.'

'Seizure?' I confirmed, 'Okay.' I hesitated slightly, 'and for how long have you noticed this?'

'When did we first notice them?' Mr Westbrook-Smith almost sneered at his wife and his round face flushed red.

'Well it was yesterday when we both saw her when we were sat at the table eating Sunday lunch,' she replied meekly.

'But you think they might have been going on longer?' her husband pressed her momentarily taking over the consultation.

'Well I wasn't sure if she was having some in the back of the car when we were driving to the shops last week.'

'But you didn't do anything about it then,' he seemed to tell her. The husband turned to face his wife who ignored his gaze and continued to stare dead ahead. 'Essentially,' he said addressing Clive more than me, 'the first I heard of it was when it happened in front of me yesterday but Amanda, on the way here this morning, mentioned that she may have been having these fits before.' The husband was like an accomplice in front of the headmaster, caught red handed and quickly absolving himself of blame by snitching on his school friend Wilkins. 'Obviously if he had noticed Wilkins sticking that fragrant cut of cod in your desk drawer he would have definitely brought it to your attention headmaster'.

She briefly fixed him in a daggered stare but said nothing. She rubbed the side of her nose in discomfort and flushed a matching shade of crimson to her husband who now looked positively bulbous. I sensed the tension and tried to defuse the situation by continuing to take the history.

'Okay, describe the seizure, what did you notice?'

'It was bizarre wasn't it,' he told her rather than asked her.

'She kind of shook all over and was grunting,' the wife added.

'And then went all red and then cried,' he chipped in.

'And you were just eating dinner?' I asked.

'Yes.'

'Did it last long?'

'Umm. Not really.' They both answered in almost unison.

'Yes, maybe a couple of minutes,' she said.

'And then it stopped immediately?' I asked.

'Yes,' the couple again chorused

'And has it happened again since?'

'Yes again in the car on the way here. That's when Amanda thought that it might have happened in the car before.' His insinuation was again evident.

'Oh I see,' I replied, 'can you describe the shaking?'

'Well it was bizarre wasn't it?' he again asked her rhetorically. 'As I say she sort of threw her arms about for a period and was rocking back and forth and grunting and then suddenly she sort of went red and became, well, a bit flushed wouldn't you say?'

'And then she cried,' his wife added.

'And it was the same both times,' I asked.

'Well yes. Although I didn't see when it might have happened before,' he added.

146

She gave him that look again. 'And as I said I was driving,' she emphasised the word heavily slowly enunciating the two syllables; dri-ving. 'So I only saw some hand motions and heard the grunting.'

'Right,' I said. A brief silence composed the room. It amplified like an enveloping vacuum sucking the noise from our vicinity.

'So what do you think is going on?' Clive asked perhaps sensing the mood. He seemed almost gleeful like he knew the answer and desperately wanted to share it.

'Well doesn't really sound like she is having fits,' I said. 'I mean unless it is a type of paediatric epilepsy syndrome.'

'Okay?' Clive said elongating the 'k' in an annoying American fashion to attempt to express reservation and request further illumination. 'Would you mind if I just clarify a couple of things.'

'Wait!' Mr Westbrook-Smith interjected, 'look,' he commanded pointing to his daughter still in the car seat. She was grunting and gyrating up and down in a bizarre fashion her arms up in the air. She waved her hands up and down the car seat rocking with the motion. 'That's it! See. Isn't it Amanda?' He was almost standing and pointing at his own daughter like some sort of exhibit. As if on cue little Clementine, stopped the gyrating, flushed red and started whimpering and crying. 'That's exactly like it was before isn't it Amanda? Isn't it?' he demanded.

'Yes,' she nodded her assent but considerably less excited than her husband.

'Tom, any further thoughts,' Clive asked.

'Maybe it is a fit?' I said. I hadn't a bloody clue.

'Okay what goes against it being a fit?' Clive enquired. I quickly glanced at the couple who sat there fixated on me. He looked irritated and twitched his red bulbous face again.

'Umm,' I hesitated under the spotlight, 'I dunno really. It certainly didn't look like the tonic-clonic seizures that adults get. And if the child isn't unwell it isn't a febrile convulsion[1]. I just wonder if it is one of the paediatric epilepsy syndromes?' I think I

---

[1] Febrile convulsion: benign generalised convulsions which occur in young children usually due to having a high fever secondary to a viral infection

fudged the answer pretty well considering I couldn't mention a single paediatric epilepsy syndrome.

'So what would you do if you were this patient's GP?' Clive asked. He seemed to be enjoying his role as tutor.

'For God's sake!' Mr Westbrook-Smith blurted out like an erupting geyser. 'Can you just tell me what is wrong with my daughter please!?'

A silence consumed the room. His wife looked at him in embarrassed accusation. The daughter who had happily resumed playing with the toys dangling from the carrying handle of the car seat started to cry Mrs Westbrook Smith picked her up from the car seat and settled her on her lap.

'I apologise Mr Westbrook-Smith, I'm just trying to get Tom to think through his management decisions,' Clive said politely. It seemed that Oliver Westbrook-Smith's outburst had probably curtailed any further educational value. 'May I be permitted to ask a couple more questions to be sure of the cause?' Clive asked. 'That seat there which Clementine is in, does that go straight into the car?'

'Yes,' murmured Amanda softly, her husband seemed to still be recovering from his unnecessary outburst.

'Ok, and the seat which Clementine had one of these 'episodes' in at home; can you describe it?' Mr Westbrook-Smith tutted and rolled his eyes. 'Is everything alright Mr Westbrook-Smith? You seem frustrated.' Clive asked graciously in false sycophancy, his face deadpan serious.

'You have seen it Dr Love. He gestured to the empty car seat to his left. I've done some research online, I think I have a pretty good idea what is going on, it is quite plain to see. If you would just refer us to a paediatric neurologist we can all carry on with our day without further undue delay,' he blurted out exasperated. 'That is what you GPs are for isn't it? To refer on to the specialist doctors? I don't see that any further discussion is relevant.'

'Humour me,' Clive said again seriously. 'The seat at home Mrs Westbrook-Smith?' Mr Westbrook Smith threw his arms up in an exaggerated sigh of protestation.

'Well it's like any baby high chair really doctor'

'Does it have a bit to stop her falling under the tray part?'

'Yes it has a strap which attaches from the seat to the underside of the tray.'

'Similar to that bit of strapping on her car seat?' Clive asked.

'Well yes.'

'Was that strap done up when the child had her 'fit'?' Clive asked raising two index fingers and wiggling them when he said fit.

'Yes. We always do up the straps.'

'I think I know what is going on,' Clive murmured. He paused briefly.

'And?' shouted Mr Westbrook Smith.

'Your daughter is displaying infant gratification behaviour.'

'So some sort of seizure then!?'

'No Mr Westbrook Smith. This is nothing to do with fits or seizures or epilepsy or anything else,' Clive said gravely.

'What? Well what is it then?'

'Another term, which might explain it better is,' Clive hesitated, 'is infantile masturbation.' Clive let the words sink in.

We both watched Mr Westbrook Smith's brow furrow, his eyes twitched from side to side as the words registered. His wife sat quietly holding the baby who was now snoozing in her lap. He stood up and glared at Clive and I, his eyes darting between the two of us. He opened his mouth and closed it and then opened it and closed it again like a funfair goldfish. He went a crimson red but remained perfectly quiet. The silence consumed the room. He stood up picked up the empty car seat. He glanced back at his wife and said in a measured voice:

'Amanda, come on we are leaving.' He walked straight past her and opened the door. She looked at me apologetically, stood up and followed him without a word. My gaze focused on the jacket which lay abandoned on his recently vacated chair. As soon as I realised it the door swung open again and the looming figure of Mr Westbrook-Smith appeared this time without the car seat. He marched to two or so paces to the chair and snatched his jacket. He turned back to face Clive, and was now visibly shaking with fury.

'You're a bloody pervert and I shall be complaining to the General Medical Council,' he barked. 'I shall expect a referral to a paediatric neurologist in the post unless you want to further your one overarching principle of being a negligent moron.'

It was now Clive's turn to do a fish impression as he marched out and slammed the door. I stared at his feet.

'I suppose we didn't meet his ideas, concerns or expectations then?' I murmured sarcastically. I couldn't help myself.

Confusion

Medical students are like learner drivers, all doctors used to be one; in fact I was one only 18 months ago. We all know they are required for the future of the profession. Consequently they should be helped and supported but when you're just trying to get on with your day they seem to persistently delay and irritate you. Work experience students are even worse; twice as keen but all completely uninitiated into the weird world of healthcare.

I was settling into life in primary care. I had navigated the computer system and I was cherry picking cases off the emergency list to see. The first Thursday session seemed to have lessened Clive's pedagogic fervour and I had mercifully managed to avoid any further sittings. It seems the complementary therapist was on holiday for 3 weeks and Clive was consequently happy for me to continue seeing patients whilst the Fridge was free. In fact I had seen very little of Clive until I was walking past him with a cup of coffee about to start the second part of the morning session.

'Oh Tom, umm may I have a quick word?' He pushed up his glasses and tickling the end of his nose in a curious circling pattern as we stood a little too close together in the corridor. I had been discussing the football with the community psychiatric nurse who had the consulting room next door to the Fridge. He saw Clive and quickly jolted with his hot mug swearing silently as he spilled it on his hand during his escape. 'How are you getting on?' Clive asked.

'Fine I think,' I replied innocently. I felt as if I had done something wrong.

'Good, good. We have heard good things from the patients about you.'

'Oh? That's great.' I smelt bullshit.

'And the weather has warmed up hasn't it? Dreadful for August wasn't it earlier?'

'Dire,' I agreed.

'All that rain.'

'Hopefully we have seen the back of it.' Classic weather small talk. I thought back to a conversation I had had with one of the other GPs, Kay, in the kitchen last week where she told me that Clive spent his weekends inspecting and categorising his expansive collection of coins. 'See you then.' I continued walking on concluding that the conversation had run its course.

'Now Tom,' he blurted as I began to walk away. I turned and looked back, 'What was it? I was going to ask you something?' He looked to the sky in this exaggerated fashion. It was like he was auditioning for the local troupe of mummers. 'Ah yes. The practice has decided to take on a medical student to, you know, help out the local medical school.' The fog of amnesia lifted. 'Doctor is Greek for teacher after all.' He chuckled rolling through his rehearsed lines. 'Did you say you had some experience at teaching medical students?'

'No.'

'Oh. I thought you mentioned you had?' As we had probably said only a couple of sentences since I started, I highly doubted it.

'Perhaps you're confusing me with someone,' I smiled. He negated to tell me how much the medical school was paying the practice for this privilege or how much he would be paid for paying little to no part in tutoring.

'Of course we are all eager to help out in the tuition but we were wondering, what with you being much closer to graduating,' he paused to let out a bizarre guffaw, 'you would also want to be involved. Good for the CV and so on?'

'Maybe,' I said, 'but to be honest I am using all the time I have just to manage the patients.'

'Right I see,' Clive soothed, 'and that must be the priority.'

'Great,' I said turning to victoriously walk off.

'Now hang on a mo' Tom, how about a compromise?'

'Compromise?' I sensed danger. He was about to unleash his actual demand. The rest had been just a preamble. I had been played like a fiddle.

'How about young Grace? Can she sit in with you?'

'Grace?'

'Yes. She is planning on applying for medicine and we agreed that sitting in a couple of times would be useful when she applied for the job.' Following our introduction on my first day I had said precious little to Grace having bashfully bustled past her on the one or two occasions our paths had crossed. Did I really want the hassle? She did look like the new blonde Carol Vorderman; I might even be able to impress her. I may not know much more medicine than a medical student but I definitely knew more than a complete muggle.

'Fine Dr Love,' I acquiesced quickly. If Grace had been a Gary I'm not sure I would have been quite so accommodating.

'You think you'll have time to throw her a few kernels of wisdom?' Dr Love relied sarcastically.

'I'll try.'

'Good. You can probably help her with the application process, we never even had an interview when I applied.'

'Really?' How unsurprising.

Grace sat in the corner of The Fridge in a large damp woollen jumper. We had been walking together along the corridor, her in the lead, both holding coffees. I was asking her questions on what she hoped to achieve today and this slight mental distraction seemed to have been sufficient to cause me to walk into her from behind as she paused to let an old lady past. My coffee went up her back all over a rather expensive cream woollen sweater. We were now running late with the clinic as she had spent the last 15 minutes scrubbing the jumper in the lavatory to attempt to remove the coffee stains. Apparently, to make matters worse, Grace was now worried about shrinking the jumper so had elected to wear it. I had lent her the fan heater directed upwards towards her back which had given the room the unpleasant aroma of a coffee soaked wet dog. I had already created an atmosphere with my repeated apologising and her repeated assertions that it was 'fine' in a way that indicated that it really wasn't 'fine'. I thought the best approach was just to try and get on with business. The most upsetting part of the whole debacle was that I had completely negated any influence I might have had in impressing her with my limitless medical knowledge. Yeah right.

'Mrs Harris is an 89 year old lady. She was seen last week by a Kay on a home visit after her niece dropped in to see her, to deliver the weekly shopping, and found her acting strangely. She had a fever, was hallucinating and confused; delirious essentially. She was sent to hospital in an ambulance. Do you know what things make an elderly lady confused?' I asked Grace.

'Stroke?'

'No, not really that usually causes a more focal problem so rather than global confusion they will lose the ability to move half of their body for example.'

'Oh.'

'A confused or delirious lady with a fever is usually due to an infection like a urinary tract infection or pneumonia.'

'I see.'

'I'll call her in and we can see how she is doing,' I confidently explained. 'Mrs Harris to Room 10,' I said now assuredly pressing the Tannoy button to call her in. We waited in awkward silence for the shuffling of feet outside the door. I tapped away a few details on the computer and continued reading about her prior visits to the GP and medication history. Grace leapt up and opened the door showing me up for my ungentlemanly conduct. In tottered an elderly frail lady whom I recognised as the old lady who had contributed to me firing hot coffee over Grace's back.

'Good morning Mrs Harris,' I hailed her loudly. She looked up and bowed her head slightly with what I presumed was acknowledgement. She continued taking awkward hesitant steps with stick towards the chair. The old lady paused when she reached the seat, made an awkward alignment before slowly descending like the Apollo moon lander: 3-2-1 touchdown, the Eagle had landed. She bowed her head in acknowledgement again, repositioned slightly in the chair, looked up and smiled slightly. Our eyes met, they were fully aware now in contrast to how they must have been, only a week or so ago, when Kay had seen her. I was momentarily transfixed by those turquoise depths. The pupils encircled by her irises were themselves orbited with a further concentric ring; a grey yellow band; a corneal arcus or arcus senilius. It is common in the elderly but in the younger it is supposed to be a sign of increased cholesterol levels in the bloodstream. I doubt whether this is actually true or whether actual clinical trial evidence supports this. It one of many archaic signs[1] of diseases taught still in clinical examination techniques to every young medical student.

'Have a quick look at Mrs Harris' eyes Grace,' I instructed whilst I tapped away on the computer. 'Mrs Harris, this is Grace she works here as a receptionist but wants to go to medical school is it alright if she sits in with me?' I asked. Mrs Harris didn't reply but Grace moved across the room and glared into her eyes.

'What do you see Grace?'

'There is a circle around her eyes.'

'Very good. That is a corneal arcus, common in the elderly.' I explained. I think she was impressed. 'Write all these down, or remember them and we can discuss at the end.' Grace made no effort to reach for a pen and paper.

Mrs Harris grasped the clasp of her bag on the lap of her pleated skirt. Her fingers, grey and gnarled, were lumped at each finger joint exhibited the signs of generalised nodular osteoarthritis. I glanced

---

[1] A 'sign' of a disease is something that the doctor notices on examining the patient. As opposed to a symptom which is something the patient describes to the doctor. Many of these signs are eponymous; named after the earliest physicians like Charcot, Virchow and Osler who meticulously dissected and categorised the human body whilst making our first furrows into the diagnosis and understanding of disease. It is the art of medicine. The bedside physician; a gentleman (or lady) scholar meticulously attending to his (or her) craft; eliciting signs, making notes and methodically creating diagnostic hypotheses. Whilst we now have advanced imaging techniques and endless blood tests that have meant these eponymous signs have, to some extent, become anachronisms which, whilst taught at medical school and consequently used to test medical students on their clinical examination skills, are rarely used in clinical practice. The clinical examination whilst still essential in many facets of medicine is now ever increasingly being performed because the patient expects it except for a few key specialties where it continues to be essential.

again at her past medical history and saw that she was severely hard of hearing but refusing to go to see an audiologist.

I leaned forward and preparing to open conversational channels. I enabled the megaphone and addressed her with a voice capable of earning me an ASBO.

'Mrs Harris this is Grace, she wants to become a doctor,' I shouted my introductions again. 'Is it alright that she sits in Mrs Harris?'

'What did you say?'

'Is that alright Mrs Harris,' I shouted.

'Yes of course.' Her grimace at me turned into a smile at the appreciation of Grace's angelic features. Grace smiled at her in gratitude.

'Mrs Harris, how are you feeling?' I continued.

'Tired...and fed up.'

'Have you been knitting anything recently?' I was quickly scanning through previous consultations where she had been labelled socially isolated as all she does is sit at home, watch television and knit.

'A scarf.'

'Is it that cold in here? Perhaps I should get Jeremy Hunt to turn the heating up?' I attempted to induce a chuckle by starting one myself like an American initiating a round of self-applause. Mrs Harris didn't join in and I turned around to see Grace looking at me like I was a moron.

'Mrs Harris, would you mind if I told Grace a little about why you were admitted to hospital last week?'

'Pardon?'

I repeated my question with appropriate pauses and stresses.

'Of course,' she gripped her handbag, turned and smiled at Grace again and re-adjusted in the chair.

'So Mrs Harris had a urine infection which had given her a fever and made her confused and delirious. This is one of the most common reasons for people being admitted to hospital, particularly in the elderly. Why do you think she became confused?'

'The infection affected her brain I suppose?'

'What do we call that...what is that condition called?'

'Not sure.'

'Delirium,' I paused allowing the word to sink in. 'Did you do Latin at school Grace?'

'Afraid not.'

'It comes from de, meaning 'from' or 'away' and lira meaning ridge. So it essentially means to go deviate off course.'

'Oh...right.' She probably wasn't impressed that I won the Latin cup, awarded to the best Year 15 Latin student either.

'Once she had attended hospital the urine dip was positive and the discharge summary gave the diagnosis as urinary tract infection with secondary delirium.'

'I see,' commented Grace.

'Now why did Kay send her to hospital?' I continued to press.

'So she could have treatment?' she replied with what I detected was just a slight edge of mockery.

'We could have given her oral antibiotics and kept her at home?'

'But she wasn't herself.'

'Who was she then?' I quipped.

'She lives alone though.'

'Exactly. She lived alone and wouldn't have been able to look after herself because she was delirious. What do you know about delirium?'

'It comes from the Latin for deviating away,' answered Grace grinning.

'Very good,' I smiled back flirtatiously. Coffee incident all but forgotten I reckon. 'Mr Harris? I'm just going to tell Grace a little about your condition,' I yelled again.

'My condition?'

'Yes,' I paused, 'why you went to hospital.' I didn't stop to check whether my bellowing had registered.

'Delirium is an acute confusion state. I say acute because it comes on quickly and should not last too long, that is, as long as you identify and fix the cause. The term confusion isn't like the type of confusion you would see, for example, if I tried to explain to you how the kidney worked. Otherwise we both would be admitted to hospital most days sharing a bay with Mrs Harris and trying out my podgy digits on her knitting patterns.'

'I know how the kidney works,' said Grace.

'Good for you,' I continued smiling.

'Confusion in the delirious sense means cognitive decline. It's a sudden drop in brain power. You are no longer orientated. You wouldn't be able to tell me the time, sometimes the day of the week or even the date of your birthday. You would not be able to tell me the prime minister at the moment or remember a simple postal address. Delirious patients can be agitated or sleepy and they often hallucinate. Do you know what hallucination is?'

'See things that aren't real?'

'Good,' I said. 'So what is the difference between a hallucination and an illusion? For example if you see a ghost is that a hallucination or an illusion?'

'Hallucination?' she guessed.

'Err, yes,' I paused for thought second guessing myself, 'for it to be a hallucination you wouldn't even question that you might be mistaken and that the ghost wasn't real. Whilst an illusion is where you think you sense something that isn't there, for example a ghost, but you have insight into the fact that you might be mistaken.'

'Hmm,' she nodded.

'So when I was at medical school they used to teach a mnemonic to remember the causes of delirium. It was HIDE MAP.'

'Hide map?' Grace repeated.

'Yes. HIDE MAP. Hypoxia, infection,' I hesitated; I couldn't remember the rest. I blushed again, looked up, caught her eye and saw a brief smirk. 'Alcohol was the 'a', and psychosis was the 'p',' I continued. 'I can't remember the rest. You can figure it out for your homework,' I said trying to cover my tracks. The expanse of medicine and my sub-par intellectual horsepower meant I relied on mnemonics as one of the few ways I can continue to pretend to be clever. My favourites included SHEEP TIT for the causes of haemolytic anaemia or SAD PERSONS for the risk factors of a psychiatric patient committing suicide. Sadly, just 18 months outside of medical school and numbed by the tedium of ward work meant that I couldn't even remember the mnemonics anymore never mind what constituted them. This somewhat defeated the purpose. I was disappointed with myself for not remembering what constituted

HIDE MAP. I thought it was permanently ingrained as it always reminded me of my dotty old aunt hiding her possessions in the freezer. Not that my dear aged Aunt had a particular fascination for hiding maps in the freezer, it was more her false teeth or glasses that were subjected to the one player game of hide and seek. But then sufferers of haemolytic anaemia don't have any particular penchant for the lactating organs of sheep to my awareness.

'So what is the difference between dementia and delirium,' asked Grace.

'Good question,' I replied, 'obviously dementia is more chronic and insidious but it is not uncommon to see patients in hospital who have dementia and a rather unfortunate superimposed delirium. Confusion does not necessarily mean delirium but certainly can be confused with it. Which can be confusing. Confused yet?'

'Not really,' answered Grace confidently.

'So Mrs Harris you're here for a check-up following your hospital admission. I have your discharge paperwork here. Do you know what happened to you? Do you know why you were admitted?'

'Well I wasn't really myself.'

'Do you remember much about it?' I shouted.

'Well not really. I remember that monstrous woman in white wouldn't let me leave before I had walked up the stairs and made a cup of tea, of all things! She seemed completely incapable of understanding that I manage perfectly well on my own at home.' I looked at her blankly and glanced at Grace. What on earth was she on about?

'Physiotherapists,' Grace mouthed.

'Oh physios?' I parroted.

'Yes the physiotherapists.' Mrs Harris affirmed loudly. 'I called them the physio terrorists.' She chuckled at her own joke and Grace and I joined in dutifully.

'You had a UTI, a urinary tract infection, Mrs Harris, it made you all confused.' I confirmed for her. She looked up from her focused expression on her hands still gripping the clasp of her bag on her knee. She glanced at me pensively. Her stern features loosened. The many wrinkles and ruts of her face slackened.

'That can't be possible,' she said softly.

'Well it's quite common in ladies of such diminished youth,' I added.

'But how could it happen?'

'It's just one of those things Mrs Harris.'

'But…but…,' she stuttered, 'I've never been with a man.' It was my turn to again look confused. Grace suppressed quiet snigger. I glanced at Mrs Harris blankly for a moment before the penny finally dropped.

'No Mrs Harris a UTI not an STI. A urinary tract infection not a sexually transmitted infection.'

It seems the Governmental sexual health advertising campaigns aren't a complete waste of money after all.

Premature Organ Failure

'Hello doctor,' she said. Her clothes were western but her heavily accented Indian voice betraying her country of birth.

'Mrs Gill please come in,' she waddled towards me. I had been expecting her, her name being the next on my computer which mercifully today, was working, albeit with the speed and efficiency of a 'no stars' McDonald's worker.

I had risen from the chair and had stepped out from behind the desk as I heard her thumping galumph up the corridor. I greeted her as she opened the door holding it open; your modern caring doctor unlocking boundaries and quite literally opening doors for his patients. Regrettably, I remembered that Mrs Gill was the size of a fully grown rhinoceros. I immediately regretted my gentlemanly conduct as she attempted to squeeze past me through the narrow door frame. I'm sure I made the same mistake last month when she came for contraception, something initially I thought was optimistic until she told me all about her obviously doting husband for which she had been blessed with 3 children, now all teenagers.

The family had moved to the area last year and had had a handful of insignificant appearances since registering. She continued to clamber beyond me but we only seemed to become locked in some mal-coordinated waltz attempting to manoeuvre around each other, limited equally by the confined room and the imaginable boundaries of our personal space. My desk pen-tidy took the brunt of this undignified shuffle catapulting a collection of drug rep pens across my desk. She mumbled apologies as I scooped around the side of the desk shepherding my drug emblazed stationary back into their tidy cubbyhole. I hoped I hadn't lost Yasmin. It was my favourite pen not only because I suspected it was the only one still functioning but also because it was given to me by an incredibly attractive drug representative who was flogging the expensive contraceptive pills. Finally Mrs Gill plonked her sizeable frame down.

'Hello doctor hello,' she said again her chair creaked its misgivings. She was visibly out of breath with exertion, hopefully from the long corridor to my remote cupboard of a consulting room, than our unsought, inappropriate, fully clothed pirouettes. I too tested the give of my leather executive. Relaxing back I took a deep breath to compose myself.

My practised poise was again shattered as the door, about to close itself with its reassuring click, swung open again. A slight pause and an emaciated fellow trailed in. He turned around, closed the door and sat down in the chair alongside Mrs Gill. I looked at him. Had he walked in by accident? Did he think he was next? He avoided my glaring efforts at establishing eye contact, my stares of social decency boring into the top of his close cropped black hair. Mrs Gill must have seen my bemusement as I stuttered in my attempts to establish contact?

'Yes…this is my husband.' Not a murmur of acknowledgement. Not even a whiff. He sat there hands in coat pockets looking at the carpet like a 14 year old being bollocked for smoking behind the bike shed.

'How can I help Mrs Gill?' Nothing followed. She hesitated. The two of them glanced at each other like naughty children caught with their hands in the biscuit jar, me an all knowing parent on my paternalistic perch wanting their guilty plea before passing penance. He continued to stare forward, fixed on a patch of carpet. She glanced to her right again and then looked at me:

'Well doctor, it is my husband really, actually he comes very quickly.'

I must have frowned, my brow furrowed with confusion. There was a momentary pause, almost a deliberate pause to allow the words to exert their maximal effect. Mrs Gill glanced toward her husband again and seemed buoyed becoming ever more expressive riding a tide of explanatory confidence sucking the sheer life-force from the man next to her who seemed to sink deeper and deeper into his chair.

'You know actually it is often over very quickly doctor and it is actually very unsatisfying for me you know.'

'Unsatisfying?' I wasn't sure I had quite grasped the point.

'Yes doctor, you know, I'm a very sexual woman.'

My eyebrows were rapidly ascending up my forehead in surprise. Sooner or later they would reach my hair line; which is some look of astonishment considering the last two years of hair recession.

'Oh…….right,' I said. The realisation swamped over me. My heart went out to him. Any initial frostiness towards this poor man melted. I empathised immediately with his demeanour. I thought back to my sessions with Clive who would constantly bang on about consultation skills and 'non-verbal cues' and then, when he attempted to show me, would proceed to ignore all of the patient's cues, verbal or otherwise.

'Sometimes it lasts, you know, seconds. Initially I ignored it you know because we used to make love for very much longer.

'Oh?'

'Yes, maybe 5, maybe 10 minutes.

'Right.' I didn't know whether to agree that that was an acceptable length of time to make love to your wife? I opted to remain quiet.

'Eventually I have asked my husband if there is anything the matter but you know doctor, I think actually he is a little embarrassed about coming to see you.'

'Mm,' I murmured in agreement, 'understandably.' Never was a more obvious statement made. I looked over at a broken man, staring at the same place on the floor, humiliated in front of this perfect stranger, half his age, by the woman he loved. No doubt forced to come and see me with consistent badgering despite arguments and protestations. He had anticipated this unrelenting torment, this perceived, slow, systematic degrading of his manhood. Now his embarrassment was nearly complete, his prediction fulfilled, his fears realised; this inability to satisfy his wife had left him feeling impotent, ineffectual, in his eyes essentially a eunuch.

'Is there maybe a tablet which might help?' she asked.

'Well let's go back a few steps,' I replied. I paused thinking how to phrase my next question. Christ. What did I even want to know? How do I even phrase a question? Do you have a problem Mr Gill? No. Don't really like the word 'problem'. Issue? Do you have an issue? What of Cosmopolitan? What Car magazine? No. I should probably go as open as possible. 'What are your thoughts on what your wife has brought up Mr Gill?' He looked up briefly and nodded and resumed his gaze fixed on the same patch of floor. Should I push for oral affirmation? Clive would tell me after asking an open question to refuse to say anything until the patient speaks. 'Silence is a powerful technique' he would say. I sensed in this case I would be losing my coffee break if I adopted that approach.

'Is there any problem with the erection itself Mrs Gill?'

'No, no. It is hard doctor. Doctor he just comes very quickly. Actually becomes too much excited.'

'And are there any problems at home, is the marriage okay?'

He looked up, for the first time fixing eye contact, steely, like a bayonet. Mrs Gill looked at him and scowled.

'No, no doctor,' a half snarl formed on her podgy face almost daring her subservient, long suffering better half to pip up. 'Definitely no. We love ourselves very much.'

'Well quite,' I replied. Who doesn't?

All the clinical staff in our General Practice had blocked off appointment slots at 1030am for a fifteen minute coffee break. Having come from hospital medicine where I was routinely forced to conduct a full morning's work without caffeine supplementation; a violation of one's human rights, this was somewhat refreshing.

The common exception, when working in the hospitals was when you were fortunate enough to be accompanying a post-take ward round with a certain consultant geriatrician[1]. Although his ward rounds progressed at the pace of sliding glaciers, he did have one saving eccentricity. Just when you thought you couldn't take anymore of trying to navigate the impenetrable hospital computer systems, just as your feet would throb and your mind seemed to exist in a permanent state of day dream he would halt the ward round with a hand signal and a declaration that it was time for 'TAB' (tea and biscuits). Not a plastic cup of lukewarm dishwater shot down at halftime like a thirsty football match spectator but a civilised sit down at the nursing station with a tea tray of Wedgewood bone china

---

[1] AKA Care of the Elderly

he kept hidden on top of the fridge in the ward kitchen on Ward 14; the apparently deemed halfway point. Beautifully intricately painted little teacups, a milk jug, a sugar bowel and a teapot complete with individual doilies. If it wasn't for the hospital teabags it would have been a cup fit for a Raj. Hospital acquired digestive biscuit were usually the biscuits pilfered and presented but very occasionally someone brought cake.

When a young doctor, such as myself, is too lazy and disorganised for breakfast, by that time of the morning, one's stomach acid was busily eroding through the pylorus and the kidney had long since gone on strike with dehydration. A digestive biscuit and a thimble of lukewarm tea in a dainty cup presented on a saucer was a blissful stay of execution. Sheer heaven.

It turned out that the coffee break in General Practice actually served more as a slush period to try and make up some lost time from the morning clinic overrunning which it almost always did. If the GPs made it down at all they usually sped in at quarter to eleven and rapidly slurping down a quick brew of variable quality depending if anyone had bought some posh stuff from the little Waitrose around the corner. This usually followed a quick gossip, a quick skim through the mail followed with a rapid demolishing of any experimental baked goods brought in by Glenys (which recently seemed to always taste of banana). As quickly as they arrived they would disappear back along the corridor, leaving a trail of coffee stains on the carpet, rushing back to start the delayed next session so as not to encroach onto the lunch break too much before the start of home visits.

It was a nice time for me, initially, to get to know the other doctors. Mercifully Clive was quite variable in his presence preferring the company of his favoured magazine; Numismatics Weekly. Usually he put in an appearance if he wanted to ask/make someone do something for him. The nursing staff rarely attended for morning coffee, perhaps they had appointments but I wasn't sure if it was an explicit rule. Angela worked part time so put in an appearance twice a week. This pretty much left, as staple regulars, Kay Thompson and Dave Simons with whom to hypothesise and pontificate with on subjects as broad as why Glenys had suddenly such a penchant for banana.

Occasionally subjects would turn medical as we opened discharge summaries on patients from hospital. The other GPs would give me the results of blood tests I had ordered as I had no access to the link system which connected with the local hospital. Every once in a while we would discuss an interesting or amusing case from the morning clinic. Clive, despite having the communicative talents of a leper with a speech impediment, had, to his credit, an encyclopaedic medical knowledge. Naturally I had told everyone about poor Mr Gill's premature ejaculation. Clive, in attendance unusually for a Monday, had blushed, rubbed his nose and wandered out with his mail without uttering a word which sent Kay into near hysterics.

Kay was a married woman from West Scotland in her early 40s. She had a wonderfully lilting accent. She had three young boys at home and a husband who she seemed, by her regular updates, to spend most of her time scolding like one of her children. This practice seemed to not only transgress to her patients but also to Dave and, lately, me too.

'I think I remember her.' Dave looked heavenward as he recalled a previous meeting with Mrs Gill. 'Big girl isn't she?'

'You didn't have to do her sodding smear test' Kay added, 'I couldn't find the wood for the trees, I had to get the nurse in to provide some retraction.' My face expressed my immediate abhorrence to the frightful image quickly conjured by Kay's statement.

'She's obviously just so amazing in the sack he can't contain himself,' Dave chuckling away at his own jest. I recoiled even further. Kay ignored him and opened another letter glanced at it briefly and placed it on the rapidly increasing junk pile.

Dave had a thick northern accent, I think from Yorkshire, which extenuated a delightfully crude and puerile sense of humour. Any coffee time conversation was short lived with him as he was consistently, at any given opportunity 'nippin' out t'back for a fag'. He was in his late 40's and overweight. So far I had gleaned that he spent his time outside of work trying to get 20 minutes in the back row of the veteran's team at the local rugby club so as to justify drinking the bar dry post-match with likeminded, team-mates.

'So what did you do with him?' Kay asked after a brief pause her interest now waning from a letter that had been finally worthy of her attention. 'Or is it her? I mean who were you actually consulting with?' Kay asked rhetorically.

'That's exactly what I thought,' I answered, 'I mean it was her name on the consultation slot! I couldn't get a twitter out of him. She'd obviously dragged him down here.'

'So what did you do?' Kay pressed.

'I said that often these problems can be psychological or multi-factorial and perhaps it would be best if I explored them with Mr Gill himself before I prescribe any pills.'

'What did she say to that? Did you ask him first?'

'She said; Doctor my husband is very busy, is there not a pill you can give us?'

'And?'

'I said I would prefer to talk to Mr Gill about these issues. So she said that she and her husband have no secrets. Meanwhile he is still looking exactly at the same space on the floor.'

'She was pushing for Viagra eh?' Dave chuckled.

'I suppose,' I replied. 'She then said she had heard about Viagra as one of her friends had bought it off the internet and if I didn't prescribe it she was going to buy it the same way'

'Manipulative,' Kay commented whilst rejecting another sheet of paper in her hands.

'Well she's desperate for a good seeing to isn't she?' Dave said smiling.

'Dave!' Kay reprimanded him.

'I'm serious I bet she does buy it off the internet and sneaks it into his evening meal,' he scoffed standing up. 'Poor bastard; sexually assaulted by your own wife,' he added putting on his coat and pulling out a cigarette packet to brave the cold early September air for his morning break nicotine fix.

'So what did you do in the end, did you give him the pills?'

'Nope, I stood firm and told him to book in with me in a couple of weeks. She wasn't happy but it isn't just her problem.'

'Well done,' replied Kay, 'I think that was the right thing to do. I probably would have done the same.'

'The drug budget doesn't extend to giving out Viagra like Dolly Mixtures,' commented Dave. Ever the practical.

A few weeks later I was first down for coffee, making it for 1030 on the dot, courtesy of a no show in the appointment slot before. The NHS are making considerable efforts to decrease the amount of no-shows. They cost millions apparently in wasted time and resource. Now you get a letter, text message, email, carrier pigeon, telegram and telepathic reminder that you have an appointment with the doctor. I hope it doesn't work because I really do enjoy a no-show, it's the only way I ever run to time and I have twice as long to see a patient than the qualified GPs. I poured myself a coffee in the kitchen and walked through to the staff room to open my mail. Kay popped her head in.

'I'm just going to have a wee and then I need to tell you about who I have just seen.'

'Okay,' I said looking up briefly from an MRI scan report I was trying to decipher. Kay always liked to keep me updated on her cycles of micturition leading to Dave teasing her on her childbirth induced stress incontinence. A ribbing which usually attracted a firm 'Fuck off Dave'. I took another sip of coffee and wondered if Glenys had made any banana bread. Maybe it was the tin she carried them in that provided the banana infusion. Oddly though, as Dave pointed out, her banana bread was the only baked good that didn't taste much of banana at all really. The conundrum continues.

'Morning,' Dave hailed. He was chewing furiously. This usually meant, according to Kay, that his wife had caught him smoking again, blown her top and he was back on the nicotine gum. Come to think of it I hadn't seen his bald spot lurking outside the back door from my window for a few days. He tended to stop drinking coffee too as he said it made him want to smoke. He grabbed his mail and plonked himself down opposite me with a sigh

'Anyway, guess who I just saw in clinic?' Kay whizzed back in, freshly relieved.

'Thor the Norse God of War?' Dave chirped. I grinned.

'No'

'Henry Kissinger?'

'Isn't he dead?'

'No idea. If he is though and still made it to come and see you this morning we could probably get it into the Christmas edition of the Journal of General Practitioners.'

'No Dave shut up and listen.'

'Tom do you remember you were saying about Mrs Gill dragging in her husband with his premature ejaculation a few weeks ago?'

'Oh yes,' I smiled reminiscently as I recalled the consultation

'What ever happened with him anyway?' Kay asked. 'Didn't you book him an appointment by himself,' she paused, 'you know, away from his wife?'

'I did, but not surprisingly, he didn't show up to it,' I explained. 'I've not heard any more about it.'

'Well I just saw Mrs Gill with her husband now. Thankfully not for a bloody smear this time.' Dave and I both grimaced. 'Wasn't she asking you for Viagra?'

'Well she was asking for a pill to fix her husband's premature ejaculation,' I corrected. 'Is that what she wanted from you?' I asked.

It was a well-known tactic by patients that if they didn't get what they wanted from one doctor they would try and see another hoping our computer notes were deficient enough not to get caught out. If Dave had seen them prior this usually resulted in success considering he typed like the keyboard was set in Russian Cyrillic mode and used acronyms that no one in the rest of the English speaking medical world used. For me, despite having twice as long as the GPs to see patients I was usually still running so late that I acquiesced to whatever the patients wanted just to hurry up proceedings.

'No, her and her husband had bought along her son. Did you know she has this 15 year old son?'

'Takes after his mum if I remember, tubby little chap isn't he,' Dave interrupted. 'In fact haven't all three of them have been at the biscuit tin?'

'I'm not sure I've met her son,' I added quickly. I sensed to tactically avoid bringing in Dave's not insignificant waistline for comparison.

'No Dave's right he is. So she drags this little lad along with her husband. And I ask what the issue is, and she says, she is worried about the size of her wee lad's penis.'

'Really?' I said.

'What did you do?' Dave asked?

'Well I had to have a look at the wee boys willy, and to be fair she has a point, it is tiny.'

'How tiny?' Dave asks.

'Massively tiny, I believe the correct terminology is a micropenis. It would look small on a 2 year only never mind a 15 year old.'

'Micropenis. Is that even a term of reference?' I enquired.

'Yep, I looked it up on Google; it can be a micropenis if it is two standard deviations from a, you know, normal willy.'

'I'm not sure I like the sound of a deviated Willy,' Dave joked. Neither Kay nor I laughed.

I pressed Kay 'So how small is two standard deviations from the norm, in terms of like centimetres of inches or another suitable term if reference?'

'Not sure maybe a couple centimetres, even smaller maybe. But essentially it was the size of half of my little finger,' Kay explained holding up her left little finger to elucidate the brevity of this little chap's member.

'They are having a nightmare in that family,' I concluded. 'So what did you do?'

'Well I wonder if it is endocrine problem or genetic or something? Maybe Klinefelters?'

'Is that where you are a boy but have two XX chromosomes from your mother and a Y from your father rather than just one X and one Y chromosome?' I thought back trying to remember back to medical school genetics lessons.

'Yes I think so,' Kay replied, 'essentially they are boys that have learning difficulties, grow boobs, don't have facial hair and have small bits. Also the wee lad doesn't seem to have started puberty yet. I'm going to refer him up to the paediatric endocrinologists.'

'Oh really,' I said.

'Anyways...' Kay paused getting more excited as she seemed to be getting to the crux of her story. 'I felt really sorry for the poor wee lad as, you don't want to get your willy out when you're 15 in front of your Mum never mind in front of a stranger. But, when I saw it, the first thing that twigged was whether this was like a genetic condition or something but I wasn't sure which one so I asked, completely without thinking, I say; 'does this run in the family?'

'Oh dear.' I saw where this was going.

'His father, who hasn't said a word since he's arrived, just stood at the back out the way suddenly pips up. He just says 'No' but quite loudly. I was absolutely mortified because for once Mrs Gill says nothing and looks at the husband who just glares. I genuinely think if she said something that would be the end of it. Especially after what he went through with you.'

'Gosh,' I said.

Dave chuckled, 'What do you think he will do now that his wife has exposed this gun slinger as having the smallest, fastest pistol in the west? I'm worried he will try and sue us for psychological damages secondary to persistent emasculation?' Dave stood up and re-loaded his nicotine gum: 'Doctor please, I beg you, I'm a very sexual women,' he imitated in a bad Indian accent rubbing his body up and down.

Kay scolded him.

Confusion +2

I yawned loudly waiting for the kettle to boil. I was half an hour late for lunch. The last patient of the morning, a tearful lady in her 60s, had been enduring bullying on her on-line knitting circle. Initially I had let out a stifled chuckle believing the whole consultation to be an elaborately staged practical joke, perhaps by Dave. When no one jumped out the cupboard yelling 'surprise' I had had to try and fabricate some empathy. She left, some forty-five minutes later with tissue in hand, me having been convinced that she wasn't going to kill herself with a knitting needle. Turns out she was quite socially isolated and this knitting group was her connection with the outside world. I managed to delude myself when she finally left, following our chit-chat, that she was feeling a little chirpier than when she arrived. I booked her an appointment for the following week to see how the knitting trolls were treating her.

I walked through into the meeting room with my cup of coffee and cellophane wrapped cheese sandwiches made in a hurry this morning before I left for work. I checked the pigeon hole for mail and picked up the letters addressed to me. It was a part of general practice I had come to enjoy. You referred a patient with a potential diagnosis for a specialist opinion and they wrote back often confirming your diagnosis. Taking a bite of my cheese sandwich, I opened the first letter:

Dear Dr Parsons,

Many thanks for referring this 15 month little girl to the paediatric neurology clinic with a possible movement disorder. I understand your thoughts were that this was infantile gratification behaviour but the parents were seeking a second opinion.

The parents describe stereotyped episodes involving the car seat and dining table high-chair seat exclusively. The parents describe a rocking motion which it would seem would be consistent with the application of pressure to the child's perineum. These 'attacks' tend to involve vocalisations, grunting, facial flushing and cease upon distraction.

I can find no evidence of any abnormality on examination. The child unfortunately didn't exhibit any behaviour today.

I have to confess, from the history, I agree with your diagnosis but unfortunately when I mentioned this to the parent's they were not open to the possibility that this was **not** an organic disease process. They referred to several pages of pre-prepared research material from the internet in reference to this. The papers were mostly regarding certain rare Epilepsy syndromes.

The parents have demanded further investigation which I was uncomfortable with requesting. Any imaging would require a general anaesthetic which carries a very small but, in my opinion, unacceptable risk. My intention was therefore to refer them to a Professor Hans Seiter a Paediatric Neurologist who has a specialist interest in this area. I advised the parents to be prepared that he may well reach the same conclusions.

However toward the end of our meeting I asked the patients to videotape their daughter which would be very helpful in giving further diagnostic clues. Unfortunately the young girl's father became rather animated at this suggestion and stormed out of the consultation soon after. He did indicate that he will be seeking a private opinion in parting so I have put this referral to Prof Seiter on hold for now.

Although normally I would be happy to see patients or their families again in clinic I fear that I too have little to offer this family. I wish them and their daughter all the best moving forward however.

Kind Regards,

Dr Alan Leeson MRCP, MRCPCH, MD
Consultant Paediatrician

Kay walked in with a steaming cup of coffee and a bundle of letters. She sat down opposite me.

'Do you remember that Westbrook-double-barrelled-smith-bigglesworth chap?' I asked her.

'Hmm' she nodded in assent, 'supercilious wanker. Came in once and demanded antibiotics for his common cold. 'Listen doctor, I know when I have a chest infection, this isn't a virus, how about you do your job, so I can go back to my job, and give me some antibiotics,' she imitated in his pompous arrogant tone.

'Sounds familiar,' I added. I slid the letter across the desk and she picked it up and started reading making confirmatory murmurs as she read through.

'Wanker,' she said, 'thing is he will find someone in the private sector who will do the scans and listen to his bleating in return for his money.' Clive walked in the coffee room and I flashed the letter his way.

'He really is a difficult man,' Clive commented, his chins wobbling remembering the verbal dressing down he received from Mr Westbrook-Smith. He passed the letter back to me and I signed it and put it in the read pile after scribbling; 'to be scanned' on the bottom. 'Tom I'm glad I have caught you, there are a few home visits I was hoping you would do for me. I have a meeting at the CCG[1] soon so I won't be available. Besides it will be good for your experience.'

Every time someone, in medicine, has said to me that something would be good for my experience it was because it was a shit task which fundamentally turned out to be of no use for my 'experience'. However Clive didn't seem to be asking me.

'I'd be delighted,' I tried to say as sincerely as possible.

'Great,' he said handing me a piece of paper with the details. 'I'll push your evening surgery back until 4pm to make time. The home visit bag is in the store room by the practice nurses room.'

'Great,' I said cheerily. I rather imagined the doctor's on-call bag to be a battered old leather case, just the right size to be shoved into the wicker basket attached to a metal framed bicycle painted in racing green. The doctor, in full tweed and trilby would slowly cycle

---

[1] Clinical Commissioning Group- commission local health care resources to provide 'the best possible health outcomes for the local population' AKA privatisation.

the cobbled streets to the sound of Dvorak's New World symphony waving cheerily at the local butcher with his rosacea[1] cheeks and ale paunch. The green grocer would be stopping Dickensian looking children from thieving the rhubarb out the front of the shop whilst the baker, a huge man, made enormous on his own produce, would run out with some baked goods for my journey. I was disappointed to find that the doctor's bag was a large black professional looking canvas rucksack with multiple compartments containing all the doctor paraphernalia, in portable form, as well as emergency medications. I sighed as I threw it into the back seat of the Skoda Labia, pausing briefly to re-fix the side mirror still only precariously attached with masking tape.

A rather uninteresting hour later of endless cups of stewed tea over trivial medical problems from the housebound, lonely elderly, had me quite convinced I wasn't a doctor but actually a visiting member of the Women's Institute. Only with the capability to prescribe lifesaving creams for persistent haemorrhoids. I was about to head back to the surgery for a break before evening surgery when Glenys phoned my mobile.

'Hello Doctor?'

'Hi Glenys.'

'How are you getting on, are you nearly done?'

'Yes just seem my last medical emergency,' I replied sarcastically.

'Oh lovely, I was wondering if you could see one more; a Mrs Wade. She is one of Dr Simon's patients. I've had a quick look at the record but it seems Dr Simons hasn't seen her for a while. The last time was 3 years ago for a referral to the audiologist for a hearing aid. She is 84 years old now.'

---

[1] Acne Rosacea Rosacea is a skin condition where there is facial flushing which usually starts on the cheeks, nose or forehead and is often made worse by alcohol. Slowly the flushing is replaced with persistent redness and sometimes what looks like spots. Occasionally, in men in particular, it develops to getting a big bulbous nose secondary to big sebaceous glands.

I swore under my breath. 'Fine Glenys, can you text me the postcode and address?'

'Ok I'll get one of the young'uns to do it, I don't get this texting business, too much like that 'twiddle'.' I had a feeling that Glenys, as part of her responsibilities, was responsible for the website and social media for the practice.

After my last set of home visits I always took the postcode. I had learnt the advantage of satellite navigation early after some early frustrating map reading resulting in getting stuck in a bog next to a makeshift Romany campsite. Although the travellers were very helpful in assisting the Labia and her complete lack of tire grip, when they discovered my profession, I felt almost compelled to hastily perform My Big Fat Gypsy Sick Parade. I considered selling the idea to Channel 4 but instead requested that they attend the practice to be registered and managed more precisely.

I sat in the car and waited for the beep. The phone rang again.

'Sorry doctor. All the young'uns have gone to lunch and I can't work it. Have you got a pen and paper? I'll have to tell you the address the old fashioned way,' Glenys said.

'Hang on,' I reaching for a chewing gum wrapper on the floor of the car, 'right, shoot.'

I plugged the postcode into my sat-nav and arrived 5 minutes later. I parked by the curve and looked for the house numbers to direct me. Identifying the correct house by elimination I hesitated slightly before ascending the path. An enormous privet hedge was slowly repossessing the pavement and front garden. The front gate, heavily oxidised to a rusty red colour, acted as the portal; the only entrance through the wilderness. I pushed it open and gained access to the front garden, an untamed inclined wilderness. A partially deflated football lay unclaimed in an apple tree half way up the steep incline. A concrete path overgrown with weeds was discernible up to the front door of the house set back some way from the road. The privet hedge blocked out the afternoon sun and I shuddered slightly as I traipsed up before re-emerging in the sunlight by the front door.

A wooded plaque shyly adorned the front door emblazoning 'Rose Cottage' in faded carved lettering. The door was a lime green colour although sun-bleached and shedding its paint like a snake's layer of skin. The chipped flaking windowsills required the attention of a double-glazing swindler.

I grabbed the rusted knocker and yanked it back. It came away partially in my hand. Whenever conducting house calls it is always important to warm up with some criminal damage before proceeding to the main event; some non-evidence based common-sense medicine. I banged hard on the front door with my fist and waited. Nothing. I banged again. Nothing. Had Glenys given me the right address?

'Mrs Wade,' I shouted banging again, 'it's the doctor Mrs Wade,' I bellowed. I paused and banged again. 'Hello,' I shouted. Again, nothing. I tried the handle and pushed against the door. It creaked with rot but remained resilient.

I peered through the window and saw an elderly gentleman sat in an arm chair in front of the TV in his coat. His mouth was open. I became immediately worried. Was he displaying the 'Q sign'? The Q sign is diagnostic of death. Essentially an open mouth formed the 'O' with the lifeless tongue lazily hung toward the bottom right corner completing the 'Q'.

I knocked on the window loudly. Not a stir. Thoughts rushed through my head. Should I phone the ambulance, or fire brigade to break down the door? And surely the police; I didn't want to add breaking and entry to my criminal damage guilt. Well a corpse is surely unable, only that morning, to book a home visit. Unless he phoned and then died. But it was a woman I was here to see. Unless she phoned for him? Or she killed him? Let's hope I can withstand her assault.

I continued my survey of the house whilst considering what to do. It was a bizarre detached cottage, tall and thin. I walked past the front window and around the side of the property, fighting off the overgrown garden, and came to a side gate separating the house from the property next door. The gate was partially obscured by a towering weeping willow tree looming between the two houses like a watchful warden. I pushed forcibly against the gate shoving my sizeable weight against it, forcing it open with a creak.

The garden behind matched that of the front; an untamed wilderness. A greenhouse roof was identifiable above the long grass and bushes showing that once it had been kept and enjoyed before nature reclaimed it. An ancient electric lawnmower sat on its side rusted and decrepit. I continued my journey into Narnia and continued to follow the path. The house had a small extension abutting the back of the house which was probably once a coal shed. Walking past I peered in through the large dirty patio doors which also led into the kitchen. A woman was pottering around the kitchen; presumably Mrs Wade. I banged on the patio doors.

'Mrs Wade,' I shouted.

She span around slowly and saw me. She tottered out of the kitchen towards the back door walking from piece of furniture to piece of furniture; like little islands which she was eager not to be caught adrift from on the open seas of the kitchen tiles. I watched her, precarious gait and felt immediately anxious that she wouldn't make her destination. The last few feet to the back door were a particular worry with no helpful handholds to support the precarious old dear. There was a pause as what sounded like 5 bolts were shot back into their housing. She tried the door although it didn't shift. A few more bolts fired. I couldn't work out if she was locking me out or letting me in. There was a further pause. I heard a key also turn in the lock. And the handle turned again with no effect.

'Try undoing the bolts Mrs Wade,' I shouted unhelpfully. Another minute of efforts seemed again fruitless. It would seem Barclay's bank had used their latest vault security system in the safekeeping of dear old Mrs Wade's back door.

I turned and looked at the patio doors on the back wall of the impenetrable threshold. I trotted over, tried the handle and to my shock opened the door walking into a kitchen. A rank smell filled my nostrils as I entered the threshold; a mustiness filled the air mixed with lavender and fusty urine. There was a loud background noise which sounded like a radio or television being played at decibels which almost certainly exceeded a European Union directive or two. There had been an attempt to keep the place tidy; the washing-up had been diligently performed although I feared would not stand-up to closer inspection. A broom, which looked like it had been stolen from the set of the Wizard of Oz lay up against the wall abandoned. The décor was so old it was in danger, if not covered by a layer of filth, of becoming imminently fashionable again. I walked through into the old coal shed which now contained a washing machine that looked as though it could fetch a pretty penny on the Antiques Roadshow.

Mrs Wade who was still busily trying to open the backdoor.

'Mrs Wade!' I shouted. She span around. She looked momentarily confused.

'Oh hello dear,' if you hold on a minute I'll get it for you now. I wasn't sure what 'it' was but I was definitely sure it was not going to be of any use.

'Hold on a minute Mrs Wade.' She ignored me and started a further precarious jaunt across the kitchen.

I pulled out a rickety wooden chair and considered sitting down until I saw the seat cushion which looked as though someone had, fairly recently, sat down to dinner and shat themselves. The linoleum floor under the table seemed to be full of partially decomposing foodstuffs which must have been nirvana to all manner of vermin. As though on cue, just to confirm my suspicions, a mouse haughtily sauntered across the floor without any deference to me.

I stood awkwardly watching the little rodent pick up an item of food, sniff it and place it down scurrying onto the next item. I tried to gather my thoughts. I hadn't even ascertained whether there was a dead man in the front room yet. Or even why someone had even phoned for a home visit.

I was going to have to speak to one of the GP's at the practice. This was well out of my depth and obviously social services needed to be involved. Mrs Wade was obviously not coping. The place was filthy. I walked over to the oven and opened it peering inside. I gagged and recoiled. Something was decomposing in a ceramic pie dish inside. Christ knows what it was, or even used to be, but it had been there for quite some time.

I wasn't sure I wanted to inspect any further. Piles of papers lay stacked on the kitchen units mostly un-opened. I realised I had been stood in the kitchen for a good 10 minutes distracted by the mess when it became quite apparent that Mrs Wade had not reappeared. A jolt of panic ensued as I realised that not only had I left a dead man in his chair for 10 valuable minutes when he could potentially have been revived but I had also contributed to his old dear falling arse over kettle by not stopping her going off on some mistaken errand. I imagined her lying on her back like an upended tortoise in the lavatory, unable to right herself and quickly raced out the kitchen.

'Mrs Wade,' I shouted entering the hall following the sound of the din. It looked as though someone had been trying to build a fort with vast quantities of unread newspapers and un-opened mail.

I turned to my right and moved into the living room where the television blared. I glanced at the old man in the chair nervously and felt instant relief as I saw him take a deep inhale, followed by an exhale of breath. Mrs Wade had sat in her chair right in front of the television and appeared to be engrossed in 'Cash in the Attic'.

'Mrs Wade!' I shouted.

'Oh hello dear. I'm sorry I forgot. She got up out of her chair with some difficulty and set off. I stood poised fearing an imminent face-plant at any point. She manoeuvred opposite her presumed husband.

'Stephen!' she shouted, 'Stephen!' The sleeping ancient oak stirred.

'The milkman is here Stephen. I need you to help me get the money.' I am embarrassed to admit that I actually looked around half expecting the local dairy worker to be stood next to me.

'I'm not the milkman Mrs Wade.'

'Of course you are you swizzler!' she replied. Stephen rose up as decrepitly as she did. He looked like the BFG; as tall, thin and slightly bowed in the back with enormous ears. Hopefully he could shed some light on the situation. He stood up slowly and pottered over. He looked even more decrepit than his wife. I was stood in the room by the door. He walked over towards me, I was slightly overpowered by the strong smell of urine that clung to him. His arm extended towards me, I thought he was going to shake my hand but he manoeuvred like a Challenger tank around me to the wall. He lifted a picture off the wall where a little recess existed behind it. Inside it was an enormous jar packed with notes and coins. He pulled out a large note and handed it to me.

I took the strange piece of paper and looked it over. It certainly did not look like any banknote I had seen. Perhaps they have a full counterfeiting press upstairs. It was for 5 pounds and had a handsome chap stood there on it, arms folded in military regalia. Next to him emblazoned on the bottom right read 'The Duke of Wellington 1769-1852'. I held it close to my face, the date of issue was 1982. This banknote was older than I was!

'Mrs Wade I'm the doctor.'

'The doctor?'

'Yes. You called for me this morning.'

'Did I?'

'Do you remember why?'

'No.'

'Brilliant,' I said aloud sarcastically. 'Mrs Wade I'm wondering whether you might benefit from some help at home. I have a feeling that you aren't managing too well?'

'I'm not unwell, I'm fine. Are you going to take the milk money or not?'

You're really scaring me now Doc

'You're really scaring me now doc,' Alex Roberts replied from one of the four chairs in my consulting room.

It was late November and my rotation in General Practice was drawing to a close. If I found the Fridge chilly in August, it was now positively Artic. I had moved into Clive's room whilst he was on holiday for 2 weeks. I very much welcomed a two week reprieve from huddling in two jumpers, the fan heater on full blast under the desk. As the senior partner it was by far the largest room and fitted with such luxuries as gas central heating. The many photos of Clive Love's slightly peculiar looking family adorned the wall but it was worth the possible mistaken association just to maintain my core body temperature above hypothermic ranges.

In my Thursday's sessions with Clive he had told me the theory of how to consult with patients in General Practice. There is lots of research which has attempted to model the interaction between the doctor and the patient. The paternalistic approach; 'Good ol' Dr Parsons, he's a lovely chap, he won't let me down, I'll just do as he says.' Here the doctor knows what is going on but shields the brutal reality from the patient. This approach was once how all medicine was conducted and so generally favoured by the old and bold. Sometimes the Doctor knows what is going on but so does the patient. Neither however indicate to each other that they know but instead opt to maintain a secretive clandestine pretence. This approach is often adopted by doctors when patients are terminally unwell and is commonly favoured by oncologists who, as far as I gather, would be happy to deliver chemotherapy to a corpse. No one wants to crush hope and doctors' first concern is generally not to do any harm to the patient so they feel they are protecting patients from the brutal reality of the truth. Usually however the patient already knows and opts to keep this from the doctor. Sometime relatives ask doctors to shield the truth from their unwell loved ones for the same reasons.

Then there is the shared approach; the doctor knows, the patient knows and both share their opinions and interests and work together to make a plan. Despite you reaching for the sick bowl this is what I should be striving for the majority of the time according to Clive.

With Alex Roberts I wasn't sure I was achieving a shared approach. He was staring intently at me, scanning me from top to toe. Intently searching for the vestige of a visual cue, any manifestation of what I was really thinking. He wanted to interpret the conclusions I had conjured and postulated to make this harrowing and stigmatising diagnostic hypothesis. He probably was thinking something close to 'what are the chances', carefully calculating his own risk assessment. An internal 'how screwed am I equation' probably based on a variety of factors; one of which had to be my clinical acumen. Probably the most fallible.

Firstly I didn't think my diagnostic hypothesis was right I am a junior doctor after all. I have fewer than 18 months experience. Consequently I wanted to mentally protect him from the agonising wait for the results which were bound to come back negative. I wasn't being completely altruistic, the thought of the poor bastard suing me for undue psychological stress had crossed my mind.

Secondly this eureka moment hadn't come to me by careful scrutiny of the available clinical literature and my in depth knowledge of infectious diseases. Oh no. It had spilled into my consulting room. A tragic soap opera played out with me an involuntary protagonist forced to tiptoe through this emotional and medical minefield.

It was afternoon surgery maybe a month back when Mrs Roberts, the wife of Alex, first popped in. I looked back at her medical record and recent consultations on the computer prior to her entrance in the hope of gleaning some background information.

When I was at medical school I had to do a GP rotation. I was assigned to a weathered old GP called Dr Dicky Flynn. Dicky was thoroughly loved by his patients. Every winter they would pile in with their coughs and colds laden with presents for dear old Dr

Flynn. I would watch him smarm the elderly ladies in the waiting room, bow with dignified respect to their elderly husbands, talk golf with the middle aged men and spew outrageous compliments to their hideous wives; waxing about their youthful splendour. A master at work was lovely old Dr Flynn doing his consultations. I still remember the first time I sat in on one of his clinics; I was in awe at his laid back repose, easily commanding the discussion like a weathered fisherman's loose hand on the tiller of his battered old boat. The patient hung on Dicky's every word. It felt like they would erupt into rapturous applause if he would do as much as break wind.

As soon as the door closed, and the patient finally left after thanking ol' Dr Flynn profusely and offering their first born in gratitude, Dicky's true persona was revealed. The façade would lift with a diatribe of verbal abuse directed at the same punters he had sycophantically smarmed earlier. He castigated them on everything from their difficulties to lose weight to their dress sense. Heaven forbid if anyone would dare to waste his time with 'banal or insignificant problems'. And those who took an active interest in their own health were all deemed to have 'an overinflated sense of self-importance'. Good old Dicky. He simultaneously showed me exactly how I wanted and didn't want to practice medicine. I did learn a few little tricks of his along the way though: 'I dunno about you Tom but I can't remember my wives irrelevant existence never mind the patients.' He would drawl, 'A little trick for you, always pop in what the patient is doing in your notes.'

'Doing?' I enquired quizzically, 'Isn't that what everyone puts in the notes.'

'No you simpleton,' he whined, 'not doing clinically, doing in real life. If the patient is going on holiday to bloody Butlin's stick it in the notes.'

'You know,' he elucidated further quoting an example, 'will review hypertension medications when patient returns from holidays in Bognor.' That way when the boring prick returns you can ask him how his holiday went in Bognor and he thinks you care and remember him. That I couldn't give two tits what their holiday plans are or give a flying fairy if it pissed it down for the entire week, is beside the point.'

No such handy hints awaited me on review of Mrs Robert's notes. She hadn't been seen for ages and the last time was to ask if there was anything she could have to lose weight. Kay had seen and given general advice on diet and exercise had referred her to a dietician.

Mrs Roberts entered the fridge sullen, quiet and purse lipped. I shook her hand and was rewarded with the flicker of a smile and a 'Good afternoon Dr Parsons'. I waved her in like Dicky would have done.

'How can I help Mrs Roberts?'

It looked as though she was fixated on something in the top right hand corner of the consultation room. I could see it coming. The tears filled her eyes. The left hand came up to her face and began flapping furiously. I was in for a meltdown. Two minutes of sobbing and tissues, tears and mucous prevailed. Sniffling, snuffling, snorting; all manner of noises for which my knowledge of onomatopoeia fails me to adequately describe. I tried to provide comfort. I had twenty minutes per consultation, most fully qualified GPs had ten minutes; some fewer. It was 10 minutes before Mrs Roberts was able to compose herself and damn the river.

'So…Mrs Roberts…how can I help?'

She dabbed the readily supplied tissue I had offered against her eye. Her mascara blotched travelled in rivulets down her sunbed damaged cheeks. Her blond hair, roots evident, seemed to have escaped its moorings becoming wild and untamed. Her still perfect lipstick gave her the impression of a rabid clown.

'Gosh Doctor I'm so sorry'

'Really don't be,' I soothed. But really, we really must get to the point. I already knew where the consultation was going. She was going to be depressed but not seriously enough for me to worry about her doing something silly. Just a feeling of insignificance or boredom or loneliness; she might have even lost her pet dog.

Carol Roberts was in her late 40s. She was probably quite the catch in her day. Alas the years hadn't been kind, her body had suffered with the environmental pressures placed upon it. Fad diets hadn't vanquished the weight she had procured through childbirth. Her skin had the orange wrinkled hue of years of sun damage.

'I think my husband is gay.'

'Oh,' I answered. Well I wasn't expecting that. More composed she calmly told me of her suspicions. I was trying to remember if I had seen her husband since I had been at the practice. 'How?' I asked.

'He has been working away a lot more recently. You know he works in sales and he has been opening up new markets, or something, in Eastern Europe. He was acting a little different I suppose looking back; just more distant. Our sex life hasn't been particularly rampant for years,' she explained quite candidly. 'In the last year, though, it has been non-existent. I thought it was because of my weight and you know how I've been trying to lose it.'

'Hmm.' It was obviously a work in progress.

'Anyway, I don't know why I did it. I've never done it before. It was just there. I picked it up and I tried to look through his phone. There was a password lock on it. He had never had one of those before. Why would he now? Thinking about it in hindsight, he would often go out in the evenings. Difficulties at the office he would say.' She paused and I let her regain her flow. 'It was then I thought he must be having an affair and I became suspicious.'

'Hmm,' I murmured.

'My plan was to try to get hold of his phone when he had put the passcode in or maybe try and learn the combination by watching over his shoulder so I could later sneak a peek. It was his work mobile though and he rarely used it in front of me and locked himself in his office when he did and said it was a business call even though he would be on for hours. Anyways I had had enough. I had asked him over and over again. Is there anything wrong Alex? You just aren't the same. You never have time for us.'

'Yeah,' I propped my elbow against the arm rest and used my clenched fist to support my chin. I found myself glancing past her focussing on the clock on the back wall and how late I was running.

'He would always reassure me, just say he was stressed and working hard because he wanted to, you, know give me everything.' My eyes jolted back to hers as she continued.

'Anyway I was due to go away for a girls' weekend to Rome last weekend with my friend Gillian. I told Alex about it ages ago and for once he remembered I was going when I reminded him earlier in the week. He made me a lovely dinner on Thursday night, told me he loved me and gave me some money to spend on the trip. He really put my mind at rest and I convinced myself that a lot of married couples have this problem and we would work through it on my return. It would probably do us some good to spend some time apart and maybe, you know, recreate the spark.'

I stifled a yawn and tried to maintain focus. Unrelenting she continued:

'Anyway I got to the airport early on the Friday and waited for Gillian. She was late of course, but then that wasn't unusual for her. Anyway I finally got a call from her, it must have been about 11 o clock because it was only an hour before we were supposed to take off. She had been in a car accident and had been taken to hospital. Don't worry doctor it was nothing severe and she is fine now,' she added waving her hand in a dismissive fashion.

Not that I would have lost too much sleep about her friend Gillian that I had never met.

'Anyway I thought well, there is no point going to Rome by myself and Gillian was definitely going to miss the flight. So we decided we would re-book it and claim off the travel insurance. I was disappointed but, you know doctor, there is very little you can do about it.'

'Hmm,' I nodded in acquiescence.

'Anyway so I drove home. I didn't think to ring Alex as it was only Friday lunchtime and I knew he would be at work late. I was a little surprised to find his car on the driveway when I got back.'

I could see the tears welling up once more. The left hand raised and began flapping away again like a bee's wing.

'What happened then Mrs Roberts?' I urged her forward, suddenly intrigued. She regained her momentary loss of composure.

'I opened the front door and walked through the hallway into the front room and, and, and, and….he was….' She hesitated her lip quibbled again, her face breaking into a frown as tears began rolling down her cheek.'

My phone rang out interrupting her latest blubber. I picked up the handset; 'Hello Doctor, sorry to interrupt, it's Glenys.'

'Hi Glenys.'

'I just wanted to make you aware you are running over 40 minutes behind.'

'Thank you Glenys. I'll err…endeavour to catch up'

'Right you are doctor. I'll get the girls to bring you up a cup of tea.'

'Thank you Glenys'

'Cheerio now.'

'Sorry Mrs Roberts, please go on.' She had managed to regain her composure.

'Well doctor, without being too graphic he was having an act performed on him by another man.'

'An act?'

'Yes doctor.' She paused wondering if that was enough information. I felt like I was on an episode of Loose Women. I wasn't sure how to ask but I really felt as though I needed to:

'What sort of act?'

'He was getting done,' she started welling up again, 'you know,' she paused again then mouthed some words which I was unable to interpret. Finally she used her finger to portray further demonstrate matters followed by breaking down in another rendition of tears.

'Oh,' I responded.

I had almost completely forgotten Mrs Robert's tale. Of course, at the time, I had mentioned it at coffee break. Kay commented that she had had a few relationship breakdowns due to one of the couples being gay. She said it was society's fault and due to inequality in sexual orientation. Nowadays being gay is perceived to be more acceptable so hopefully youngsters won't try and hide it by entering into loveless marriages. Dave attacked the story with homophobic rigour.

Mrs Roberts didn't return to see me after I recommended that if her husband was gay then perhaps they should consider separation but it was important to talk it through and I gave her a leaflet for a relationship counsellor. This was a suitable turf for something that really wasn't a medical problem I thought. I wasn't an agony aunt, interesting though the tale was. But what did she expect me to do? Despite what Dave and the Catholic Church preach homosexuality isn't a disease. I wrote a rather non-committal entry into her notes: 'Marriage difficulties- recommend marriage counsellor. No risk of suicide presently. No psychiatric illness.'

Alex Roberts was in his late 40s. He had thinning dark hair which he attempted to hide by slicking it back. I bet he once had a pony tail. His skin was well tanned and, by his appearance alone he looked like he worked in sales. He attempted to portray erudition and wealth in his bearing and wanted you to recognise it. He also, like his wife, looked sun-kissed; perhaps there was a couple's offer at the local fake tanning salon. He wasn't in the slightest effeminate but appeared arrogant and masculine. He came to the practice for review following a recent hospital stay. I had forgotten all about his wife's revelation until half way through the consultation when the penny dropped.

He had been ill for a couple of weeks previously; vomiting, diarrhoea, coughing, sweaty yet cold, tiredness and off food. He had come to the practice a week before and seen Kay who thought he had had a bad case of influenza and sent him on his way with advice to take regular paracetamol and rest. It was the right time of a year for flu and Alex wouldn't have qualified for the flu jab. He obviously ignored this and when his condition had become protracted he went to A&E and got admitted to hospital. A lengthy discharge letter sat in front of me which I read in the patient's presence. He seemed to have been submitted to a barrage of investigations which is usually brought about when there is no diagnosis.

'I still don't really know what was wrong with me,' Alex said, 'those useless tossers at the hospital didn't have a clue either.'

I continued to leaf through the discharge letter. Mostly normal bloods on admission, normal CT scan, normal heart trace and a normal lumbar puncture. The auto-immune screens were normal and there was no evidence of glandular fever. His liver function tests had shown some liver damage later in the admission and this had fitted with a probable viral picture.

189

'Well how do you feel now?' I asked

'Better but still a bit grim,' he answered. He looked expectantly at me for answers. Having looked through the discharge letter I really had no way of giving a definitive answer to his problem if the hospital lot hadn't been able to with all their resources. I did what all self-respecting doctors would do in the situation:

'It looks like you've caught a virus Mr Roberts'

'A virus?' That's what they said in the hospital.

'Yep, it's given you the flu.'

'The flu? That's what Dr Rapley said before I went to hospital. But I felt like shit.'

'Hmm.'

'How did I get the flu?' he asked.

'A virus.'

'Oh.'

I could sense his scepticism. Incompetent doctors and their 'it's a virus'. The magical all-encompassing diagnosis; undetectable, unprovable and ultimately recoverable.

'The discharge letter has asked me to repeat your liver function as it showed some inflammation in your liver from the virus. It is important that we check that has resolved and not worsened again.'

'Ok,' he agreed.

'Who is at home with you?'

'No one now, the wife and I have separated. I've moved out.'

'Sorry to hear that,' I paused and something fired in my brain. 'Carol wasn't it?'

'That's right.'

'Hmm,' I mused. I thought back to my consultation with his wife and I felt a moment of revelation. Was it that he might be gay? He was statistically more at risk I suppose. I couldn't ask him outright. It would breach the confidentiality his wife had entrusted in me. I didn't want to open a can of worms by flatly asking him either. He might still be in denial. He might smell a rat. I paused a moment to think. He looked at me quizzically and spoke the immortal line:

'What's up doc?'

'There are some viruses we haven't tested for yet,' I continued, 'some affect the liver directly. Have you heard of Hepatitis A or B or C?

'Yep,' he replied quietly. I had his attention. Maybe he wasn't letting on all he knew.

'Some viruses can also affect the liver indirectly and I shall test for them too if that's okay'

'Fine.' He looked away briefly. I continued regardless.

'Now one of these viruses is HIV[1],' I paused allowing my words to take effect, 'do you know what HIV is Mr Roberts?' He fixed me with a stare for a few seconds.

'Yes,' he stated softly. He paused for a moment, swallowed hard. 'You're really scaring me now doc,' he said.

Alex stared intently at me, scanning me from top to toe. Intently searching for the vestige of a visual cue, any manifestation of what I was really thinking. He wanted to interpret the conclusions I had conjured and postulated to make this harrowing and stigmatising diagnostic hypothesis. He probably was thinking something close to 'what are the chances', carefully calculating his own risk assessment. An internal 'am I fucked equation' probably based on a variety of factors, one of which had to be my clinical acumen. Do I know what I'm talking about?

'Mr Roberts as you know we have yet to find a clear diagnosis for why you were so unwell. All I'm doing is ruling out one more cause.

---

[1] HIV or the human immune deficiency virus attacks a type of white blood cell called the T helper cell. T helper cells play an essential role in the immune system. The T helper cells are destroyed over time and the body is unable to compensate. As the immune system weakens it becomes susceptible to several infections including those caused by invasive fungus. Other viruses play a role in cancers to develop including of the blood and skin. When the immunity drops to a certain level and these opportunistic infections appear the patient is said to have AIDS. AIDS is now an entirely preventable illness with the advent of HAART or highly active antiretroviral therapy. Whilst the first anti-retroviral was used in the mid-1980s, several classes are now used in combination to supress the virus.

I can say to you now, quite candidly, that I have no great expectation the test will come back positive.

'The HIV?'

'Yes.'

'Good.'

'We can do all the tests at the same time we repeat your liver function tests,' I attempted to placate him.

'Well you must think it's a possibility or why would you take it.' I had to hand it to him. His logic was watertight. 'Besides doc, I feel much better.'

'Of course it is a possibility Mr Roberts, but so is winning the lottery.'

'Well this doesn't feel much like a lottery win to me mate.' Probably not my best turn of phrase.

'Indeed,' I soothed, 'but let me just arrange to have the blood taken, send the test off, and then please put it to the back of your mind.'

'How long 'till it's back doc?' It was Friday afternoon and I had no idea where this had to be sent to get processed.

'The next week or two.'

I was sat in the coffee room a week or so later opening my mail. I leafed through a letter, skimming through to quickly attempt to assess whether it could be immediately disregarded to the rubbish pile. 'Alex Andrew Roberts test results' I read. I skimmed down the page reading several negative results and improved liver function. I read on: 'HIV p24 positive.' I had no idea what that meant and skipped to the, rather helpful, explanatory text below: 'in keeping with sero-conversion and acute HIV infection.' For the first time, as a doctor, I felt the strange dichotomy of making a satisfying but unwelcome diagnosis.

Accident and Emergency

(AKA Emergency Medicine)

People have access to health care in America. After all, you just go to an Emergency Room.

President George W Bush

Heartsinking

I walked through the staff entrance of the A&E department with the gentle grace of a grazing gazelle. I had a notable spring in my step. As of last week I was an Emergency Department doctor; previously known as an Accident and Emergency doctor before the re-branding exercise. Whatever I was to be called, I was, at least in my eyes, George Clooney.

I had survived the local induction: the takeaway message seemed to be that the overwhelming priority of the department was to, at all costs, avoid 'breaches' with the safe, empathetic (and rapid) discharge of patients a close second. I thought breaches (especially when described by one of the senior nurses in the department in her strong Glaswegian accent) were short trousers worn by chinless morons who go galumphing around the country searching for Fantastic Mr Fox. Turns out it is a violation of Tony Blair's 'four hour rule' where (cue your best Tony Blair voice) 'by 2004 no one should be waiting more than 4 hours in the emergency department from arrival to admission, transfer or discharge'. This was quickly modified from 100% of patients seen in 4 hours to 98% to allow for clinical exceptions. This dropped again to 95% by the time I had started. Our hospital seemed to be struggling to achieve that, such was the demand[1].

My last week in general practice had been gripped by some sort of seasonally affective depressive epidemic. I had been through a bumper box of tissues which I handed enthusiastically to the patients. There had also been a big argument at the practice when Clive, a keen horticulturist, had got back from holiday and found that that his house plant, pride of place in the corner of his office, had all but perished. He blamed Glenys the receptionist in a foot-stamping tirade and a mutiny seemed to be afoot. I had been feeling guilty having

---

[1] I worked as an A&E doctor in 2010. As of Christmas 2016 only one department in the entire country was meeting the 4 hour rule.

used the senior partner's office whilst he was away and not thought twice to water the plants.

Being the junior doctor with only a week left in the job before my next rotation I was hoping to keep my head below the parapet. As the receptionists had stopped talking when I entered reception and stared silently into their coffee I was beginning to think the battle lines had already drawn. By virtue of my middle class upbringing, a medical school education and a complete inability to notice a parched *calathea ornata* plant I was on the wrong side of the trenches. To complete the misery every single heartsink patient in the practice had booked in my clinic. One patient with a rather anxious disposition and chronic fatigue syndrome[1] on two consecutive days. My clinics had overrun by hours.

The heartsink is a descriptive but pejorative term where the patient is like an annoying distant relative who feels the need to frequently drop in to see you uninvited. They always overstay their welcome, make requests you feel obliged to fulfil and just as you feel as though you have expunged them from your consciousness they drop in again to further exasperate, overwhelm, defeat and depress you. Upon seeing the patient's name on your clinic schedule, immediately recognisable from your numerous previous inconclusive encounters, one usually unleashes an audible groan.

So what does a patient have to do to gain this formidable title; this accolade of persona non grata? I'd say the only definite criterion is that they must attend frequently enough to be recognised with a semi-medical quirk significant enough to frustrate. They do not fall into the traditional model of patient comes with problem, doctor diagnoses problem, doctor provides treatment and information for problem and patient goes away happy and cured.

---

[1] Chronic Fatigue Syndrome. Also known as ME or myalgic encephalitis. A syndrome of persistent fatigue unrelieved by rest. It can be following a viral infection such as glandular fever. It can also be seen in the generally odd. Indicators include dark tinted glasses, a soft neck collar and the use of one crutch. You are in for a long consultation and a list as long as your arm worth of complaints which are largely uninvestigable and untreatable.

Many of you will be appalled by this. How can a doctor, a caring and empathetic professional, label patients and trivialise their problems in such a callous and demeaning fashion? Well you can either ignore your abject disdain for the heartsink and pretend it doesn't exist, or accept it. However, before you start to write your strongly worded letter to the GMC about Dr Parsons' disgraceful attitude let me say this; there has been research on the heartsink. Furthermore it has been recognised that one in ten of you might display qualities of the heartsink. They have even been categorised in medical journals as 'the heartsink'. JE Groves[1] described four types:

1. The Dependent Clinger:
Grateful for all the care the doctor provides but always returning with an array of new symptoms.
2. The Entitled Demander:
Full of complaints, regarding the doctor as a barrier to services when these complaints cannot be satisfied.
3. The Manipulative Help-Rejecter:
Returns repeatedly to tell the doctor the treatment is not working, but looks more for emotional support than to complain formally.
4. The Self-Destructive Denier:
May well suffer from serious disease but makes no alteration to his lifestyle and seems hell-bent on defeating any attempt to help him.

I had really enjoyed my time in GP but, even four months was enough to attract some of the practice heartsinks who, having long ago exhausted and exasperated the GPs had now latched on to the foundation doctors as easy prey. Naturally I had stayed resilient and given in to their every demand.

Not any more though. Now I was an A&E doctor. I had, by the grace of the Labour government, just four precious hours with a pa-

---

[1] Groves JE. Taking care of the hateful patient. N Engl J Med 1978; 298: 883–7.

tient. Even the most tedious patient can't possibly cause one's heart to sink in four hours? Besides A&E was for accidents and emergencies right? Broken arms and legs and lifesaving interventions. Yesterday I had diagnosed several fractured bones and helped the registrar resuscitate a patient who had been involved in a car crash. I was George Clooney.

After dropping off my coat and bag in the staff room I walked onto the 'shop floor' (a bizarre and slightly annoying word used by A&E people to describe their department). I picked up the first set of notes and read the demographic information on the top. Mabel Hoare, born 1915, I read her cubicle number on the computer and calculated her age on the way to see her. I opened the double doors at the end of the corridor and was greeted to the chorus of some 1940s war-time song:

'All the nice girls love a sailor, all the nice girls love a tar. For there is something about a sailor. Well you know what sailors are,' sang a shrill reedy voice. The singing emanated from behind the curtain 12. I glanced at the top of the notes. My fate lay, as clear as day, in a scrawled scribbled '12' imprinted in spidery writing and re-enforced with a circled finishing flourish.

'Hello,' I greeted as I pulled the curtain back and replaced it. An elderly lady sat on the hospital gurney in a red cardigan and floral skirt. Her white long hair clung thinly to her head, bordering her thin gaunt face. Her small beady eyes peered at me through thick lenses. Immediately she stopped singing and smiled to reveal her real teeth; brown, frequently missing and fixed loosely in her receding gums. I looked at the top of the clerking notes again and silently read her last name; Hoare. I hesitated briefly. How is one supposed to even pronounce that?

'How do you pronounce your last name is it Horaaarree?' I asked overly pronouncing every syllable and probably adding a few more to boot.

'What dear?'

'I said how do I pronounce your last name?'

'You'll have to shout dear I'm a touch deaf.'

I had been a doctor for nearly 18 months and already I felt like writing a strongly worded letter to someone about the standard of audiology services in this area. Someone at the Clinical Commissioning Group had obviously spent that pot of money on an espresso machine.

'How do you pronounce your last name?' I bellowed.

'Whore,' she replied quite bluntly,'

'Whore?' For some reasons I was continuing to shout.

'Pardon?' she winced her hand behind her ear.

'Whore?' I said louder.

'Sorry dear you'll have to shout, I'm a bit deaf you know,' she repeated as though on a loop recorder.

'WHORE!' I shouted hearing the nurses sniggering from behind the curtains. Obviously repeatedly shouting whore at a nonagenarian was not ideal in a crowded department.

'Yes alright dear there is no need to shout it so loudly. How do you think I feel?' asked Mrs Hoare in response. 'I've had to live with it for 97 years.'

'I thought you might, you know, call a bucket a bouquet?'

'What's that dear? Pardon?' I couldn't face repeating myself.

'Were you ever married Mrs Hoare?' I shouted still phonetically emphasising the 'a'.

'That's right, rub it in further. You don't think I didn't try? If only to get rid of my name?'

I found her bluntness amusing, if not mildly uncomfortable, but she seemed to be taking no offence to my questions.

'How can I help then Ms Hoare?' I asked perching on the yellow bin no doubt breaking half a dozen infection control regulations. 'I heard you singing,' I continued.

'When you live by yourself, you enjoy a good sing-song.'

I smiled humouring her. Enough of the pre-amble I had severe traumas to manage. I was George Clooney. Besides I didn't know how many years she had left and I was worried she might expire before I managed to, at least, work out why she was here. There might even be a government target for that.

'What brought you to hospital Ms Hoare?'

'An ambulance,' she answered quite plainly.

I smiled. I was going to have to stop asking that question. My first week and I had already heard it a dozen times.

'Ok,' I asked, 'how can I help?'

'I don't really need any.'

'Why, are, you, here?' I loudly enunciated with pauses.

She hesitated looking at her withered feet and shifted her posture uncomfortably.

'Oh I felt all anxious again,' she confessed sheepishly.

'Anxious?'

'Yes, I sometimes get anxious.'

'Do you?'

'It's the loneliness,' she added.

'Loneliness?' I parroted.

'I live alone you see.'

I was a bit confused. Patients usually come to A&E because they are unwell. They want something or are in pain. Unless of course they have just made the mistake of overriding common sense and called NHS direct. 'So what do you want us to do about this anxiety my dear?' I asked persistently.

'Nothing dear,' she smiled.

I felt angry. All of last week I had looked forward to be an A&E doctor as I dealt with heartsink after heartsink. I had heard endless bleating, whinging and whining: 'Why am I still in pain? Why did you send me to that doctor? He just completely ignored me. Why haven't you fixed it yet? I feel so down. I hurt all over. I'm really tired all the time. What do you mean it is all in my head? I have this strange feeling just at the tip of my middle finger. I've left my husband and I feel sad. I was leant over doing yoga and my nose bleed and I'm worried I might have cancer of the nose.'

I was now supposed to be George Clooney running from lifesaving emergency to lifesaving emergency. Instead I was faced with a choral coffin dodger who had wasted five hundred pounds of the taxpayer's gold pieces on an ambulance to come to hospital for a chit-chat with me. I wasn't sure how even to proceed. Should I tell her off?

'Knock, knock?' a voice announced their presence at the cubicle entrance. The cubicle twitched as though to simulate the knock.

'Yeah,' I answered. I hopped from my seat on the clinical waste bin and walked over and pulled back the curtain. A healthcare assistant stood there with the tea trolley.

'Sorry Doc,' she genuinely apologised. She winked at me, glanced at the patient and then back at me. 'Just seeing if Mabel wants a cup of tea?' The healthcare assistant boomed.

'Oh,' I hesitated. I looked around. Mabel Hoare obviously pre-empted my question.

'Yes please dear.'

'White no sugar?' the healthcare assistant confirmed as she pulled out the ready loaded plastic cup and poured in the hot water. She picked up the cup and delivered it to its anticipant owner who grate-fully received it in both hands.

'Would you like a sandwich too Mabel?' she shouted.

'Yes please.'

'I think we've only got egg mayo.'

'Oh I don't mind that dear.'

I stood perplexed, scratching my head in a comedy baffled pose; less George Clooney more Oliver Hardy. I was momentarily per-plexed by the exchange which just took place before me. Was I a doctor, in an A&E department, delivering lifesaving treatment? Or supervising a coffee morning at the Women's Institute? The healthcare assistant sauntered off. I excused myself from Mrs Hoare and ducked out the paper curtain as she tucked into the egg mayo and gratefully slurped her tea. I caught up with meals-on-wheels at the next cubicle. I didn't want to be indignant I mean I am a junior doc-tor with only 18 odd months on the job but I was feeling a little ag-grieved.

'Hi...,' I hesitated. I couldn't remember her name. I tried to sur-reptitiously look at her ID badge. It was upside down in its plastic covering. 'Err hi,' I continued.

'Hi,' she countered with a smile. I felt any self-righteousness I had mustered quickly evaporate

'Do you know that lady?'

'What Mabel?' I looked again at my clerking sheet to remind me of her first name.

'Yeah that lady in the cubicle there,' I said with a remonstrating point.

'Mabel is always in, she's a frequent flyer,' she giggled at me in an almost condescending fashion. 'She gets anxious and calls an ambulance, comes in, gets a cup of tea and a sandwich, sings a few songs and then goes home.'

'What?' I asked incredulously, 'that is insane.'

'Here,' she said snatching the clerking documents from my left hand. She pointed at the front clerking sheet with her felt pen. It contained the demographic details which I had yet to properly review. She circled a small box with a number in it. Above the box read 'number of visits', in the box the number: 384. 'The most important box Doc,' she smiled again.

'What?' I was astonished, 'She has been to A&E three hundred and eighty four times.'

'Well three hundred and eighty five now,' she explained, 'it doesn't count the current one.'

'No way.'

'Way,' she giggled, 'and we have only been using that computer system for about three years too.'

'But that is nearly a visit every three days then?'

'Yep. At least.'

'Why don't the ambulances stop bringing her?'

'I said that but apparently if they do miss something the paramedic will be in deep shit. Still the egg mayo sandwiches are disgusting and usually get binned anyway, even the staff don't touch them.'

I quite liked egg mayo.

'But this is ridiculous, that is nearly 200 grand in ambulances alone in the last two years never mind the sandwiches'

'Hmm, but what are you going to do about it?' the healthcare assistant seemed to be baiting me. Fair question. What was I going to do about it? Remonstrate loudly in the corridor? Barge in and bollock a lonely anxious 97 year old lady for the inappropriate use of the very resources that she has paid into her whole life? No I would fold like the yellow bellied, dastardly, lily livered poltroon that I was.

'I'll write to the GP, they should be looking into this.'

'A strongly worded letter is it?' she mocked walking off.

201

'Yes.' The irony that I had, only last week, been exasperated by exactly this type of patient in General Practice was quite lost on me.

The A&E computer system was actually quite user friendly for the NHS. Every time a patient was seen a 2 page clerking sheet was generated. There was a space for initial observations, nursing triage and then a space to write the notes, prescribe some medication and list the patient's disposal. The documents were then scanned forming part of the patients enduring medical record. When the patient is discharged home a letter is computer generated which is sent to the GP. From what I could see for the past year, although the system acknowledged her attendance only a few admissions had clerking notes attached and no GP letters had been generated for months.

'Who is that? What Mabel? Oh that one,' the sister chortled when I questioned the dearth of clinical notes. 'Yeah, she usually discharges herself after a couple of hours, and because of her frequent admissions she is usually triaged last in the queue so often doesn't even get seen.'

'Really?'

'I'm surprised you saw her Tom. All the other doctors leave her to the bottom of the pile as she usually just gets herself home.'

'Well I'm going to write some additional choice comments on her computer discharge asking her GP to pull his finger out and manage this lady properly in primary care,' I said with as much menace as I could muster.

'I bet that will show him,' she cooed at me mockingly.

I wasn't to be distracted:

'Dear Doctor,

This lady has presented over 300 times to A&E by ambulance with anxiety attacks. She is not receiving any treatment in A&E and her attacks seem to be self-terminating. Could you review her with regard to appropriate management in primary care?'

I glanced at the registered GP name. It was Clive at my old practice. I thought for a moment and quickly deleted the letter. What harm can a cup of tea, a bit of reassurance and a sandwich do? Besides I didn't want to piss him off any more following the death of his pot plant; he had yet to do my educational supervisor's report. No one really likes Egg Mayo anyway.

Mentalists

'No! Fuck off.'

'Sir! There is no need to swear,' the exasperated nurse pretended shock indignation. 'Apologise?' she demanded, 'we are only trying to look after you.'

'Fuck off,' the patient screamed again. He continued shouting obscenities. I could hear him from the central sanctuary of the Emergency Department. I exchanged knowing looks with my colleagues as we listened to the din of the commotion from the doctor's desks. The senior nurse grabbed her clipboard and purposefully marched down the corridor to reprimand the patient in the way only a senior nurse could. I finished writing my notes and nosily thought I would see what all the hubbub was about. I went through the door into the resuscitation bay. An unkempt, scrawny young man with a matted, blond, wispy pubescent beard was being rather ineffectively restrained by hospital security.

Whilst hospital security wear stab proof vests and black issue military boots they are probably the last people you want to call in a crisis. Firstly, they are unlikely to come at all, even when called, being too busy plastering young doctors' cars with parking tickets. That the aforementioned junior doctor pays 30 pounds a month for the privilege to park somewhere (just about) within walking distance of the hospital does not appear to lessen their fervour.

My usual routine was to drive around for half an hour competitively hunting, against a dozen small hatchbacks, for an empty space. 'Is he going into work or leaving' you would ask yourself? Just when you think you've found one some arsehole has parked a motorbike in the space. Or worse still, spotting a space through the cars and racing there, only to be snuffed at the last moment. The final common endpoint was mass anti-establishment abandonment of vehicles outside the management block. As you locked your car door you would see other frustrated hospital workers following suit and abandoning theirs; swearing under their breath as they glance at their watches, questioning, like me, why they pay 30 pounds a month for the privilege of this morning charade.

'What's going on?' I quietly enquired to the weary paramedic who was writing up his notes on the desk a few metres from the ensuing confrontation.

'What the scrawny fella going mental in there?' he clarified.

'Hmm.'

'Heroin[1] overdose in Tesco toilet. Usual story really,' he explained. 'We gave him the naloxone[2] and saved his life and now he's pissed off because he has wasted his hit. Looks like his groin is infected though.'

'You think he has been injecting in the groin?' I asked.

'Undoubtedly.'

This addict had been found collapsed in the ladies' toilet by some poor elderly pensioner, who was spending a penny, after picking up her Fray Bentos tinned steak pudding and frozen vegetables. She had raised the alarm and the supermarket staff had diligently provided first aid. Quite impressively, in these times, the ambulance had got there quickly enough to save his life. He thanked them by attempting to punch one of the paramedics for wasting his hit. He had some horrible groin infection or venous clot or something from attempting to inject into his deep veins. Consequently he would need to be admitted. Heroin addicts often use non-sterile needles and the junk is

---

[1] Heroin is the street version of the powerful medical drug diamorphine. It is a strong opioid analgesia. The term 'opioid' refers to the receptors spread throughout the body which these painkillers act on to exert their effects. They stem from opium which is harvested from the opium poppy; the primary source of opioid analgesics. One of the side effects of activating the opioid receptors with a powerful drug like diamorphine or heroin is respiratory depression. If you take enough, you stop breathing and die. As you never know how much street heroin has been diluted you never know quite what dose you are injecting. You also don't know what it's been diluted with.

[2] Naloxone blocks the opioid receptors and rapidly halts the effects of the diamorphine. This rather abruptly wakes the patient. It is commonly used in overdose whether the patient causes it, or we inadvertently do.

cut with all sorts of muck. The effects of continually injecting this into your body can be quite striking. That's before you even start thinking about all the blood-borne viral infections[1] transmitted or received from needle-sharing. This chap would need to be referred to the physicians for antibiotics and further investigation. Intravenous drug users can be challenging personalities to manage as inpatients, especially if they are actively withdrawing from heroin addiction. I remember I had to look after a similar patient last year. He was an unmitigated nightmare. He had been a heroin addict for 20 years and had absolutely no peripheral veins left. He had developed an infection on the valve separating the right side of his heart[2] which required 6 weeks of intravenous antibiotics[3]. I remember one afternoon after a long morning ward round spending the entire afternoon, at the expense of all the other jobs I had to do, trying to find a small, pathetic vein in his hands or arms, even his feet. The patient sat there tolerantly enduring failed attempt after failed attempt. Eventually I had to phone the anaesthetic registrar[4] and beg her to come to the ward and put a line in. She managed to get a small cannula in the patient's wrist. I thanked her profusely and got on with my neglected jobs. It was about two hours later when the patient was found collapsed at the front of the hospital outside WH Smiths' having scored some heroin and shot up through his newly inserted cannula.

---

[1] Classically HIV and Hepatitis C

[2] Known as infective endocarditis

[3] Intravenous antibiotics are delivered through a plastic cannula which is put in the vein.

[4] Anaesthetists (or anaesthesiologists as the Americans say) are the doctors who deliver the anaesthetic for operations. They put in cannulas all day and are usually very proficient at finding a vein to stick a needle into. They are consequently often pestered for difficult ward patients. Occasionally between operative cases they will come to the ward and grudgingly help out a useless pleading junior doctor. This anaesthetist obviously could sense the desperation in my voice and came.

'What's next?' I asked the sister with the clipboard. Clipboards mean power in the NHS. She held it firmly against her shapely hips. A shield to deflect the ambulance drivers trying to offload patients. Or perhaps a lead screen to block out the radiation emanating from the eyes of angry relatives: 'Well it has been 20 minutes and my mother still hasn't had her heart tracing the doctor wanted,' you would hear a concerned relative cluck to no one in particular. Adopting the tell-tale stance, standing outside the patient cubicle with their arms folded with occasional exasperated noises, foot tapping and hand gestures. The clipboard; chief buffer of the government's four hour wait rule. The pressure to see and discharge patients in 4 hours was ever omnipresent. I had been an A&E doctor for 6 weeks and so far my conclusions are, whatever Tony Blair thinks, if you are stupid enough to pitch up to A&E with a two year history of finger pain, as the patient I saw last night had, well then you deserve to wait in the waiting room until you mummify.

'So why did you come tonight, of all nights in the last 2 years?' I had asked. Maybe it had got a lot worse? Maybe the finger had fallen off? Maybe they had been attempting to get an appointment with their GP for the last 2 years?

'I was bored really', he explained, 'I thought it would be quiet.'

I felt like slamming his finger in the door. The medical hierarchy didn't quite share my view. If the department didn't see 95% of the patients who attend A&E in four hours then the hospital loses money. All patients must therefore be seen in time order unless they are at death's door. I don't know what was written on the nurse-in-charge's clipboard or whether it was there merely to increase her authority. A badge of merit perhaps; the doctor has the stethoscope, the senior nurse has the clipboard. Her authority was enhanced further with a green bib emblazoned on the back with 'senior nurse' and below 'co-ordinator'. Whilst having the very useful purpose of allowing her very quick identification by ambulance drivers, other staff or relatives, it did have the unfortunate effect of making her look like she worked on the fish counter at Morrison's.

'What's next?'

'Chest pain, cubicle 4,' the Morrison's fish supervisor said. She directed my gaze to cubicle 4 using the clipboard of power.

'Can I have the next one Sister? That will be the third chest pain I've seen today, I can't face another one.' I don't know why I was complaining; I remember last year I saw six anal abscesses in a row. The great arse inspection of 2009.

'Okay, but it is either that or some lady acting odd in cubicle 5,' sister replied they are both on equal waiting times.

'I'll have the chest pain please.'

'You'll have the odd women,' she commanded shoving the notes in my chest. 'She's on 2 hours and 34 minutes wait already so don't dick around like usual.'

Odd lady it was then. I never thought I would be one of those doctors, when I was at medical school, who referred to patients by their medical condition. It had already thoroughly permeated into my practice; the last thing I remember is the names. When working on the medical wards, due to the vast amounts of patients, and huge volumes of work, you would often tip up to evening handover late, tired and flustered. The handover would quickly degenerate into a game of 'Guess Who', discriminated not only by their ginger hair or their several chins but their medical condition and location on the ward: 'Oh you know, that chap on the gastro ward with decompensated alcoholic liver disease who keeps drinking the alcohol hand cleansing gel. That one, the fatty, the one on ward 4, third bed on the left, Type 1 diabetes who keeps stuffing her face with chocolate and her blood sugar levels are so high you could make marmalade with her piss.' Always met with a smile, a nodding acknowledgement and usually: 'I know the one, I saw her last week.'

I poked my head around the curtain. An attractive middle aged lady sat on the trolley. A younger chap was sat in the chair alongside the gurney.

'Hi, I'm Dr Parsons, please call me Tom, I'm one of the A&E doctors,' I introduced myself. I glanced at the top of the notes. 'You must be Mrs Cooper?'

'Missed'

'Pardon?'

'Missed?'

'Missed what?'

'I'm not married, so it's Miss,' she explained, 'Miss Cooper.'

'Oh, right, I do apologise.' So far she was showing me up on the cognitive front.

I had learnt not to assume…'So when are you due?' They look at you rather quizzically and then when the penny drops I might as well have walked in the cubicle with my left testicle dangling out of my fly. I remember I once introduced myself to an old chap, in his seventies, who had a lady perhaps forty-five with him. It was quite obvious to me that she was his daughter. But Parsons, the old charmer said: '…and this must be your granddaughter then Sir. I'm his wife,' she replied with intent disgust.

'Miss Cooper,' I started again, 'and may I ask who you are Sir?' I looked inquisitively at the other gentleman in the chair whilst offering my hand.

'I'm her partner James.'

He was deathly thin, emaciated, and it looked terminal, like he had been on some sort of hunger strike. His T-shirt billowed out like the sail of a Napoleonic warship whilst his jeans remained fixed mid abdominal position, by virtue of a tightened belt like rigging to the mast. It made me wonder whom I should be diagnosing.

'Would you like to stay sir?'

'Yes, if that's okay?'

We all looked at each other sharing, what I hope was, a mutual nod of agreement and consent. I quickly scanned the GP letter. Some GP letters are remarkably detailed and helpful, considering the 10 or so minutes they would have had to see the patient. Understandably some GPs prefer, what one would call, a more minimalistic approach to letter writing. Occasionally the patients just seem to be delivered by an ambivalent ambulance driver into your lap with no one quite knowing why they have come to A&E other than that their GP sent them. This one read:

'Dear Dr, Please see this 46 year old lady who had a sudden onset headache ten days ago and has been acting strangely. Please see to rule out an intracranial event[1]. Yours sincerely...' There was a rather unremarkable, computer generated, past medical history attached. Acting strangely is something my dotty Great Aunt does when she puts her TV remote in the dishwasher not a 46 year old who has never had anything wrong with them before.

'So...tell me in your own words what's been going on?'

'Well,' Miss Cooper paused, rolled her eyes and smacked her lips. She rolled her eyes again and pouted at me. 'I feel odd. I can't seem to recognise people at work and I can't remember people names.' She looked sharply left with her eyes keeping her head very still.

'How long has this been going on for?'

'A while,' she pouted again then smiled.

'How long exactly?'

'Umm 3 err days or a week or maybe 3. Anyways...'

'Well hang on a minute, is it 3 days or weeks,' I interrupted, 'when did it all start?'

'I had a headache three weeks ago and my nose was running. I often get headaches. I have had four antibiotics for sinus infections you know. Then I got another headache and another. Then I couldn't remember things,' she looked away and pouted her lips again.

'Do you have a headache now?'

'No.'

'Okay.' Taking a thorough history is the key to forming a differential diagnosis. So far I had drawn a blank. 'Anything else?' I fished.

'Not really.' She looked away again to the left staring at the dividing curtain and then re-focussed on a spot over my left shoulder. 'I don't really feel real. I don't feel myself,' she stated.

'I'm not sure I'm getting to the bottom of this Mrs..Miss Cooper. Shall we start again?'

Second time round I was none the wiser. Her fella chipped in a bit to try and clarify the history. She seemed to have had a bad headache

---

[1] Intra-cranial event basically means something bad going on inside the head.

and seen her GP who thought her sinuses[1] were inflamed. He gave her some antibiotics. She went to see another doctor at the emergency walk in centre when the headache began to really deteriorate and worsen who changed the antibiotics and gave some pain relief. She then went back to another doctor with a change in personality who thought that was due to the morphine in the painkillers. She then went to her usual GP who thought she had had some sort of intracranial event and sent her to A&E with a covering letter. I should have gone for the chap with chest pain. Even the heroin addict would have been simpler.

I made my excuses to go and get some examination tools; a tendon hammer, a pen torch and a fundoscope to look in the back of the eyes. James, the cachectic boyfriend headed me off as I drew back the curtains.

'Actually doc....do you mind? You know...if I could just fill in the blanks?'

'Is that Miss Cooper?'

She nodded and pouted again. I led him from behind the curtain to conduct a whispered meeting and elucidate the fruits of his espionage in the corridor outside the disabled lavatory.

'She has been acting oddly Doc, I think she might have lost it.'

'Ok. How? Can you give me some examples?'

'Trying to put books in the tumble-dryer, umm not recognising our neighbours even though they have lived next door to us for 6 years. I asked her to change the TV channel last night, you know, with the remote control.' He used his fingers to imitate changing the channel on a remote control and then paused to summon his thoughts.

I considered why he felt he had to explain to me how a television remote worked but continued to nod.

---

[1] Sinuses are little air filled spaces within the bones of the face. Occasionally they can become infected: known as sinusitis, which usually brings headache, facial pain and lots of greeny snot comes out one's nose.

'So she went upstairs turned on the upstairs TV to the channel we wanted,' he continued, 'and just lay on the bed, like this was a completely normal thing to do'.

'So you asked her to change the channel on the TV downstairs and she went upstairs and changed the channel on the TV upstairs?'

'Absolutely,' he confirmed, 'that's when I thought we should see our doctor in the morning.'

I thanked him for the clarification and made my excuses to go again to fetch the clinical examination tools. He grabbed my arm as I took the first step of my small re-supply mission. I stopped dead and looked at his hand lightly grasping my forearm. He immediately withdrew it and looked apologetic.

'Doc, is she going mental?'

'Mental isn't really a medical term,' I responded. 'Do I think this it is all in her head, that is, a psychiatric problem?' I asked rhetorically, 'no, I don't.' The malnourished one looked immediately relieved. Is the stigma of mental disease so powerful that he would rather his sweetheart had some sort of rotting brain malady? I continued. 'I think your wife...'

'Partner,' he interjected.

'Sorry, partner,' I apologised, 'so I think your partner, Miss..,' I hesitated, looking at the top of the clerking sheet to remember her name, 'Cooper,' I regained, 'has something neurologically wrong; either a bleed, or a growth or an infection on the brain or in the brain tissue itself. Now what it is I'm not sure but we shall see whether I can try and find us all some answers.'

'Thanks doc.' He looked at my arm again apologetically and I gave what I hoped was a sympathetic smile. He was obviously worried about her. I strolled leisurely in full contemplation back to the nurse's station.

Ten minutes later I was still opening drawers in a fruitless search with various bits of cylindrical steel tubes and a dozen flat batteries. Why is it that the NHS trust with a budget of over a hundred billion pounds per annum can't seem to provide one functioning fundoscope[1]? Walking back I tried to remember all the words to describe the many bizarre neurological signs and symptoms. There was a fantastic book 'The Man Who Mistook His Wife for a Hat' by an American neurologist, Oliver Sachs, who beautifully describes these bizarre neurological signs and symptoms including a man who actually did mistake his wife for a hat.

I had a good look at Miss Cooper and put her through my examinational rigours. There was no hint of weakness or numbness, the reflexes and sensation seemed entirely normal. I looked, with my acquired fundoscope, into the back of her eyes. Sometimes when there is an increase in pressure inside the head the disc can look swollen. I could, as per usual, make out only what looked like a pizza. All the cranial nerves looked normal, all twelve of them. They can be remembered rather easily by the mnemonic Oh Oh Oh To Touch And Feel Virgin Girls Vaginas And Hymens. Something I still use (and try not to mouth or count on my fingers) to remember the order of Olfactory, Optic, Oculomotor, Trochlear, Trigeminal, Abducens, Facial, Vestibulocochlear, Glossopharyngeal, Vagus, Accessory and Hypoglossal cranial nerves[2]. The partner looked at me expectantly as I hesitated. Nothing found yet. I showed her a biro.

'What is this called Miss Cooper?'

'Um it's a, what do you call it, a pencil'

'A pen', the partner said. I looked at him despairingly. It isn't a pub quiz you fool.

'Just Miss Cooper thank you Sir.' He smiled and looked somewhat sheepish.

'And this,' I said showing my ID card.

---

[1] A fundoscope is used to look at the optic disc and retina at the back of the eye. It is very much a piece of kit where experience of use increases the sensitivity and specificity. I was just getting to the point where I could reliably see the optic disc rather than initially where everything resembled a rather sparse pizza. Practice makes perfect.

[2] The cranial nerves control your sense of smell, control eye movements, sensation to the face, facial movements, speech and the ability to cough as well as palate and tongue movement amongst many other functions.

'A, err,' she hesitated, 'a plastic.' More rather bizarre mouth pouting and eye movements followed. I glanced up at the partner who stared at me. I broke away from his gaze as she tried again, 'no a thingy.'

'Okay,' I said calmly taking off my stethoscope, 'and this?'

'Err tubes,' she looked confused momentarily, raised her eyebrows and then returned to normal fixed on something obviously interesting on the inside of the curtain.

'So what does that mean?' the beanpole asked me.

'It means we need to get a scan.' It also meant I needed to try and remember what the words were for these signs so I could reliably inform the radiologist in 'doctor speak' of what I had found when requesting a CT scan of her head[1]. I picked up the phone and organised the scan.

'Who's looking after cubicle 5?' the sister's voice rang out.

'That's me.' I was writing up the notes having requested the scan.

'First of all, you are at 3 hours and 20 minutes. What are you doing with your patient?'

'Getting a CT scan of her head.'

'Can that not happen after she is referred?'

'Probably but there is a CT scanner in the department.'

'If she breaches......,' the Morrison's supervisor threatened.

'Fine I'll bleep the radiology registrar.' I punched the keys into the phone next to me, hung up and waited the short moment before the radiology registrar rang back.

---

[1] Incidentally the terms are:

    1) Prosopagnosia- the inability to recognise familiar faces despite having normal vision.

    2) Depersonalisation- a subjective feeling of altered reality of self.

    3) Paraphasia- the inability to speak properly, substituting one word for another. In semantic paraphasia the substituted word is related to the intended word e.g. leaf and tree.

    4) Anomia- a type of speech disorder characterised by the inability to recall words or names

(I looked it up on Wikipedia).

'Hello.'

'Hi Radiology Reg.'

'Hi this is Tom in ED?'

'Is this about that Cooper lady?'

'Oh that was quick.'

'Yeah I was actually in the scan room when she went through and it looked a bit funky so I looked at it there and then and repeated the scan with contrast.' I waited in silent anticipation. 'There is an area of low attenuation in the left temporal lobe, some mild mass effect. After the contrast there was some odd gyriform enhancement but no real focal enhancement.'

'Ok,' I said in an anticipatory fashion. I had no idea what that meant.

Predicting my internal monologue the radiologist replied without requiring a prompt: 'I think the differential diagnosis could be a malignant process[1] which is less likely or maybe herpes simplex encephalitis[2]. Although you did mention that she had been having trouble with her sinuses and I suppose it could be an abscess[3].'

'So what do you think I should do now?' I asked.

'Dunno mate, I'd speak to your boss. You should definitely get a neurosurgical opinion though.'

'Right. Thanks.' I hung up the phone.

I found the A&E consultant in his office. He was halfway through a round of NHS toast and nearing the completion of a game of minesweeper on his computer.

'Mike?' I asked.

---

[1] A malignant process is doctor speak for cancer. In this case: brain cancer.

[2] Herpes Simplex encephalitis is a viral infection that effects the part of the brain involved with visual memory, language comprehension and emotions. Herpes simplex is the virus that gives you cold sores and genital herpes.

[3] An abscess is a ball of infection that usually contains pus

'Yeah,' he answered. 'Come on in…err,' he hesitated and glanced at my name badge which was hanging upside down so precluding Mike 'remembering' my name.

'I'm Tom, one of the FY2 doctors,' I reminded.

'Of course, of course. Come on in,' he repeated.

'I've got this patient…'

'Shoot.'

I told him the story and scan results. He sat back in his chair, his scrub top littering with crumbs and a fairly sizeable nob of semi-melted butter on his chin.

'Hmm have you spoke to the medical doctors?'

'No not yet.'

'When does she breach?'

'15 minutes or so.'

'I would speak to the medical doctors,' he shrugged.

'Not the neurosurgeons?'

'Sure,' he shrugged again, 'but they are based at another hospital and we don't want to transfer her from A&E she'll be here for ever. Send her to the medics, they can sort it out.'

I could tell his main effort was just to make her someone else's problem. Maybe he was right. After all, isn't that what A&E is about? They are only yours for four hours.

I watched over the top of the computer sat behind the desk as Miss Cooper was wheeled past me out of the Emergency Department and into the bowels of the hospital. The trouble is you never know what happens to these patients when they leave the department. It was like seeing the first part of a film trilogy or only reading the first chapter of a gripping novel. Would she get better? Do any of them get any better? Did she have a brain infection? Or was it a tumour? What will the medics do with her? Will she just sit there and rot waiting to be transferred to the tertiary neurosurgical centre down the road? Would they even operate? I wouldn't know. I suppose I could find out but tomorrow would bring fresh challenges and today would blur into insignificance.

I walked out of the hospital that night, in pitch darkness, and made my way to the management block where I had abandoned my car 10 hours earlier prior to starting my shift. I greeted the plastic wrapper stuck to my windscreen containing my £50 parking ticket with a resigned shrug. I ripped it off the windscreen and shoved the ticket and plastic wrapper in the glove compartment with the others. I was nothing like George Clooney. He would never have put up with this shit.

What is wrong with these people?

'How did it happen?' I asked. His nose was obliterated and already his eyes were turning a shade of purple and slowly closing shut. His oozing nose had been self-stymied with rolled-up wads of bog roll which made him look mildly ridiculous. The formally white canvas of his tracksuit looked like a crimson inspired Jackson-Pollock painting. In response to my question he glanced up at the police officer, who was accompanying him, who stood bored in the corner of the cubicle.

'Fell over Doc.'

'You too?' I responded wearily with heavy sarcasm. 'I can only presume this was some sort of syncope[1] virus which had briefly stricken one pub in middle England?'

It was nine o'clock in the evening and anyone would think we were giving out free hot-dogs. The department was rammed and I was sat in minors simultaneously dealing with the fallout of a motorway coach crash and the Saturday night amateur Fight-club that had erupted in the pub around the corner.

'A what doc?'

'Never-mind, you've broken your nose. I'll send you an appointment for ENT clinic,' I said peeling off my latex gloves and throwing them in the wrong coloured bin in the corner. 'Stay there whilst I do the paperwork please.' I walked out the cubicle into the furore. I don't believe in God but I believe in purgatory; it is an Accident and Emergency department on a late Saturday afternoon. In the most part it doesn't even seem to be the punters who are suffering in expiating their sins. It is the staff, and more importantly; me. It was worse than Christmas shopping on Christmas Eve or a budget long-haul airline flight with a '2 for 1 sale where toddlers can

---

[1] Syncope; collapse with transient loss of consciousness.

go free'. In fact if someone offered me the opportunity to work every Saturday afternoon in our Emergency Department for the rest of my life I wouldn't do it for a golden duck that shits Fabergé eggs.

The fight in the pub, as far as I could tell, seemed to have occurred as someone's football team had unreasonably beat someone else's. Not that anyone was being particularly forthcoming with details. Perhaps this was due to the heavy police presence in the department. Or maybe they were just obeying the first rule of Fight club?

I scurried past the throngs of infirmed and their pissed off relatives. I looked continually at my feet as I walked to avoid any eye contact. I quickly typed the three line discharge letter for the chap with the broken beak which would be automatically sent to the patient's probable fictional GP address he had given to accompany the fictional name he had registered with. I circled the ENT[1] follow up box knowing full well he would DNA[2] it. I shoved his paper work in the 'discharged' pile and picked up the next piece of paper work for the next punter waiting. I walked to the minor's cubicle and introduced myself as I pulled the curtain back.

'How can I help?' I asked.

'I was in the coach accident on the motorway too,' said a somewhat overweight balding middle-aged man in a striped polo shirt.

'Ok,' I paused. This was the third injured patient I had personally seen in the last hour or so from this particular low speed coach accident which had bumped into a lorry when the driver was trying to change the radio station. The prior two were a mild head injury and a twisted ankle; the latter wasn't even injured during the crash itself but on disembarking from the coach following the accident. 'So how can I help?'

'Well I thought I should get checked out.'

'Oh,' I paused, 'are you in any pain?'

---

[1] Ear Nose and Throat surgeons who oddly specialise in ears, noses and throats (as well as necks). Also known as otolaryngology.
[2] DNA: did not attend

'Not really, I mean I feel a bit sore.'

'Anywhere in particular?'

'Not really, my neck is a bit stiff.'

'Ok. Did the ambulance bring you?'

'No but I thought I should follow it here when they took away the sick-uns.'

'Follow?' I asked, 'follow in what?'

'My car.'

'Your car?' I said surprised, 'were you not in the coach then?'

'No. I was behind the coach when it drove into the back of the lorry.'

'Oh. Could you still drive your car, wasn't it damaged in the crash?'

'No I didn't crash. I did have to stop quite suddenly though.'

'So you were in the coach crash but you weren't in the coach and you didn't crash?

'Well yeah. But, as I said, I did stop suddenly. I'm worried about whiplash aren't I?'

I let out a little chuckle in retort. 'Come, come now Sir', I said dripping in patronage, 'we both know the reason you are here?' This fraudulent little weasel was trying to pull a fast one from the insurance companies for his supposed neck injuries. He'll be straight on to an ambulance chaser for hyper-exaggerated 'no win no fee claim'. But being too tired (and too conflict averse) to argue I quickly prodded his neck, wrote a couple lines in his notes and discharged him.

'Well what about work Doc?'

'What about it?' I replied antagonistically.

'Well I think I'm going to be in too much pain?'

'Really?' I commented derisively, 'what is it you do for a living?'

'Security.'

'Hmm,' I nodded allowing my lip to curl as I looked at his rotund form sat in the chair, 'what sort of security?'

'Building sites mostly, I do the night shifts, stop the tools and plants being nicked?'

'So you're sat down most of the time?'

'Well, yeah but I have to patrol around too.'

'Do you really,' I sighed.

'So any chance of a sick note?'

'We'll see how it goes,' I mollified, 'if it's still painful go and see your GP.' I drew the curtain back and walked away from the curtain.

'But I'm at work tonight Doc?' he hollered after me as I walked off. 'Can you at least make sure it gets in my medical notes so I can claim on the insurance?'

Most Accident and Emergency Departments are split into Majors and Minors. This terminology is supposed to reflect the degree of accident or emergency that the patient is suffering. There is also a Resuscitation department or 'Resus' which takes the extremely sick patients who require very close monitoring. Often departments also have a Paediatric Emergency Department or occasionally, in some hospitals, this is co-located with paediatric wards. As a general rule minors patients usually needed discharging, majors patients are usually admitted and resuscitation patients are always admitted.

Bored and fed up I left Minors and walked through the adjoining corridor to Majors. A further corridor attached Majors and the Resuscitation department to an outside door where the ambulances parked. A line of stretchers loaded with patients queued down the hall and outside the door of the ambulance entrance. Bored ambulance drivers yawned and read newspapers, tinkered on their mobile phones and drank gulps of indeterminate brown fluid from disposable cups as they stood guard alongside their festering patients, waiting to hand them over to the frenetic nursing staff. The rule was that if there wasn't a cubicle for the patient they couldn't be offloaded from the paramedics to the department. Patients had been lying on hard stretchers for hours and they were all quite keen to regularly update any poor bastard in scrubs, like me, unfortunate enough to pass in close proximity to them, about how royally pissed off they were with their situation. Usually I would dodge this by walking along the back corridor adjacent to the Paediatric Emergency Department and CT scanner but even that was full of patients awaiting a hospital bed.

The department had reached gridlock. Even patients who had already been seen, treatment started, partially investigated and now just awaiting an admission to their appropriate department were stuck in their cubicle, or the corridor, as there was no bed in the hospital for them to go to. The Acute Medical Unit, Surgical Assessment Unit, Gynae Assessment Unit even the Orthopaedic Assessment Unit were full. The whole hospital had become constipated. The bowels of this gargantuan, megalithic beast of a care had become obstructed. Nothing was coming out and consequently everything you tried to put in came spewing out in bilious vomit sprayed all over the floor of the A&E department. I was faced, as far as I could see it, with two possible options; the first was to use the only viable remaining space and start consulting in the staff lavatory or even set up a minor injury clinic at the hospital Costa coffee shop. The second was to just sit and drink tea and watch the wailing and gnashing of teeth as it played out before my very eyes. It was a crisis. What does one do in a crisis? They shine the bat sign into the sky and hope the caped crusader arrives. Unfortunately for us, this hero; this saviour, this guardian angel who had descended to solve this calamity was a podgy red faced manager in a suit. I wasn't sure who he actually was or what he was doing other than running laps of the department spasmodically yelling out words like 'black alert', 'level 3' and 'resource diversion' as he rather ineffectually flapped his arms and clucked like an old mother hen. Two minions orbited around him like insignificant electrons occasionally being ineffectively unleashed from the unstable nucleus of a radioactive atom. 'Lead Nurse' emblazoned their tunics. I wasn't sure if this meant that they were some sort of radiation shield, if they were in first position of all the nurses or whether they were on some sort of leash controlled by the fat manager. I suspected the later. They occasionally bumping into one another shouting 'breach, breach' and harrying the clinical staff to decide what they were going to do with Mrs Fudge who had been waiting in the department so long she had managed to get hold of some slippers, a bedspread and her fractured neck of femur, for which she had originally attended for, was showing signs of uniting in protest to the unacceptable delay.

'Chuck, what are you doing with the lady in cubicle 7?' Chuck looked up from furiously writing his notes, shook his head in a dismissive fashion, sighed heavily and continuing to write. Even he had stopped smiling.

'Chuck?' she repeated loudly and looked at him as though talking to a simpleton, 'The lady in 7?' repeated the minion. Chuck signed his name, raised from his chair and walked past the senior nurse to the sister running the department.

'This lady in cubicle 7 is to be admitted under orthopaedics,' he said in his deep Ghanaian tones. He walked past the manager's harem and relinquished a quick glare of disapproval. He picked up the next set of notes from the in tray and walked to the next cubicle whilst the harem stamped off to go and find a consultant to piss, snitch and whine to about the insolence of his staff.

I made myself a cup of tea from the 'patient only trolley' in the corridor and sat down at the Doctor's station to spectate the catastrophe unfolding in front of me. Nurses continued to race up and down the Majors corridor whizzing around the patients, their relatives and the ambulance drivers who blocked the department with their trolleys. The manager had taken off his suit jacket, rolled up his sleeves and was protesting at the computer screen with Mike the ED consultant for the day. The computer ran the programme which displayed the tragic state of play in the department. The manager, red faced and fraught, kept on reaching his hand behind him and inserting it into his bum crevice.

Annie, one of the other ED SHOs came and stood next to me with a bottle of water.

'I wonder when they will just accept defeat and close the doors,' I said gesturing towards the manager.

'Who is he anyway?'

'Dunno, could be the chief executive for all I know. I wouldn't know what he looked like if he kicked me between the legs.'

'I've just had to fish out a tampon from between a girl's legs. It had probably been up there for months?'

'What!?'

'I shit you not.'

'How the...,' I stopped myself and shook my head.

'That wasn't even why she came.'

'I'm not sure I want to know.'

'It was her boyfriend that made her,' she explained taking another swig of water and leaning against the desk. We both stood side by side watching one of the lead nurses trying to move a hospital bed with an elderly lady lying on it. She kept on crashing into other gurneys, walls and members of her staff like she was wrestling with a defective shopping trolley.

'Made her what?'

'Come to ED. He said his willy smelt whenever they had sex.'

'I might have to ask you not to tell me the rest of this story.'

She smirked and me and took another swig from her bottle. 'She didn't even known it was up there. I got her on the bed and flopped her legs open and it smelt like something had crawled up there and died. I mean I actually gagged. I even stopped what I was doing to reach for another pair of gloves to, you know, double glove.'

'Sounds like her fella should have done the same thing.'

'Quite,' Annie said.

'So what happened?' I asked after a pause. Curiosity killed the cat.

'Well I shoved my hand up. And I have to say that it was like opening the window and sticking my hand into the night.'

'Nice.'

'I was surprised more wasn't lost up there.'

'What like the lost Ark of the Covenant or the Mary Celeste?'

She laughed. 'Anyway did you ever wonder what a tampon looks like when it has fermented in a vagina for a couple of months?'

'No.'

'Cottage cheese.'

'Tom?' I span around to see Mike the ED consultant who had left the manager by the computer. 'What are you doing now?' he said sternly as though to insinuate that I was doing bugger all. He was right, obviously.

'Just been in minors but there is no room to see anyone at the moment; all the cubicles are taken,' I explained. He glanced back at the computer.

'Can you quickly see the girl in the triage room? I think it should be a quick one for you.'

'Of course,' I turned to Annie. We both raised out eyebrows at each other.

'Better keep going,' I said.

'Yep.' She sat down in my vacated seat and started doing the tampon girl's discharge paperwork.

The triage room was supposed to be where patients had a quick assessment, usually by a senior nurse, so as to quickly direct the patient's care to the appropriate area of the department. Rather than being a cubicle with a curtain, the room was a walled off space located near the entrance to the department close to the waiting room and ambulance unloading bay. In the state of chaos, the triage room had now turned into a clinic room to see patients in, start treatment and then send the patients back to the waiting room. Mike handed me the notes and, without looking at them, I made my way to the triage room. I negotiated myself around the loaded trolleys and knocked on the door of the triage room and let myself in.

'Hi. Tom is my name. I am an A&E doctor.' I glanced up and saw a teenage girl lying on the trolley. She didn't look much older than 15. She was thin with, what seemed to be dyed black hair. She had dark leggings on and a dark T-shirt on top covered with a chequered shirt. She had a ring through her bottom lip and wore dark eye shadow.

'Hi,' she replied quietly. She briefly glanced at me and then focussed on the wall in front of her.

'What is your name?'

'Amy.'

'Hi Amy. So how can I help?' I glanced at the top of the notes and saw written in the 'presenting complaint box' on the admission sheet 'paracetamol overdose'.

'You can't,' she replied sulkily.

'Oh?' I paused, 'well why is it that you are here?'

'Why are you even asking me? You already know,' she whined, her eyes remaining focussed on the wall. 'The nurse has already taken all my details.'

'Remind me. What have you taken?'

'Paracetamol.'

'Only paracetamol?'

225

'Yes

'And what did you want to happen following taking the paracetamol?'

'What do you think?'

'Did you want to kill yourself?'

Amy glanced back at me and hesitated. 'No,' she said sulkily.

'So why?'

'To teach him a lesson?'

'Who? Your boyfriend?'

'Yes. He was cheating on me with my best friend and I wanted him to know how much he hurt me.'

'By hurting yourself?'

'He did this, not me, he drove me to it.'

'I see. Do you know how paracetamol kills you?'

'Not particularly no.'

'Well allow me to tell you. For the first day or so you will typically feel very little except some nausea, occasional vomiting and tiredness. But as the liver injury progresses you will typically develop pain here,' I said pointing to my liver just below the lungs o the right hand side of the abdomen. 'When that happens often your kidneys pack in too. At around 3-4 days you will go yellow as a result of the jaundice from advancing liver failure. You typically become confused and occasionally bleed heavily. Death is common at this stage and sometimes fulminant liver failure occurs requiring transplantation. All in all it is a pretty dire way to go.'

'Great,' she replied sarcastically, 'I'll keep that in mind.'

'So how many do you think you have taken?'

'Of the paracetamol?'

'Yes'

'Five.'

'Five packs?' [1]

---

[1] In 1998 legislation came into force that restricted pack sizes of paracetamol sold over the counter. Packs were restricted to a maximum of 32 tablets in pharmacies and to 16 tablets for non-pharmacy sales. This resulted in a significant reduction in deaths from paracetamol overdose.

'No just five.'

'What five tablets?'

'Yeah.'

'Five?' I repeated. Christ that's only 3 more than what you would take for a bloody headache. 'Did you take anything else? No other tablets or recreational drugs or alcohol?'

'No?'

'And have you ever harmed yourself before?'

Before she could answer we were interrupted by a knock on a door. A spotty gangly face peered around.

'Amy?' he said. I glanced back to Amy. Tears had begun to form in the corner of his eyes.

'Go away Si,' she said loudly, 'I don't want to see you'.

'Amy,' he repeated, opening the door.

'Can you give us a minute buddy okay?' I more told than asked the acne-ridden youngster as I pushed the door closed on him. I turned back to see Amy.

'We are going to take a blood test 4 hours after you took the tablets and that is going to decide what we need to do. If you have only taken five and nothing else then we should be able to let you go home once you have had a chat to our psychiatric liaison nurses. Sound okay?'

'I guess.'

'What do you want me to say to your fella?'

'Send him in,' she said quietly.

I exited through the door and walked back to the doctor's station. I sat down and started writing my notes. I faintly heard a shout for help with a buzzer sounding. I looked up nonchalantly. Buzzers seemed to go off in ED all the time and could indicate anything from burnt toast to a chemical weapon strike.

This is likely to be because the majority of people who overdose on paracetamol do it impulsively and therefore take what is available in the household. If people do plan the overdose it takes them longer to get hold of significant enough amounts to cause severe liver failure.

'It's coming from the triage room,' a nurse said walking briskly in the direction.

'The triage room,' I said, 'but that is my patient. She has only had 5 paracetamol?'

'I raced back to the triage cubicle and swung open the door to find a red faced frenetic nurse trying to hold an oxygen mask to a flailing body shaking away on the couch. The gangly spotty boyfriend stood ashen in the corner?

'What happened?' I said struggling to keep the panic out of my voice.

'We were just talking, she was upset, and,' he paused, his voice cracked, 'her eyes rolled back and she went unconscious and started fitting,' he blurted.

'Can we have some help please?' I shouted at the door.

Mike the ED consultant appeared at the cubicle. He stood at the entrance to the cubicle and surveyed the scene.

'Ah fitting[1] is she?' Mike said nonchalantly, 'I thought she only took 5 paracetamol Tom?'

'She did! I only just left her,' I attempted to explain and obviate blame.

'Oh dear,' said Mike calmly, 'do we have intravenous access?'

'No,' said the nurse.

'Okay get the rectal diazepam[2],' said Mike. There was a brief pause and a further nurse ran into the room. The girl was still shaking

---

[1] Fits or seizures are due to an abnormal excess in neuronal activity in the brain. Whilst fits can be partial, people are normally referring to a generalised tonic clonic seizures when they describe a fit. Having a fit does not make you epileptic. Whilst anyone can have a fit under certain circumstances (if they have a head injury or are deprived of oxygen for example) epilepsy is a neurological condition where patients have recurrent unprovoked fits with no immediately identifiable cause

[2] Diazepam is a benzodiazepine drug also known as Valium. In tablet form it is used to reduce acute anxiety, for insomnia as well as alcohol withdrawal. It essentially acts like a 'brake' on the brain by slowing it down. In intravenous or rectal form it is used to sedate patients or to terminate seizures.

violently on the bed her head arched back. I stood like a lemon next to the gangly boyfriend as helpless and useless as he was.

The nurse yanked down the girl's leggings and attempted to insert the rectal diazepam applicator. One of the girls shaking arms moved slowly down to the top of her leggings and tried to pull them back up as the nurse continued to try and yank them down to access her bottom and insert the medication into her rectum. The nurse continued to struggle against the seizing girl's tight grip on the top of her leggings. It was a few seconds before she realised.

'What the…,' the nurse said still holding the diazepam applicator in her gloved hand. She looked at me.

'You can't perform purposeful actions when having a seizure,' I said confused. I looked at Mike.

'No, it isn't a real seizure,' Mike said slowly shaking his head. He turned and walked out of the cubicle and back into the chaos. 'What the fuck is wrong with these people?' he exasperatingly muttered. Bugger all evidently.

Signing Off

I had come in, on my day off to see Dan; my consultant supervisor. My time in Accident and Emergency, and Foundation training, was coming to a close which meant that we needed to have an educational meeting to 'reflect' on my experiences. Or something.

'I am pleased with how you have performed in the last three and a half months Tom.'

'Thank you.' I was a little taken a back. I would have been pleased if he had remembered my name never-mind been able to comment on my performance. I'm pretty sure he only had to glance at my open online e-portfolio, displaying my name, details and passport photo briefly to remind himself too.

'So what are you going to do next year? What have you applied for?'

During the last few months of Foundation training doctors apply for their next jobs which ultimately sets their career trajectory. Doctors who want to go into medical disciplines such as Gastroenterology or Rheumatology or Haematology apply for Core Medical training; a further two years of rotations but this time just medical disciplines. Those who wish to do surgery in the future whether General Surgery or Orthopaedic Surgery choose Core Surgical Training which, like Core Medical Training, is a further two years of rotations around Surgical disciplines. In fact the majority of mainstream specialities have a further two years of Core training. When the Core Training is finished, trainees commonly apply for speciality training and at that point become a specialist registrar where they have anything from 3-5 years of further training until they can apply for Consultant jobs. For General Practice there are two more years of General Practice focussed hospital rotations followed by a year of training as a GP registrar before you are a GP. Many don't choose to jump straight on the escalator to consultancy or General Practice and instead decide to take what is colloquially known as an FY3 year (Foundation Year 3 year if you excuse the tautology) also known as an 'F-off' year. This essentially means you are going to go to Australia or New Zealand to be treated like a proper healthcare professional. Those that miss their family and friends come home, those that don't usually stay and live happily ever after.

'I'm going to take a year out,' I responded. The fact was I had not the first inclination what I wanted to do, but, what the last three and a half months had told me was that I definitely didn't want to do Emergency Medicine.

'So, would you consider a career in Emergency Medicine when you come back into training?'

I hesitated. What would be a suitably non-committal answer? 'Maybe,' I answered. Maybe when hell freezes over. Don't get me wrong I enjoy seeing patients. I enjoy seeing sick patients and I enjoy trying to make them better. I enjoy interacting with the thankful masses too, in the most part. And I certainly like the matching scrubs; it makes it so much easier to decide what to wear in the mornings. I would be amiss not to point out that the reason one wears scrubs to work in the ED department is because they at least provide some consolation when some well-oiled entertainer thinks it will be a great wheeze to piss up your trouser leg; an act which may result in an even more calamitous sense of humour failure if one was wearing their finest Italian suit. It is perhaps ironic that, during the 12 hour night shift, you commonly stop just once to dribble out a drop of acrid concentrated urine. Patient after patient back to back and still they come. I am not scared of hard work but I am also not keen on ritualistically thrashing myself shift after shift on account of the masses who are either too ill-informed or feel too entitled ('it is their taxes that pay my wages don't I know?') to figure out that the funny rash they have had for a few months is neither an accident nor an emergency. But when your own Health Secretary cannot, or chooses not to, make this distinction what hope can one expect from everyone else? No wonder that trainees leave Emergency Medicine training in droves. The specialty runs on locums; commonly non-training doctors working for money grabbing agencies who use the department's desperation for staff (it's not as if you can run an ED without doctors) to charge a fortune for often shoddy, lazy doctors to do half as much for four times the money. Why the hell would I want

231

to bust my balls in an Emergency Department only to see the locum doctor next to me doing my job less well than me whilst earning as much in one shift as I would take home in a week?

'I think the thing I enjoy most about Emergency Medicine is,' Dan paused leaned back in his desk chair and clasped his hands together. His index fingers were outstretched and touching his bottom lip as though considering a complex physics theory, 'it's probably the variety. We literally see everything. Children, the elderly, surgical, medical, orthopaedics,' he paused again, 'gynaecology,' as if this exemplified the diversity of his specialty. 'Everything,' he added again.

'I think the thing that puts me off Dan is the lack of continuity of care,' I said meekly.

Accident and emergency physicians are exposed to a wide variety and maybe even diagnose a multiplicity of disease but they don't necessarily fix it. What they see, fix, diagnose and send home is a smattering of minor cuts and broken bones. The rest you diagnose, stabilise and give to the specialists to ultimately fix. You don't put in the stent for the myocardial infarction. You don't put on the external fixator for the open femoral fracture. You don't perform the dilatation and curettage when a young lady presents with a miscarriage, nor hold their hand and comfort them after. You don't sort out the Parkinson's medications or social circumstances of an elderly lady who lives alone. You don't perform the laparotomy to fix the perforated duodenal ulcer or remove and repair the lacerated viscera of a severe trauma. You literally spend four hours with someone and then try make it someone else's problem.

'I think that is a good thing,' Dan replied, 'you see sick and desperate people, make them well but don't have the long term dramas. Do you know when I last did a ward round or did an outpatient clinic that was packed to the gunnels?'

I stayed silent.

'No staying late to get through bloated email inboxes for me. I turn up, do my shift and go home.'

Most of the Emergency Department consultants espouse that the beauty of A&E medicine is the random assortment of patients; the department in-tray (where the triaged patient's notes sit prior to them being seen by a doctor). Our department referred to it as the 'a box o' chocolates' often said with a deep south United States drawl. Having worked in ED for nearly four months, I suppose, theoretically, you could get anyone with anything wrong with them. But this box o' chocolates is not quite as arbitrary as Forrest Gump's container of highly randomised assorted Belgian cocoa deliciousness. This was more a tub of Roses left at the nurse's station about 5 days after Christmas. With the menu long lost, coupled with a few days of concerted cherry picking you face increasing odds of a coffee cream (now abandoned I note) or one of the disgustingly sickly strawberry flavoured efforts. I would liken the Emergency Department patient in-tray to be like the magic porridge pot; as soon as you get near the bottom, in stomps the receptionist and throws in another few. Not a lot, just enough to continue the illusion that getting to the bottom is achievable and you can reach that hallowed oasis, the Promised Land; an Accident and Emergency department with no one left to see.

The metaphorical coffee creams are quite obvious. Humans have a natural instinct in avoiding these type of people. And doctors are nearly human I assure you. The drunks who have cracked their heads is an illustrative example. Most of us cross the road when they see a drunk individual shouting and swearing whilst ataxically[1] drifting and swerving towards them with a large blunt object in their hand. However in the Emergency Department there is no crossing the road. Not only can you not avoid them you have to actively involve yourself with them. You have to ask yourself such questions like; are they being loud and abusive because they are a debauched old drunk or are they being loud and abusive because they are a debauched old drunk who has fallen over or taken a crack around to the skull where underneath lies a slowly developing sub-dural haemorrhage which will in a few hours have a somewhat life-

---

[1] Ataxia is a constellation of symptoms due to an inability to coordinate movements. It is commonly secondary to damage to a primitive part of the brain called the cerebellum. It can most effectively simulated by drinking too much; staggering walk, slurred speech, poor coordination.

limiting impact on their meagre cortical function? Almost impossible to take a history from, or even examine, without being punched, had aspersions cast over your sexuality (or is that just me?) or hit with a wave of four letter expletives. But you must try and differentiate whether you can wave your pen and discharge them back to the local boozer (with the promise of organising alcohol abstinence assistance through their GP that they never attend) or whether you must keep hold of them and tolerate their glowing banter and the smell of piss (and if you're lucky shit too) just a trifle longer. The media generally paints a somewhat malign portrait of the arrogant and dismissive A&E doctor who sent home that dear old chap, stalwart of the local community, nearly a pensioner, who had just been out celebrating the evening and when he accidently fell over and hit his head only to return home where he sank into a coma and died leaving behind 6 (illegitimate) children and 3 (ex) wives.

There are those little treats who think that 2am, when you are up to your eyeballs in metaphorical chocolate, would be a good time to come to A&E with that one toenail that has been a strange colour now for a few years. You don't even have to self-present. Why not drag along another: 'My child has a rash and I'm worried it is meningitis.' Classically the rash of meningitis, as far as I'm aware, doesn't smell of magic marker and isn't ably washed off with a wet-wipe. Despite the general consensus that children should be fast asleep at that time, toddlers really are just as delightful at 3am, in the short instances that they stop screaming.

'Well think about it. A&E always needs more doctors,' Dan said. So I'll just have a quick look at your reflective practice,' he added turning his attention to my e-portfolio.

I imagine the portfolio started out as a good idea. These sorts of ideas always do. I imagine doctors previously would carry around their certificates and logbooks as pieces of paper. They would turn up to interviews with these dog eared and coffee stained records of their achievements. The e-portfolio turned this into an electronic resource. This was taken hold of, with gusto, by the health education boards and rapidly turned into some sort of confused, unnavigable, proxy marker of competence and assessment. The e-portfolio expanded and bloated and became not just a peculiarity of keeping an eye on us baby Foundation Doctors but used by all doctors until they finish their training. For a hospital consultant this could be for 12-13 years. And the final kick in the testicles is that we have to pay for the privilege of using it. On the face of it an e-portfolio seems quite useful. You can record all the procedures you perform appropriate to your level of training. When you see a patient with an interesting disease you can sit down with your consultant immediately afterwards and discuss the complexities of their diagnosis and learn new facts. You can get feedback on your performance; hear what you did well and what you can improve on. There is even a tool where the consultant can watch you perform a consultation and give feedback on your capability to perform a diagnosis.

Here's the kicker though: It never, ever, happens. What feedback you get on your patient interaction is rarely contemporaneous and rarely useful. Why is this you may ask? Simple: time. No one except the most zealous pedagogue has anywhere near enough time to watch a young doctor examine a patient's heart properly from start to finish as described in the textbooks and then in true Pendleton's[1] form of non-judgemental immediate feedback 'ask them what they thought went well' and 'what everyone else thought went well' and 'what they thought they could have done better' and 'what everyone else thought they could have done better' followed by logging onto their e-portfolio and formalising this is a 'mini-CEX'[2]. Not when they can quickly listen themselves and move onto the next patient and stand a chance of making it back home in time for their children's bedtime.

---

[1] Dr David Pendleton was a social psychologist that came up with some rules for giving feedback. I can only presume that he worked with a room of trainees with impressive persecution complexes as his method is the most long-winded, inoffensive, delicate and tedious way to receive feedback that anyone could conceive.

[2] Mini clinical evaluation exercise- where someone watches you take a history or examine a patient and provides instant contemporaneous feedback.

You have to collect evidence on a plethora of conditions to show evidence of learning on the multitude of disease processes in medicine. Why? Medicine is a vast occupation and one of the key principles is that of *primum non nocere*; first do no harm. There are many things that I don't know in medicine but fabricating some tenuous half-baked evidence in collusion with my consultant just to show that I am learning is ridiculous. If I don't know I ask someone who does and then if suitably interested I read the evidence and learn and then I know. That is medicine. Why this process has to be formalised I cannot fathom.

And I've not even mentioned my favourite; the 'reflective log'. This is not, as it sounds, when one takes a somewhat insightful and introspective turd but a way of formalising and documenting what, for anyone with a modicum of insight, comes naturally. Anyone without insight will not learn from their 'log' so rather obviating the purpose. Say I prescribed a medication wrongly; easily done, you were in a hurry and scribbled the wrong dose of a blood pressure tablet. This was picked up by the pharmacist the next day (who, by the way, embody the peculiar paradox of saving your registration daily but doing it in the most irritating way) but not until the nurse had given the patient double the dose. This will, in all likelihood, have no particular short-term or long-term effects to the patient, which you would explain to them with your apology, except for maybe making them feel a little light headed for a few hours or so. Lesson learnt; be more careful when prescribing medications. Perhaps use quick reference guides like the British National Formulary application on your smart phone. Why this has to be written down, like some sort of confessional purging, I have no idea? What if I thought that it was not my fault but the nurses fault for not checking, or the patients fault for being hypertensive or the pharmacists fault for not being there, on the spot, to green pen your prescription (for some reason all pharmacists write in green). You are not going to realistically write this in your reflective log to be scrutinised by your superiors. And if you lack such insight surely you would be too set in your ways to change anyway. So what is the point?

Dan nodded reading through some of my forced reflections as I sat slightly behind him feeling awkward at his appraisal of my forced self-analysis.

'Good. Fine,' he commented. 'And the 360 degree? You did that here did you?'

'Yep,' I swallowed hard.

The 360 degree review or multi-source feedback is an interesting tool which aims to identify the junior doctor who is charming, diligent and knowledgeable to his consultants but rude, arrogant and lazy to his fellow junior doctors, nursing staff, pharmacists, receptionists; basically everyone who works in the hospital. It is colloquially known as the 'slate a mate'. One has to select 20 or so colleagues who fill out an online feedback questionnaire about your performance. For those who lack a little insight into their manner it can be the bitter pill of reality that one must swallow. For those who completely lack insight it is water off a duck's back. For those who have complete insight into what an arsehole they can be to work with it is a time of nervousness as they desperately try and find enough people who they haven't offended to fill out the questionnaire. The surgeons generally struggle with this. For those who want to be a new age, caring, considerate team player it is a valuable tool and for that reason I think it a useful exercise to complete yearly along. That along with some sort of procedural logbook with competence sign off to ensure you don't take out a fallopian tube instead of an appendix would be enough for me. Make it useful to show procedural proficiency, that you aren't a total narcissistic psychopath and leave it there. The rest is a total waste of time. I don't believe this to be just my opinion; all but the most ardent of pedagogic windbags feel that the whole debacle is an exercise in tick boxing.

Dan read through the comments and smiled. 'You take too many 'unofficial breaks',' he smiled raising his index fingers to indicate a quotation.

'Oh?' I replied. I felt a trifle riled by this comment and immediately found myself questioning which nurse or doctor I had asked to provide feedback would have made this suggestion. And what the hell is wrong with making a cup of tea?

'Other than that; pretty good. A word of advice if I may before you leave Tom.' His indexed fingers returned to his lips, his elbows resting on the arm rests of his office chair. 'Make sure you don't slack off for the remaining 4 weeks. We have found previously that the Foundation Year 2 doctors get a little too big for their boots and become complacent either with the staff or patients. Make sure no mistakes creep in. Always ask if you don't know. Don't feel too bad about going for a cup of tea every now and again though. This is a difficult demanding job and if I was Health Secretary it would be different.'

'Thanks Dan,' I smiled.

'All signed off then,' he smiled making a tick motion with his hand.

A Doctor's Mess

'Well it's my guts Doc.'

'Oh?' I asked.

'It's been giving me some right grief.'

'How so?'

'My arse Doc, honestly, it's been falling out of me like shoes out of a loft.' He rubbed his sizeable gut over a giant shiny black polo shirt that made him look like a professional darts player.

'I see.'

His name was Gary and he was a 50ish year old bloke. He was lying propped up on one of the ED gurneys in a cubicle in the majors department. It was a busy Sunday evening and I was in my last week in the job. I had a long weekend to look forward to before two final night shifts next week. I was counting down every shift left in Emergency Medicine and of my time as a Foundation doctor.

Now all I had to do was decide what type of doctor I was going to be. What did I want from a specialty? Well instead of selecting what I was going to be I was deselecting what I definitely was not going to be. Accident and Emergency was out, we had clarified this: one should always have time for a cup of tea. I was definitely not going to be a Paediatrician; there appears to be nothing more stressful than treating sick children, except for managing their parents. GPs just seemed to get continuously shafted from politicians, condescended by the rest of the profession and abused by their patients. Patients seem to have no idea what anaesthetists do all day and frankly neither do I. Definitely not Obstetrics and Gynaecology; nothing worse than wailing women and old vaginas. Radiologists seemed to be deficient in vitamin D and I just wasn't sure I could ever be that obstructive. Pathologists only seem to deal with dead people or bits removed from soon to be dead people. Psychiatry was interesting but no one had any idea what was the actual pathophysiology of any of their diseases and, no doubt, the patients are extremely challenging. So that left Medicine or Surgery; the art of diagnosis or the art of treatment. I was veering towards surgery despite Buzz Lightyear and having to throw away my socks due to them being caked in shit.

'So some loose stool?' I clarified.

'Yeah Doc, it's not diarrhoea; not water,' he explained,' just loose.'

'For how long?'

'A few days now?'

'Anything else you've noticed?'

'Stomach cramps Doc. Oh my days Doc I was up all last night with it. The cramps Doc, I've never had pain like it.' He rubbed his abdomen in a circular motion as though massaging the pain away.

'Anything else?'

'Bit a blood Doc.'

'From below?'

'Yep.'

'With the poo or on wiping?'

'Both.'

'How much?'

'Only a little. It was last night.'

I went through the remainder of his story. He had no real past medical history apart from some high blood pressure and borderline diabetes. He had had no previous operations and took only a blood pressure medication. I examined him and he had a bit of pain in his abdomen when I pushed deep and had just the slightest sheen of sweat on his bald forehead. I glanced at his observations chart, other than raised blood pressure and a slightly high respiratory rate, all observations were in normal parameters.

'Sounds like a bit of gastric flu but the bleeding from below is a bit of a worry. I'll send you for a few blood tests and X-rays and see where we are. If they all look okay I'll send you home and you can pop in to see your GP if the bleeding doesn't settle. You might need a pipe up the bum.'

'Right-o Doc. You're the boss. Any chance of some pain killers though?'

'Sure I'll write you up some antispasmodics. It will help with the cramps.'

'Thanks Doc.'

'Cubicle 4 needs some Buscopan[1], bloods and X-ray please,' I told the sister in charge; a thin aggressive senior nurse with a moustache who always looked like she had drank a cup of coffee too many.

'Who's that?'

'Cubicle 4.'

'He's already on 2 hours and 35 minutes, there won't be time to get the bloods back. Can he just have a venous gas[2]?'

'Umm,' I hesitated.

'Well you're not keeping him in are you,' she glanced up from the screen and stared at me accusingly.

'Not sure yet,' I murmured. I felt like asking if she wanted to see the patient and I'll stand next to the computer being a massive pain in everyone's arse. I hesitated again. She continued to stare at me. 'Fine, I'll just do a venous gas and some X-rays,' I sulkily agreed.

'If you need lab bloods then you should ask for the surgeons to admit the patient,' she commented sensing my agitation.

'But I need more time and more information to decide.'

'Time is not something we have in ED poppet now write the X-ray forms and I'll get one of the nurses to do a venous gas so you can see the psych patient in the cubicle 12 quickly?'

'Psych?'

'Yeah...also on 3 hours,' she said robotically reading from the master screen.

'Great,' I said sarcastically.

---

[1] Buscopan- hyoscine butylbromide- apparently provides relief for patients with crampy abdominal pain

[2] Venous gas- a blood test which can be acquired quickly without waiting for full laboratory testing. The gas analyser can take venous or arterial blood. Arterial blood (arterial blood gas or ABG) is used to determine levels of carbon dioxide and oxygen in the blood. A venous gas is often just used for simple haemoglobin, electrolytes such as potassium and sodium as well as serum lactate- a marker for shock or poor perfusion to important organs.

'Chop, chop,' she said not looking up from her computer screen.

I picked up the notes, reading the nursing triage as I walked around the corner to cubicle 12. 'Acting strangely' was all that was scribbled. I pulled back the curtain to be greeted by what looked like a Guinness book of Records attempt; how many Asian men can one fit into an A&E cubicle.

'Hello,' I said a little taken aback

'Hello doctor, hello,' they all replied in chorus.

'I'm Tom, one of the A&E doctors. Sorry for your wait,' I added, 'all of your waits.' I glimpsed up and looked into the eyes of at least 7 men surrounding a hospital gurney. Their collective gaze was fixated on me. In the middle, sat on the gurney was a slightly unkempt teenager who was staring intently at his own feet. He was wearing dirty jogging bottoms, a grey jumper with a fleeced gilet over the top. On his feet were big dirty white trainers. His hair was frizzy and unruly, and despite his youth he had a good going stubble. His shoulders were being massaged from behind by a broad man with a wispy beard and skull cap who stood behind the hospital bed.

'So,' I said not sure how to proceed. Everyone turned to the far corner of the room where an elderly male was sat on the only chair in the cubicle. He had a thick white beard and wore traditional Pakistani dress. He slowly stood with the aid of a stick and shuffled towards me. The crowd flattened themselves against the walls of the cubicle to allow him past. He slowly advanced towards me. I watched him curiously as approached, closer and closer. Just when I thought he was going to walk straight into me he halted, a foot away, and slowly rocked backwards and forwards as though he was still trying to get his balance. He bowed his head as though paying his respect to a passing hearse. He stood there silently.

'Hello Sir.'

'Hello,' he replied heavily accented.

'So how can I help?' I asked the elderly gentleman.

'He doesn't speak much English I'm afraid,' interjected a thin man to my left with a clipped moustache, a rather ridiculously loud shirt and heavily greased hair combed in a side parting.

'Ah,' I replied.

'The problem though is with my nephew Faizal. He has been acting a bit oddly, saying some strange stuff doctor.'

'And is this Faizal?' I addressed the elderly man as well as jazzy shirt whilst pointing to the quiet teen on the bed who said nothing.

'Yes,' a chorus of male voices said.

I hesitated for a moment, 'Well perhaps I best speak to Faizal alone,' I said glancing up at everyone.

They all glanced at each other and there was a smattering of Urdu for the elderly gentleman. They all slowly filed out of the cubicle with the elderly gentleman leaving last. I walked towards the curtain and glanced behind to ensure no one was waiting within ear-shot.

'So what is the problem,' I asked addressing the patient for the first time.

'No problem,' he snarled looking straight ahead.

'Listen,' I said quietly, 'my name is Tom, I am a doctor. I am only here to help you. You don't have to talk to me but if you do I can try and help you.'

He glanced at me intently looking deep into my eyes. After a brief pause he broke off my stare at glanced to the other wall.

'I can't talk to you.'

'Why?'

'Not here.'

'Why?' I repeated.

'They are listening to me,' he whispered suddenly fixing me with a deep stare.

'Who are?' I replied softly.

'The police.'

'Oh?'

'They know what I have done, but I haven't done it.'

'What haven't you done?'

His eyes furtively leapt from side to side and he glanced again at the empty wall. He looked pre-occupied. 'They think I've raped my sister. They all do. But I haven't.'

'How do you know they know?'

'The signs, I've seen them.'

'Signs?'

'They are trying to control me. They are trying to frame me.'

243

'Who? The police? About raping your sister?'

'Yes and raping my mother and cousin.'

'Raping your mother?'

'I can't say anymore, they know.'

'How do you know that they know?'

'I can hear them talking about me. I know what they are trying to do. My family are trying to get me caught. My uncle knows everything, he is working for them.'

'How do you know?'

'The films, haven't you seen them? They know.'

'I haven't seen them.'

'They have everything bugged, they have bugged me, they know my thoughts,' he continued tapping the side of his head.

I considered the situation. I had seen psychosis whilst at medical school and I could tell immediately that Faizal's thought processes and beliefs were completely deranged.

'Listen Faizal I'm going to get someone to come and speak with you, a professional, someone you can trust who can help you. Is that okay?'

He glanced at me wearily, said nothing and stared over my head resuming his gaze on the curtain separating us from the corridor.

I walked outside the cubicle and was accosted by the throng of relatives.

'Doctor have you spoken to him, what is going on do you think?' asked the uncle with the oily hair and jazzy shirt.

'Well, it's complicated."

"Will he be alright Doctor?' a few voices asked.

'Well I think he is having a psychotic episode,' I said frankly, 'I'm going to call the psychiatrists to come and assess him.'

'Psychosis? What is this?' the thin man asked.

'Schizophrenia,' I said, 'he is having paranoid thoughts. He thinks he has raped family members.'

A cacophony of Urdu could be heard as my conclusions were translated.

'Thank you Doctor for your help,' the old gentleman said bowing his head again.

'I'm going to speak to the psychiatrists but if they confirm my suspicions they might want to admit Faizal to a psychiatric hospital for further assessment.'

'I understand Doctor, thank you for all your help.'

I returned to the computer and typed in 'Schneider's[1] First Rank[2]' and 'Schizophrenia' into Google. I clicked on the Wikipedia link. This young lad had the full shebang. I took some time writing my notes and phoned the on-call psychiatrist who actually seemed interested for once; a welcome interruption from the usual risk assessments of young women and aborted paracetamol overdoses.

'Tom what are you doing with cubicle 4 he's only twenty minutes to breaching?' the senior nurse yelled from behind her computer.

I had forgotten about Gary and his rotten guts.

'Sorry just dealing with the psych patient.'

'Have you discharged him?'

'Who?'

'The psych patient.'

'No!' I said infuriated, 'He's psychotic. Needs psych assessment.'

---

[1] Kurt Schneider was an early twentieth century German psychiatrist came up with the 'first rank' symptoms of schizophrenia that is symptoms that are particularly characteristic for the disease.

[2] Schneider's first rank symptoms are, to save you the Wikipedia review:

1) Third person auditory hallucinations: hearing voices conversing with one another often about the sufferer.

2) Delusions of passivity: the patient feels that some external force or agency is controlling them.

3) Thought delusion: belief that thoughts are being taken out of the patient's head or conversely that thoughts are being forcibly inserted into the patients head. Sometimes the patients feel their thoughts are broadcast to everyone.

4) Delusional perception: normal patient sensations are interpreted with a peculiar conclusion.

'Have you called them?' I felt like I was fourteen being asked whether I had picked up my dirty washing.

'Yes!' I said back huffily. I picked up the notes for Gary out of the rack and replaced Faizal's notes in the cubicle 12 slot. I loaded up the radiology system and looked at the abdominal x-ray. There were multiple bowel loops visible but they didn't appear to be dilated in keeping with bowel obstruction. The chest X-ray looked as though he hadn't taken a breath in when they were taking the film. The venous gas had been printed out and stuck to the front of the notes. The haemoglobin and electrolytes were all in the normal range. The lactate, a marker of poor perfusion or shock was mildly raised and probably reflected dehydration secondary to the diarrhoea. I thought I should probably at least discuss his case with the surgeons but opted to see how he was getting on first:

'How are you Gary?

'Blood hell Doc, I thought you had forgotten me.'

'Afraid not', I smiled, 'how is the pain, are you feeling better?'

'Bit better I reckon Doc,' he said. He still had a sheen of sweat on his brow. I glanced at his observation chart. Everything was in the normal range except his blood pressure again and a mildly raised respiratory rate.

'Have you been drinking much fluid?'

'Trying to Doc.'

'So what do you think we should do with you?' I asked smiling.

'Send me home Doc, I'll be alright.'

'Who's at home with you?' I asked.

'Trouble and strife and my teenage daughter. It's only because of them I came today.'

'Nice, how old is your daughter.'

'Nearly sixteen.'

'So here's the thing, there were a couple of things that were a bit odd on your blood tests.'

'Oh?'

'I'm just wondering whether I should discuss your case with the surgeons?'

'Surgeons Doc? I don't need surgery.'

'I'm not saying you do but…'

'I think I'll be alright Doc.'

'Are you sure?'

'I reckon.'

I hesitated for a moment. 'Alright then boss, I'm happy for you to go home but if things aren't getting better you need to see your GP. Promise?'

'Ok Doc, thanks now,' he said slowly getting his big frame of the ED couch.

With that he was off.

'Tom may I have a word,' Dan my educational supervisor sauntered over. I had just finished handing over my last patient in the morning after my penultimate night shift in Emergency Medicine. I was putting on my coat in the staff room ready to go home for a sleep before coming back for my final shift. I was feeling good about my career. I had a plan. I was going to take a well-earned holiday. Do some locum work to raise some cash before applying for a clinical assistant job at the local medical school to prepare for my future as a surgeon. I reckoned I was good at it.

'Sure Dan.'

'Would you mind coming to my office,' he said softly.

'Now? I've just finished a night shift.'

'If you wouldn't mind, it shouldn't take too long.'

'Sure,' I said. I felt my pulse quicken as I sauntered behind him down the back stairs to his office. He opened the door with a key and motioned for me to sit down in a chair opposite his desk. Dan sat down behind it and plucked some papers off, one of several, large stacks.

'Do you remember that chap you saw last week, he came in with some abdominal pain?'

'Dan I can hardly remember the patients I saw this evening,' I smiled pulling up the zipper on my jacket.

'I have the notes here, if you have a minute?' Dan said offering the papers over to me. I took the notes from him and glanced at the opening computer generated demographic sheet 'Gary Doherty' I read on the top of the remainder of his demographic data. I flipped over to the second sheet to see my scrawl. With that I remembered Gary, with his shiny black polo shirt, sheen of sweat and gut pain.

'Oh yes,' I said, 'I remember, middle aged chap with abdominal cramps and diarrhoea. I sent him home with GP follow up. Everything looked okay I thought,' I explained.

Dan paused for a moment and nibbled his lower lip. 'He came in in cardiac arrest over the weekend.'

I felt as though I had been hit by a sledgehammer. It took a moment for the weight of Dan's words to hit full impact. 'How?' I blurted.

'Looks like maybe a ruptured aortic aneurysm or perhaps ischaemic gut. He will need a post mortem to be definite.'

'Post-mortem!? You mean he fucking died!?'

'He couldn't be resuscitated.'

'Fuck,' I exclaimed, 'but he looked okay.' I repeated. The whole consultation with Gary played over again and again in my mind, on fast forward, as I tried to make sense of my catastrophic mistake.

'I dare say. Listen we will need to touch base again when all the facts are back in. Obviously his family are really upset and angry so we will need sit down with them too.'

'He had a sixteen year old daughter,' I blurted. I thought I was going to cry. My right hand was shaking and I felt an overwhelming urge to vomit.

'Listen, go home and rest. We can talk about this when we have all the facts.'

'Should I speak to them,' I asked.

'Who?'

'His family?'

'No I think that would be inadvisable.'

'So what should I do?'

'Nothing, put it out of your head, you will be asked for a statement.'

'I can do it now,' I pleaded. I wanted to do something, anything, to try and make it right again.

'No, no. Go home. We need you back tonight.'

I stared at the carpet, my thoughts in a maelstrom. 'Okay.'

'There is something else I should probably let you know about,' Dan's voice tailed off.

'What?' I glanced up at him pleadingly.

'This will probably go to the Coroner's court so you will probably be called up as a witness.'

'Court?'

'I'm afraid so,' he looked at me sympathetically.

'Fuck,' my voice faltered. I rubbed my hands against my face and felt the cold sweat on my palms. I felt like I was in a nightmare and any moment I would wake up and this wouldn't be happening. I tried to stand up to leave. I appeared to have temporarily lost control of my legs.

'Listen you need to go home, put this from your mind, get some rest make sure you finish on a high tonight. I guarantee when you wake up you'll feel better about it all.'

'Okay, okay, you're right. I'll go.' I managed to force my legs to stand up. I staggered towards the door.

'Tom, did you know about the raised lactate.'

I glanced back at Dan. 'It was only slightly raised, I thought he was dehydrated,' I pleaded.

'Okay. Don't worry, we all have our battle scars,' Dan smiled again sympathetically. 'Go and sleep.'

I didn't. Sometimes I still don't.

19072529R00146

Printed in Great Britain
by Amazon